New Frontiers in Translation Studies

Series Editor

Defeng Li, Center for Studies of Translation, Interpreting and Cognition, University of Macau, Macao SAR, China

Translation Studies as a discipline has witnessed the fastest growth in the last 40 years. With translation becoming increasingly more important in today's glocalized world, some have even observed a general translational turn in humanities in recent years. The New Frontiers in Translation Studies aims to capture the newest developments in translation studies, with a focus on:

- Translation Studies research methodology, an area of growing interest amongst translation students and teachers;
- Data-based empirical translation studies, a strong point of growth for the discipline because of the scientific nature of the quantitative and/or qualitative methods adopted in the investigations; and
- Asian translation thoughts and theories, to complement the current Eurocentric translation studies.

Submission and Peer Review:

The editor welcomes book proposals from experienced scholars as well as young aspiring researchers. Please send a short description of 500 words to the editor Prof. Defeng Li at Springernfits@gmail.com and Springer Senior Publishing Editor Rebecca Zhu: Rebecca.zhu@springernature.com. All proposals will undergo peer review to permit an initial evaluation. If accepted, the final manuscript will be peer reviewed internally by the series editor as well as externally (single blind) by Springer ahead of acceptance and publication.

Yasir Alenazi

Exploring Lexical Inaccuracy in Arabic-English Translation

Implications and Remedies

Springer

Yasir Alenazi
Arts and Education
University of Tabuk
Tabuk, Saudi Arabia

ISSN 2197-8689   ISSN 2197-8697   (electronic)
New Frontiers in Translation Studies
ISBN 978-981-19-6389-6   ISBN 978-981-19-6390-2   (eBook)
https://doi.org/10.1007/978-981-19-6390-2

© The Editor(s) (if applicable) and The Author(s), under exclusive license to Springer Nature Singapore
Pte Ltd. 2022
This work is subject to copyright. All rights are solely and exclusively licensed by the Publisher, whether
the whole or part of the material is concerned, specifically the rights of translation, reprinting, reuse
of illustrations, recitation, broadcasting, reproduction on microfilms or in any other physical way, and
transmission or information storage and retrieval, electronic adaptation, computer software, or by similar
or dissimilar methodology now known or hereafter developed.
The use of general descriptive names, registered names, trademarks, service marks, etc. in this publication
does not imply, even in the absence of a specific statement, that such names are exempt from the relevant
protective laws and regulations and therefore free for general use.
The publisher, the authors, and the editors are safe to assume that the advice and information in this book
are believed to be true and accurate at the date of publication. Neither the publisher nor the authors or
the editors give a warranty, expressed or implied, with respect to the material contained herein or for any
errors or omissions that may have been made. The publisher remains neutral with regard to jurisdictional
claims in published maps and institutional affiliations.

This Springer imprint is published by the registered company Springer Nature Singapore Pte Ltd.
The registered company address is: 152 Beach Road, #21-01/04 Gateway East, Singapore 189721,
Singapore

Contents

1 **Introduction** 1
 1.1 Background 2
   1.1.1 English Language in the Kingdom of
     Saudi Arabia (KSA) 2
   1.1.2 The Status of the Translation Industry in KSA 3
   1.1.3 Language Proficiency and Translation Competence 4
   1.1.4 The English Language and Translation Programmes in
     Saudi Public Universities 5
   1.1.5 English Departments and Translation
     Course Description 7
 1.2 Statement of the Problem 7
 1.3 Goals of the Study 9
 1.4 Questions of the Study 10
 1.5 Significance of the Study 10
 1.6 Organisation of the Book 11
 References 12

2 **Literature Review** 15
 2.1 The Significance of Lexis 15
   2.1.1 The Relationship of Lexical Knowledge to Successful
     Communication Through Translation 16
   2.1.2 The Nature of Lexis and Lexical Knowledge
     Acquisition 17
 2.2 The Teaching of Lexis 19
   2.2.1 Lexical Chunks 19
   2.2.2 Classifications of Lexical Chunks 20
   2.2.3 Approaches to Teaching Lexical Chunks 21
 2.3 Lexical Errors 22
   2.3.1 A Critical Overview of Language Errors 23
   2.3.2 Approaches to Examine Language Errors 24
 2.4 Sources of Language Errors 32
   2.4.1 Interlingual Influence 32

	2.4.2 Intralingual Influence	33
	2.4.3 Interlingual Errors or Intralingual Errors	34
2.5	A Brief Overview of Arabic Lexis	35
	2.5.1 Characteristics of Arabic Lexis	36
	2.5.2 Similarities Between the Arabic and English Lexical Systems	36
	2.5.3 Differences Between the Arabic and English Lexical Systems	37
2.6	EA Studies on L2 Learners' Lexical Errors	38
	2.6.1 A Review of Previous Studies Investigating Lexical Errors in EFL/ESL Contexts	40
2.7	Summary of the Identified Gaps in the Literature	48
	References	49

3 Research Design and Methodology 55
    3.1 Introduction 55
    3.2 Theoretical Framework 55
        3.2.1 Error Analysis 55
    3.3 Conceptual Framework 57
        3.3.1 Shalaby Et Al.'s Lexical Error Taxonomy 58
    3.4 Research Design 58
        3.4.1 Quantitative Analysis 58
        3.4.2 The Data and Participants 59
        3.4.3 Data Collection Procedure 63
        3.4.4 Ethical Considerations 63
        3.4.5 The Validity and Reliability of the Data 64
        3.4.6 Corpus Data Analysis Procedures 65
    3.5 Summary and Conclusion 71
    References 72

4 Formal Lexical Error Analysis 75
    4.1 Introduction 75
    4.2 Quantitative Analysis and Description of Formal Lexical Errors 75
        4.2.1 Formal Lexical Errors 77
    4.3 Discussion and Explanation of Formal Lexical Errors 86
        4.3.1 Analysis of Interlingual Errors 88
        4.3.2 Analysis of Intralingual Errors 92
        4.3.3 Comparison of the Study's Findings with Previous Studies in relation to the Frequency and Sources of Formal Lexical Errors 94
    4.4 Conclusion 95
    References 96

5 Semantic Lexical Error Analysis 99
    5.1 Introduction 99

5.2	Quantitative Analysis and Description of Semantic Lexical Errors.	99
	5.2.1 Semantic Lexical Errors.	101
5.3	Discussion and Explanation of Semantic Lexical Errors.	118
	5.3.1 Analysis of Interlingual Errors.	120
	5.3.2 Analysis of Intralingual Errors.	123
	5.3.3 Comparison of the Study's Findings with Previous Studies in Relation to the Frequency and Sources of Semantic Lexical Errors	128
5.4	Conclusion	129
	References.	129

6 Implications for Language Learning, Translation, and Language Teaching 131

6.1	Introduction	131
6.2	Implications for Language Learning	132
	6.2.1 Implications of Error Analysis for Language Learning	133
	6.2.2 Positive and Negative Transfer in Language Learning	134
	6.2.3 The Implications of a Systematic Error Taxonomy for Language Learning	136
6.3	Implications for the Translation Studies	137
	6.3.1 Impacts of Lexical Errors on Translation Quality	137
	6.3.2 Impacts of Lexical Errors on Translation Practice.	139
	6.3.3 Impacts of Lexical Errors on Translation Principles	144
6.4	Implications for Language Teaching	145
	6.4.1 Content.	147
	6.4.2 Assessment: Evaluation and Learning Outcomes	150
	6.4.3 The Teaching Process.	151
6.5	A Summary of the Analysis Impacts on Language Learning, Translation Studies, and Language Teaching.	153
6.6	Conclusion	155
	References.	156

7 Summary, Conclusion, and Recommendations 159

7.1	Introduction	159
7.2	Overview of the Research Project	159
7.3	Summary of the Major Findings	160
7.4	Contributions of the Study.	162
7.5	Recommendations for Teaching Vocabulary and Alleviating the Related Language Errors	163
	7.5.1 Pedagogical Strategies for Remedying Lexical Errors	164
7.6	Limitations of the Study.	171
7.7	Suggestions for Future Research	171
	References.	172

Abbreviations

*	Signals lexical errors and misspelled words (errors at the phrase and sentence levels are underlined)
< >	Angle brackets are used to refer to orthographic letters
C	Consonant
CA	Contrastive Analysis
CAH	Contrastive Analysis Hypothesis
EA	Error Analysis
EFL	English as a Foreign Language
ESL	English as a Second Language
FL	Foreign Language
GTM	Grammar Translation Method
IL	Interlanguage
Italics	Indicates the corrected word and sometimes are used when presenting examples of lexical items
KSA	Kingdom of Saudi Arabia
L1	First Language
L2	Second Language
SL	Source Language
SLA	Second Language Acquisition
STEMM	Science, Technology, Engineer, Mathematics, and Medicine
TBA	Task Based Approach
TL	Target Language
V	Vowel

List of Figures

Fig. 2.1	Aspects of lexical knowledge (Based on Nation, 2001)	18
Fig. 2.2	Fossilisation-determining processes (Adapted from Krzeszowski, 1977).	25
Fig. 3.1	Taxonomy of lexical errors (Based on Shalaby et al., 2009).	59
Fig. 3.2	Microsoft excel spreadsheet of errors categorisation	66
Fig. 4.1	Formal lexical error classification	76
Fig. 4.2	Types of formal lexical error overall percentage	77
Fig. 4.3	Sources of formal lexical errors.	87
Fig. 4.4	Percentage distribution of formal lexical errors based on their possible sources	88
Fig. 5.1	Semantic lexical error classification	100
Fig. 5.2	Types of semantic error overall percentage	101
Fig. 5.3	Types of confusion of sense relations error frequency distribution	103
Fig. 5.4	Sources of semantic lexical errors	119
Fig. 5.5	Percentage distribution of semantic errors based on their possible sources	120
Fig. 6.1	Influence of negative transfer on the process of translation	134
Fig. 6.2	Summary of the current study lexical error taxonomy	137
Fig. 6.3	Implications of the analysis of lexical errors for language learning	138
Fig. 6.4	Implications of lexical error analysis for translation studies	146
Fig. 6.5	Implications of lexical error analysis for language teaching	154
Fig. 6.6	Impact of lexical error analysis on language learning, translation studies, and language teaching	154
Fig. 7.1	The frequency distribution of the major types of lexical errors.	161
Fig. 7.2	The proposal of "ERROR"	165
Fig. 7.3	A proposed writing pedagogical strategy	168

List of Tables

Table 1.1	Examples of the English language and translation programme courses	6
Table 2.1	James's (2013) lexical error taxonomy	40
Table 2.2	Summary of major findings of previous studies on the written production of non-Arab EFL learners	42
Table 2.3	Summary of major findings of previous studies on the written production of Arab EFL learners in the Saudi context	44
Table 3.1	Lexical error taxonomies and their classification criterion	57
Table 3.2	Taxonomy of lexical errors with coding scheme for analysis purposes	67
Table 4.1	Length of the corpus texts and number of formal lexical errors	77
Table 4.2	Types of formal lexical errors and their frequency percentage distribution	78
Table 4.3	Misselection error subtypes frequency percentage	78
Table 4.4	Misformation error frequency percentage	79
Table 4.5	Percentage frequency distribution of distortion error subcategories	81
Table 4.6	Types of capitalisation errors in the translation texts	82
Table 4.7	Types of omission errors in the translation texts	82
Table 4.8	Types of substitution errors in the translation texts	82
Table 4.9	Types of impeding comprehension errors in the translation texts	83
Table 4.10	Types of addition errors in the translation texts	84
Table 4.11	Types of unique errors in the translation texts	84
Table 4.12	Types of word segmentation errors in the translation texts	84
Table 4.13	Types of transposition errors in the translation texts	85

Table 4.14	Types of grapheme substitution errors in the translation texts	85
Table 4.15	Types of L1 transfer errors in the translation texts	86
Table 4.16	Types of inappropriate meaning errors in the translation texts	86
Table 4.17	Total percentage frequency distribution of formal lexical errors based on their possible causes	89
Table 4.18	Different forms of capitalisation errors	90
Table 5.1	Length of the corpus texts and number of semantic lexical errors	101
Table 5.2	Types of semantic lexical error frequency distribution	102
Table 5.3	Types of stylistic errors frequency percentage distribution	115
Table 5.4	Total percentage frequency distribution of semantic lexical errors based on their possible causes	121

Chapter 1
Introduction

The English language holds a high status in the education system of the Arab world due to its significance as a language for scientific development and economic globalisation. English is becoming a lingua franca in the Middle East for various reasons, such as academic, vocational, and business. Translators as mediators between Arab countries and international professionals need to be particularly proficient in their English. However, many university students of translation in the region have difficulties to communicate in written language while translating from their first language (Arabic) to the second language (English) and mainly in the accurate use of English lexis. They produce various types of lexical errors that negatively impact on the quality of their translations. This problem calls for English language teachers and translation trainers in the Arabic-speaking countries to have a better understanding of the types of errors EFL learners produce in their written language while translating. There have been a few recent error analysis studies concerning the lexical errors of Arab EFL students' writings. However, no study was found that endeavoured to provide a comprehensive analysis of lexical errors in the translation texts of Arab English major students. The analysis of lexical errors in the learners' language production could facilitate the understanding of theoretical implications in EFL/ESL learning and vocabulary acquisition. It is necessary to explore the English language learning process of Arab university English major students to help enhance their learning outcomes. Examining the students' lexical errors in their language production can yield significant insights into problematic lexical aspects in writing.

This chapter provides a description of the context of the study and its basic aims, and lists the research questions. It investigates the current status of the English language in the education system of the Kingdom of Saudi Arabia and its impact on the translation industry. Saudi students need to be proficient in the English language since it is increasingly an essential employment requirement in several professional domains in the Middle East. However, Saudi learners find writing in English a challenging task and particularly in the appropriate use of

---

© The Author(s), under exclusive license to Springer Nature Singapore Pte Ltd. 2022
Y. Alenazi, *Exploring Lexical Inaccuracy in Arabic-English Translation*,
New Frontiers in Translation Studies, https://doi.org/10.1007/978-981-19-6390-2_1

lexis. This chapter illustrates this problem and discusses in detail the research gaps in relation to Saudi English learners and lexical errors. It indicates the plans this book aims to achieve. It explains the significance of the study to the fields of SLA, translation, and language learning. At the end, the chapter concludes with a summary about the structure of this book.

1.1 Background

1.1.1 English Language in the Kingdom of Saudi Arabia (KSA)

English plays a significant role in the education system of KSA, because of its importance as a language for scientific and technological advancement. Even though Arabic is the official language and the primary medium of communication, for many Saudis and Arab people, English is becoming a lingua franca in the region for various reasons, such as academic, vocational, and business. For academic-related purposes, Saudi learners enrolled in the different university programmes in science, technology, engineering, medicine, mathematics (STEMM), and specifically in English as an academic programme need to be proficient in the English language in order to experience success with the academic requirements of their courses, given English is used as the medium of instruction in many of these programmes (Alshahrani & Al-Shehri, 2012; El-Dakhs, 2015). For vocational-related purposes, English continues to be the official language of communication in both the private and public sector in KSA. Saudis need to be proficient in the English language, since it is increasingly an essential employment requirement in several professional domains in the country. For example, Aramco, a major petroleum and natural gas company, requires employees to have a good command of both spoken and written forms of the English language. In the health sector, the English language is the main language used for communicative purposes between employees, which emphasises the importance of the English language in KSA (Alshahrani & Al-Shehri, 2012).

There is a growing need for Saudis to be highly proficient in English in the fields of STEMM and business so that they can interact globally. Translators as intermediaries between Saudi and international STEMM and other professionals need to be particularly proficient in their English writing. Since writing is one of the primary tasks of a translator, English language and translation students should become familiar with the different writing genres in both first and second languages. Translation students should also have a good lexical knowledge of both First Language (L1) and Second Language (L2). In other words, they should be able to use various expressions, idioms, and specific vocabulary correctly when translating different texts of different genres (Awadalbari, 2015).

Saudi learners of English are expected to be able to use the English language in spoken and written forms. However, generally Saudi students find writing in

English a challenging task and they usually perform poorly in that area, even after graduation despite many initiatives to improve their writing (Rahman, 2011). Studies by a number of scholars over the years (e.g., Alharthi, 2011; Al-Jabri, 1998; Javid et al., 2013; Rahman, 2011; Shalaby et al., 2009; Sheshsha, 1993; Shukri, 2014) indicate that Saudi university students' English writing is riddled with grammatical and lexical errors. To address this issue, Javid et al. (2013) claimed that there is a great need for error analysis research to raise English language teachers' awareness about their learners' common weaknesses in writing.

Several studies have shown that the most significant aspect affecting written language is lexis. Every word in a sentence plays a significant role in which all parts of the sentence support each other to form a comprehensible message and errors can be an irritation that hampers effective communication (Maniam, 2010). Even errors that are often classified as grammatical usually relate to lexical errors (Hemchua & Schmitt, 2006; Shalaby et al., 2009). The appropriate selection and use of lexis in written texts have a positive impact on the quality of writing and on the learners' language proficiency level (Llach, 2005). Thus, it can be said that lexis is the fundamental element, which is very important to communicate, especially in written communication through translation. In short, lexical errors are an urgent concern of language learning and teaching (Hemchua & Schmitt, 2006; Llach, 2011; Shalaby et al., 2009).

Khalifa (2015) stated that Saudi university students make lexical errors when they are writing or translating in English language because of a lack of vocabulary. Many university students use the first meaning of the word that comes to their mind without trying to determine appropriate word choice based on the context and the type of text. Many university students appear to be unaware of the many synonyms a particular lexical item may have, and seemingly make uninformed choices when selecting what they consider to be appropriate vocabulary. In translation from one language to another, an idea cannot be transferred without the lexis, and by learning lexis, we can comprehend a text or communicate with others (Awadalbari, 2015). Moreover, there is a strong relationship between an individual's language knowledge and comprehension of lexical items. The more lexical items acquired and comprehended, the broader the students' knowledge of the language because they are able to convey and receive information more easily. Recent error analysis research has focused on the use of English lexis by students studying different disciplines (e.g., Hemchua & Schmitt, 2006; Shalaby et al., 2009). This study will focus specifically on students of English language and translation.

1.1.2 The Status of the Translation Industry in KSA

English language has a high status in the translator training industry in KSA. There is a growing demand on translation services in KSA with its entry into the international business sector which creates outstanding career opportunities for trained translators (Alshaikhi, 2018; Fatani, 2009). The establishment of new economic centres in many parts of the country and the different and large number of professional sectors that have lately joined into strategic partnership with foreign parties are additional factors behind this growth (Fatani, 2009). Furthermore, the Saudi government has contributed significantly to the translation profession by creating an international award for distinguished translation works, the King Abdullah Bin Abdulaziz International Award for Translation (also known as the KABAIAT). However, the demand for professional translation services in KSA has led to a need for effective academic English and translation programmes that can meet the challenges of the Kingdom's public and private sectors. ElShafei (2014) argued that the lack of well-designed translation courses is the reason behind the weaknesses university students have in their translation products which in turn affects the quality of preparation for the labour market. Furthermore, recent research has indicated that many university translation students face difficulties translating from Arabic to English and vice versa (Elmahdi, 2016; Khalifa, 2015). According to Khalifa (2015), Saudi students find translation a challenging task due to the differences between Arabic and English structures. They produce different translation errors that negatively impact the quality of the translation. It is important to identify these difficulties in order to design an effective translation course programme for positive outcomes.

1.1.3 Language Proficiency and Translation Competence

Sufficient language proficiency, that is being able to read and write in both the L1 and the L2, is essential in translation. Language learners should expand their lexical knowledge in order to have better access to languages. Previous research (e.g., Baker, 2011; Masrai & Milton, 2012; Milton, 2009; Schmitt, 2008) has shown the significance of lexis and its relationship between language proficiency and translation competence.

'Translation' has been delineated differently by different scholars. Recognizing the ambiguity surrounding the term, Hewson and Martin (2018) claimed that the term denotes both the notion of translation product and that of translation production and hence any appropriate definition of the term has to take into consideration this duality. They nonetheless regard translation as a process that involves either the instrumental practice or the "actual cognitive operations" through which "a translated text" is produced from "a source text" (Hewson & Martin, 2018, p. 1). Melby and Foster (2010) regarded translation as a complex perceptive process in which context is integral; save for instances where the L1 and the L2 have identical ambiguities. Tymoczko (2014) argued translation as a transfer in that the L2 text is not only subject to translator agency but also to influences of context inflection and cultural realities on the L1 text meaning. Thus, translators should obtain full access to the L1 original text in order to comprehend it. They should also acquire the skills to reproduce this text in the L2. According to Eszenyi (2016), the translator language competence has an influential part in determining the quality of his or her translation. It is impossible to translate without having an adequate language proficiency in both the L1 and the L2.

The proficiency of L1 and L2 is crucial in the translation profession along with several other translation competences. The different translation processes of texts "encoding and decoding, rewriting, analysing and synthesising" (Alshaikhi, 2018, p. 36) cannot be achieved without an advanced level of language proficiency in both L1 and L2. This affirms the significance of language proficiency in the translation process. As a result, translation training programmes at the university level should pay more attention to the language learning section of the programmes and the difficulties students have in order to improve outcomes.

1.1.4 The English Language and Translation Programmes in Saudi Public Universities

Each public university in KSA aims to be a comprehensive institution of higher education that is developed by productive community partnerships and research in focused areas that are of identified importance to the future of KSA, and to the world. To maintain excellence in education, these universities aim at offering certified academic programmes and distinguished scientific research that address the needs of the community, expectations of the local market, and the country's Vision 2030.[1]

The English language and translation programmes were established at the Saudi universities to equip students with the fundamental knowledge, essential skills, and high values that contribute effectively to the development of the local community. In addition, one of their main goals is to enhance students' prospects in employability in areas that require mastery of the English language. Since this kind of programme was established, it has been a requirement that all admitted students take different English courses in the field of linguistics, translation, and literature and successfully complete the required programme courses by attaining a minimum Grade Point Average (GPA) of 2 (out of 5) in order to be able to graduate. Students can successfully complete the programme across eight academic semesters. Admission into this programme is based on the placement capacity and on the students' total scores in secondary school and the National Centre for Assessment tests (General Aptitude Test and the Achievement Test). These two educational tests presented by the centre measure the analytical and deductive skills of high school graduates planning to pursue their studies in Saudi universities. Holding a secondary school certificate that is not older than three years is an additional admission requirement.

---

[1] In 2016, the Kingdom of Saudi Arabia announced its Vision 2030 which is likely to transform Saudi society. Saudi Vision 2030 intends to make huge investments with different international organisations and the English language would be the common commination tool to achieve the Kingdom's goals and ambitions. http://vision2030.gov.sa/en. Retrieved on 10/08/2018.

Table 1.1 Examples of the English language and translation programme courses

English language and translation programme		
	Domain	*Example of courses*
1	English language skills	Essay writing (2 levels), Advanced Grammar (2 levels)
2	Linguistics	Introduction to Linguistics, Language acquisition, Phonetics (2 levels), Syntax and Morphology, Semantics, Error Analysis, Stylistics
3	Translation	Principles of Translation, Translation Practice (4 levels)
4	Literature	Introduction to literature, History of English Literature, Applied Criticism, Theoretical Criticism, Civilisation (2 levels), Novel (4 levels), Drama (3 levels), Poetry (4 levels)

The programme provides university students with the necessary background about English language in different areas such as linguistics (phonology, syntax, morphology, semantics, pragmatics, grammar, language acquisition, and language theories), literature (including drama, poetry, and novels, theoretical and applied literary criticism), and translation (translation principles, practices, and theories). With regard to the translation training studies, the programme is dedicated to training students to translate literary and non-literary texts in Arabic or English in the fields of literature, science, medicine, journalism, education, and others. Thus, graduates of this programme are expected to be qualified and prepared for professions in the translation industry as translators, the education industry as English language teachers, and other work fields where an excellent command of English is required since they are supposed to be exposed to both language knowledge and translation training.[2] Table 1.1 illustrates examples of the courses taught in the English language and translation programme at a Saudi public university.

Saudi English major students, however, have difficulties communicating in written language while translating from Arabic to English language and particularly in the appropriate use of English lexis (Elmahdi, 2016; Khalifa, 2015). In my personal experience as an English lecturer at the Languages and Translation Department (English Language and Translation programme) at a Saudi public university, lexical errors are problematic and pervasive in the written language of Saudi English major students, which negatively affects their translation quality. Most students do not pay enough attention to the lexical aspect. They still frequently make errors in their written language. They presume that lexis is not a complicated problem, since they can easily look up words in a dictionary. However, lexical aspects are important as translators need to choose words appropriately to convey their intended meaning and to facilitate communication. Therefore, this problem calls for English language teachers and translation trainers

---

[2] Language Studies undergraduate programmes (Majors Guide, 2017) retrieved from https://hesc. moe.gov.sa/Pages/Downloadvk.aspx?t=t. Retrieved on 01/05/2019.

in KSA to have a better understanding of the types of errors English major students make in their written language while translating. For this purpose, this study aims to identify the lexical errors in English major students' translated English texts at the university level.

1.1.5 English Departments and Translation Course Description

English Departments at Saudi public universities offer a four-year undergraduate programme, which is usually divided into two stages, the foundation stage (first year) and the advanced stage (the second, third, and fourth years). The foundation stage focus is on four basic English language skills: listening, speaking, reading, and writing, all of which are taught in a comprehensive English course across two academic semesters. Students at this stage will have the opportunity to develop and improve their English language skills. In addition, this compulsory course aims at encouraging the use of specific grammatical rules, promoting fluency, and enhancing communication skills. With the basic language skills presumably learnt by the students at the foundation stage, the advanced stage offers several courses in the field of literature, linguistics, writing, and translation.

As a part of the translation courses requirements and objectives, students in their second and third years are first introduced to the basic principles and methods of translation. Once the students have a strong background on translation methods, they will start to practise basic translation to develop some awareness on some of the language problems that are likely to occur during translating different genres in, for example, education, literature, politics, journalism, and science. In addition, the translation courses at this stage focus on improving the students' basic linguistic skills and enriching their vocabulary knowledge of the L1 and the L2.

Having provided second- and third-year students with basic vocabulary and an understanding of the possible linguistic differences between the L1 and the L2, the fourth-year translation courses aim at training students on how to deal with various syntactic and textual problems that could be encountered during the process of translating from Arabic to English and vice versa.

1.2 Statement of the Problem

In the field of second language acquisition (SLA), procedures for identifying, classifying, and interpreting errors systematically are continually being established to address the different errors that L2 learners produce (Crystal, 2008). Creating taxonomies of errors relies on the analysis of lexical errors, that is, classifications that can describe and explain the occurrence of incorrect word choice. Quantitative studies of language learners' errors can also decide which errors are more frequent and typical of non-L1 users.

There have been a few recent error analysis studies concerning the lexical errors of Saudi EFL students' writings (e.g., Al-Jabri, 1998; Shalaby et al., 2009; Sheshsha, 1993). To my best knowledge, no study has endeavoured to provide a comprehensive analysis of lexical errors in the translation texts of Saudi English major students. The analysis of lexical errors in the learners' language production could facilitate the understanding of theoretical implications in ESL/EFL learning and vocabulary acquisition (Belz, 2004; Hunston & Francis, 2000). It is necessary to explore the English language learning process of Saudi university English major students to help enhance their learning outcomes. Examining the students' lexical errors in their language production can yield significant insights into problematic lexical aspects in writing. For teachers and syllabus designers, an exploration of lexical errors could potentially enhance course and material design (Chapelle, 2004; Krishnamurthy & Kosem, 2007).

Although the effect of L1 on L2 has been investigated in some of the literature on English foreign language learning in KSA, this process needs more exploration when it comes to the use of English vocabulary. L1 interference /negative transfer phenomenon (interlingual influence), which is known as "the use of a negative first language pattern or rule which leads to an error or inappropriate form in the target language (TL)" (Richards et al., 1992, p. 205), is considered one of the critical factors influencing the English learning process of Arabs. However, the word (interlingual) has been used to refer to the transfer of learners' L1 knowledge while learning an L2. Therefore, as an outcome of such interference, errors might occur in the L2 language written or spoken production which includes the application of learning strategies that are equivalent to those established in the first language (Lim, 2010; Richards, 1971).

Interference or misperception within the L2 is called (intralingual influence). This type of interference does not relate to the L1 and can show a unique error type of the learner or, generally, a language proficiency issue, which is considered a part of L1/L2 universal processes (Ellis, 2008). In this respect, there should be more research to scrutinise the nature of lexical errors and investigate the extent to which these errors occur interlingually (L1 influence) and intralingually (L2 influence) in learning English by Saudi English major students.

While there is a growing body of research exploring lexical errors made by L2 learners of English in other contexts, differences in the first language backgrounds and other learning settings limit the applicability of the findings of these studies to the Saudi context. It is clear that the quality of the learning opportunities shaped for learners and the ways in which these opportunities are acquired by the learners influence the language learning outcomes. Research asserted that the learning environment, the types of language input used, the quality of language instruction, and available opportunities for language practice influence the L2 learner performance (Khamkhien, 2010; Littlewood, 1984; Moeller & Catalano, 2015; Weismer

& Hesketh, 1996). Hence, to develop a more precise understanding of the main areas of problems in the lexical use of Saudi English major students, analytic and comprehensive studies in the Saudi context are needed.

The research gaps which are mentioned above and related to Saudi English major students can be summarised as:

- There is still lack of research about the problematic lexical aspects in the written production of Saudi learners of English;
- There is a lack of studies that examine lexical errors in the translation texts of Saudi English major students;
- The current studies on Saudi English major students' lexical errors do not provide adequate and comprehensive linguistic analysis of the identified lexical errors in the written production (translation texts) of this group of students;
- Previous studies do not consider the issue of L1 influence or L2 influence in the occurrence of lexical errors in the translation texts of Saudi English major students; and
- Most of the existing error analysis studies that examine lexical errors in the written language of ESL/EFL learners of English have been undertaken in non-Saudi contexts.

Taking into consideration the research gaps mentioned above, there is a need for an empirical study to investigate lexical errors in the translation texts of Saudi English major students. Consequently, this research aims to fill these gaps in the literature and provide a deep analysis and explanation of the types, nature, and reasons of the lexical errors in the Saudi students' English language production.

1.3 Goals of the Study

The study intends to fill the gaps in the literature on lexical errors in the written production of Saudi students majoring in English. It aims to investigate how Saudi English major students at the English language and translation programme deal with their L2 lexis by (a) analysing the types of errors in lexis selection by students in translation tasks, (b) determining the frequency distribution of the types of lexical errors identified, and (c) identifying which of these errors can be traced back to interlingual/intralingual influences. The lexical errors are inappropriate because they form a deviation between a lexical item and its context despite the language rules (Martin, 1984). Quantitative research of errors could be useful for language teaching by identifying the problematic aspects of lexis for L2 learners, and examining precisely why native speakers may perceive L2 vocabulary in a specific context, despite the correct grammar, as foreign (Hasselgren, 1994). In addition, the study plans to gain a better understanding of the students' lexical errors as an attempt to contribute to the improvement of English language education in the Saudi context.

1.4 Questions of the Study

The main research question guiding this study is:

What are the characteristics of the lexical errors in the translation texts produced by Saudi English major students?

In error analysis studies, error taxonomies are used to determine the types and frequency of the errors distributed in a written text (Llach, 2011). Thus, the main research question can be more comprehensively answered by several sub-questions:

1. *What are the types of lexical errors distributed in Saudi English major students' translation texts?*
2. *What is the frequency distribution of lexical errors prevalent in the students' translations?*

These questions do not entirely cover the question of the source of errors. A third sub-question of interest is therefore:

3. *What are the reasons behind the occurrence of these lexical errors in Saudi English major students' translation texts?*

To answer the research questions, this study follows the main steps in the error analysis approach, (EA) approach, as originally suggested by Corder (1974) and acknowledged mostly by SLA researchers (e.g., Ellis, 2008; Gass & Selinker, 2008; James, 2013). These main steps are collection of a language sample, identification, description, and explanation of errors. To collect language samples, as appropriate to the goals of this research, the study utilises a corpus of translation texts upon which a linguistic analysis is based. For data analysis, a quantitative analysis method using frequency statistics is adopted to analyse the data necessary to address the research questions above. Lexical errors identified in the language samples collected are examined from a quantitative perspective to describe them and reveal their sources, and additionally, their frequency distributions are calculated. The use of quantitative analysis provides the researcher with both depth and breadth of insight into the data.

1.5 Significance of the Study

The research contributes to the field of SLA research, particularly to the body of knowledge on lexical errors of L2 learners, by providing information about lexical errors made in the language production of Saudi learners of English which has, up until now, received little attention in published research. For that reason, this research provides an in-depth and statistical analysis of the lexical errors made in the learners' translation texts. The findings of the study provide significant insight into the problematic features in the language production of ESL/EFL students.

In addition, the research findings shed some light on gaps in the L2 knowledge of Saudi students with respect to vocabulary. Since the study takes into account learners' L1 and its influence on their L2 performance, the findings of this study extend the growing body of literature on the phenomenon of first language interference or negative transfer. The study makes an important contribution to adding to research on Saudi learners' English performance cross-linguistically.

At the pedagogical level, the findings of this study can contribute to the enhancement of ESL/EFL teaching in the Saudi context as well as in other Arabic-speaking contexts and the improvement of English major students' writing and translation quality. The study provides detailed analysis and explanations about the main lexical areas that cause specific difficulties for Saudi English major students in their written production while translating, as well as the potential sources of the problems. This would be useful for educators and curriculum writers in designing materials since it discusses important information about the key problematic lexical areas that should be given more attention in the course syllabus. It can benefit language teachers by raising their awareness of the common lexical errors made in students' language production. Knowing the language features that cause problems for students and the sources of those problems helps language instructors in using more effective teaching techniques and developing more suitable strategies to address learners' needs and weaknesses, which, consequently, can improve their learning outcomes.

1.6 Organisation of the Book

This chapter described the context of the study and its basic aims, and listed the research questions. In addition, it provided a brief overview of the research design and the data analysis approach and the rationale for its use. It also illustrated the problem that this book investigates and the suggested solution. The chapter explained the significance of the study to the field of SLA and language learning.

Chapter 2 reviews the relevant literature concerning lexis and error analysis in SLA research. It deals with lexis and its significance in various academic and professional contexts. It discusses the relationship of lexical knowledge to successful communication. In addition, it presents a brief explanation about the nature of lexis and lexical knowledge acquisition. It also focuses on the pedagogical issues in regard to lexis, lexical chunks, classification of lexical chunks, and the approaches of teaching lexical chunks. The notion of lexical errors and a critical overview of language errors are discussed in this chapter in addition to the common approaches to examine language errors. Furthermore, it illustrates the common sources of language errors and how interlingual and intralingual influences play a major role in the occurrence of errors. A general overview of the Arabic lexis is also presented. At its conclusion, a review of previous EA studies concerning the lexical errors of L2 learners is provided.

Chapter 3 introduces and discusses the research design and methodology employed in this project. It includes a description of the setting of the study, and the participants, followed by an elaboration on the data collection and analysis procedures. The study utilises a quantitative method to analyse the lexical errors in the corpus texts. Furthermore, the study follows the main steps in the EA approach as acknowledged mostly by SLA researchers. The approach is used to examine the different patterns of lexical errors and provide a detailed analysis of the lexical errors made by students and identify the possible reasons behind these errors.

Chapter 4 presents the results of formal lexical error analysis of the collected corpus data in relation to the aims and questions of the research and its interpretations. It provides a linguistic description of the formal lexical errors made in the translation texts, along with detailed statistical analysis. Furthermore, the chapter presents a discussion of formal lexical errors and explains the potential sources of the errors made by Saudi English major students.

Chapter 5 presents the results of semantic lexical error analysis of the translated corpus texts with respect to the research aims and its questions. The chapter presents a description of the semantic lexical errors identified. It provides a linguistic description of the semantic lexical errors made in the translation texts, along with detailed statistical analysis. It also focuses on explaining the potential sources of semantic errors made by Saudi English major students.

Chapter 6 discusses the implications of the findings for ESL/EFL students, teachers, and SLA researchers. It illustrates the contributions to linguistics and implications of the study analysis for the field of SLA. The chapter also discusses the contributions of the study analysis to the field of translation. It provides pedagogical implications for the teaching of English language with respect to vocabulary.

The book concludes with Chap. 7, which presents the conclusions reached in this study, acknowledging some limitations and suggestions for further research. It provides a brief overview of the research project. The chapter demonstrates a summary of the major findings and contributions based on the research questions and analysis. It offers two pedagogical frameworks as a set of recommendations to improve ESL/EFL teaching/learning with respect to language errors and writing skills. The chapter then concludes with identifying limitations of the current study and suggests areas for future research.

References

Alharthi, K. (2011). *The impact of writing strategies on the written product of EFL Saudi male students at King Abdul-Aziz University* [Unpublished PhD thesis]. Newcastle University, UK.

Al-Jabri, Samia M. H. (1998). *An analysis of lexical errors in written English of Saudi college freshman female students* [Unpublished master's thesis]. Girls College of Education, Makkah, Saudi Arabia.

Alshahrani, K., & Al-Shehri, S. (2012). Conceptions and responses to e-learning: The case of EFL teachers and students in a Saudi Arabian university. *Monash University Linguistics Papers, 8*(1), 21.

References

Alshaikhi, T. (2018). *Bridging the gap between translation profession and translation programmes in Saudi universities* (pp. 1–348). [Unpublished PhD Thesis].

Awadalbari, M. (2015). Translation as an aid to enhance students' writing skills at university level. *SUST Journal of Humanities, 16*(4), 241–252.

Baker, M. (2011). *In other words: A coursebook on translation* (2nd ed.). Routledge.

Belz, J. A. (2004). Learner corpus analysis and the development of foreign language proficiency. *System, 32*, 577–591.

Chapelle, C. A. (2004). Technology and second language learning: Expanding methods and agendas. *System, 32*, 593–601.

Corder, S. P. (1974). Error analysis. In J. P. B. Allen & S. P. Corder (Eds.), *Techniques in applied linguistics (The Edinburgh course in applied linguistics: 3)* (pp 122–154). Oxford University Press (Language and Language Learning).

Crystal, D. (2008). *A dictionary of linguistics and phonetics*. Blackwell Publishing.

El-Dakhs, D. S. (2015). The Arab university students' use of English general service and academic vocabulary: A lexical development Study. *English Language Teaching, 8*(6), 32–49.

Ellis, R. (2008). *The study of second language acquisition*. Oxford University Press.

Elmahdi, O. E. H. (2016). Translation problems faced by Saudi EFL learners at university level. *English Literature and Language Review, 2*(7), 74–81.

ElShafei, N. (2014). Implementing a professional approach within translation. *International Journal of Applied Linguistics and English Literature, 3*(2), 145–154.

Eszenyi, R. (2016). *The modern translator's profile*. In I. Horvath (Ed.), *The modern translator and interpreter*. Eotvos University Press.

Fatani, A. (2009). The state of the translation industry in Saudi Arabia. *Translation Journal, 13*(4), 1–8. Retrieved December 20, 2020, from http://accurapid.com/journal/50saudi.htm

Gass, S., & Selinker, L. (2008). *Second language acquisition: An introductory course* (3rd ed.). Routledge.

Hasselgren, A. (1994). Lexical teddy bears and advanced learners: A study into the ways Norwegian students cope with English vocabulary. *International Journal of Applied Linguistics, 5*(2), 237–260.

Hemchua, S., & Schmitt, N. (2006). An analysis of lexical errors in the English compositions of Thai learners. *Prospect, 21*, 3–25.

Hewson, L., & Martin, J. (2018). *Redefining translation: The variational approach (ePub)*. Taylor & Francis.

Hunston, S., & Francis, G. (2000). *Pattern grammar: A corpus-driven approach to the lexical grammar of English*. John Benjamins.

James, C. (2013). *Errors in language learning and use: Exploring error analysis*. Routledge.

Javid, C. Z., Farooq, M. U., & Umer, M. (2013). An investigation of Saudi Efl learners' writing problems: A case study along gender-lines. *Kashmir Journal of Language Research, 16*(1), 179.

Khalifa, M. (2015). Problem in translating English and Arabic languages' structure: A case study of EFL Saudi students in Shaqra University. *European Journal of English Language and Literature Studies, 3*(4), 22–34.

Khamkhien, A. (2010). Factors affecting language learning strategy reported usage by Thai and Vietnamese EFL learners. *Electronic Journal of Foreign Language Teaching, 7*(1), 66–85.

Krishnamurthy, R., & Kosem, I. (2007). Issues in creating a corpus for EAP pedagogy and research. *Journal of English for Academic Purposes, 6*(4), 356–373.

Lim, J.M.-H. (2010). Interference in the acquisition of the present perfect continuous: Implications of a grammaticality judgment test. *The Open Applied Linguistics Journal, 3*(1), 24–37.

Littlewood, W. (1984). Foreign and second language learning: Language acquisition research and its implications for the classroom. Cambridge University Press.

Llach, M. P. A. (2005). A critical review of the terminology and taxonomies used in the literature on lexical errors. *Journal of English and American Studies, 31*(1), 11–24.

Llach, M. P. A. (2011). *Lexical errors and accuracy in foreign language writing.* Multilingual Matters.

Maniam, M. (2010). The influence of first language grammar (L1) on the English language (L2) writing of Tamil school students: A case study from Malaysia. *Language in India, 10*, 1–209.

Martin, M. (1984). Advanced vocabulary teaching: The problem of synonyms. *The Modern Language Journal, 68*(2), 130–137.

Masrai, A., & Milton, J. (2012). The vocabulary knowledge of university students in Saudi Arabia. *Perspectives (TESOL Arabia), 19*(3), 13–19.

Melby, A. K., & Foster, C. (2010). Context in translation: Definition, access and teamwork. *The International Journal for Translation & Interpreting Research, 2*(2), 1–15.

Milton, J. (2009). *Measuring second language vocabulary acquisition.* Multilingual Matters.

Moeller, A. J., & Catalano, T. (2015). *Foreign language teaching and learning.* https://digital-commons.unl.edu/cgi/viewcontent.cgi?article=1199&context=teachlearnfacpub

Rahman, M. M. (2011). English language teaching (ELT) in Saudi Arabia: A study of learners' needs analysis with special reference to community college, Najran University. *Language in India, 11*(4), 367–461.

Richards, J. (1971). A non-contrastive approach to error analysis. *English Language Teaching Journal, 25*(3), 204–219.

Richards, J. C., Platt, J., & Platt, H. (1992). *Longman dictionary of language teaching and applied linguistics.* Longman.

Schmitt, N. (2008). Instructed second language vocabulary learning. *Language Teaching Research, 12*(3), 329–363.

Shalaby, A. N., Yahya, N., & El-Komi, M. (2009). Analysis of lexical errors in Saudi college students' compositions. *Journal of the Saudi Association of Languages and Translation, 2*(3), 65–93.

Sheshsha, J. A. (1993). Lexical error analysis in learning English as a foreign language. *Social Science Research Series, 24*, 5–30.

Shukri, N. A. (2014). Second language writing and culture: Issues and challenges from the Saudi learners' perspective. *Arab World English Journal, 5*(3), 190–207.

Tymoczko, M. (2014). *Enlarging translation, empowering translators.* Routledge.

Weismer, S. E., & Hesketh, L. J. (1996). Lexical learning by children with specific language impairment: Effects of linguistic input presented at varying speaking rates. *Journal of Speech, Language, and Hearing Research, 39*(1), 177–190.

Chapter 2
Literature Review

This chapter reviews the literature concerning lexis and EA in SLA research. The chapter consists of six main sections. First, lexis and its significance in various academic and professional contexts is broached. It discusses the relationship of lexical knowledge to successful communication and offers a brief explanation about the nature of lexis and lexical knowledge acquisition. The second section focuses on the teaching of lexis, lexical chunks, lexical chunks classification, and the pedagogical approaches towards lexical chunks. Third, the notion of lexical errors and a critical overview of language errors are discussed in addition to the common approaches to examining language errors: interlanguage, contrastive analysis, and EA approaches. Fourth, the chapter illustrates the common sources of language errors and how interlingual and intralingual influences play a major role in the occurrence of errors. A general overview of the Arabic lexis is presented in the fifth section. In the sixth and final section, a review of previous EA studies concerning the lexical errors of L2 learners is provided.

The chapter concludes with a summary of the gaps identified in the literature regarding the particular focus of this study.

2.1 The Significance of Lexis

Lexis plays a significant role in the language learning process. It is the key for every language. According to Michael Lewis (1993), lexis is an essential part of every language. It is important for language learners to learn because it provides the building blocks of the language (Milton, 2009). Moreover, Wilkins (1972, p. 111), highlighted the significance of lexis, stating that "without grammar very little can be conveyed; without vocabulary nothing can be conveyed." Specifically, even if language learners do not have sufficient grammatical knowledge, they can convey their messages by using the appropriate vocabulary. Thus, limited lexical

---

© The Author(s), under exclusive license to Springer Nature Singapore Pte Ltd. 2022
Y. Alenazi, *Exploring Lexical Inaccuracy in Arabic-English Translation*,
New Frontiers in Translation Studies, https://doi.org/10.1007/978-981-19-6390-2_2

knowledge is more critical than grammar. Consequently, learners should develop their language knowledge focusing on lexis, since the level of language accuracy and fluency of an individual depends on his/her depth of lexis.

In learning English language, lexical items are essential elements in language reception and production skills (Nation, 2011). Lexis is an important linguistic element for effective language use whether in or out of the school environment. In schools, competent language learners often possess sufficient vocabulary to experience scholastic success. Without sufficient lexis, an L2 learner will find difficulties in the use of the L2 structures (Nunan, 1991). The lack of lexical knowledge is very difficult for L2 learners to overcome since they depend heavily on vocabulary (Huckin & Coady, 1999). According to Meara (1980), lexis is perceived to be the L2 learners' real source of difficulty while learning the L2. This statement may possibly reflect the unsystematic nature of a lexical item. In other words, lexis does not follow systematic rules that a learner can rely on to develop his/her language knowledge.

Regardless of the complications that language learners encounter learning and using L2 lexis, accuracy in using lexical items is an important factor in exams. According to Schmitt (1999), in language examinations, vocabulary is one of the language elements that is usually measured. Moreover, many L2 learners attempt to memorise hundreds of words and use several reference materials such as dictionaries for the purpose of communication. Thus, the importance of learning lexis is generally admitted by most language teachers and now studies are investigating effective approaches towards the teaching of vocabulary (e.g., Hemchua & Schmitt, 2006; James, 2013; Lewis, 1993; Milton, 2009; Nation, 2011; Richards, 1976; Schmitt, 2010; Shalaby et al., 2009). Some of these studies take the form of EA of learners' language production with respect to vocabulary, which is the focus of this research.

2.1.1 The Relationship of Lexical Knowledge to Successful Communication Through Translation

According to Schmitt (2000, p. 55), lexical knowledge is crucial for L2 learners since the lack of that knowledge of the L2 hampers "successful communication." Moreover, SLA research claims that acquiring lexis is necessary for the successful use of the language and it is essential in producing spoken and written texts (e.g., Barcroft, 2004; Huckin & Coady, 1999; Laufer, 1986; Ramos & Dario, 2015). In addition, Nation (2001) stated that there is a correlation between lexical knowledge and effective language use; the more an individual uses the language the more lexical knowledge he/she gains and vice versa. Therefore, lexis can be considered as a crucial tool for individuals to express their thoughts and ideas.

In translation, research has emphasised the importance of lexical knowledge and its relation to language proficiency (e.g., Masrai & Milton, 2012; Milton, 2009; Nation, 2006; Schmitt, 2008) and to successful translation (e.g., Baker,

2011; Eszenyi, 2016; Hatim, 2001; Munday, 2012; Robinson, 2004). A professional translator must be able to deliver the source text's intended meaning by choosing the correct lexical expression in the L2 (Hatim & Mason, 2005). Obtaining sufficient lexical knowledge in both the L1 and the L2 is crucial for translators to maintain full comprehension of the L1 message and to be able to analyse its features. In addition, accuracy in lexical choice is significant in producing adequate translation that conveys the L1 text style and meaning. According to Nida and Taber (2003/1969), "translating consists in reproducing in the receptor language the closest natural equivalent of the source language message, first in terms of meaning and secondly in terms of style" (p. 12). This study focuses on university students of English language and translation in KSA. The focus, however, is mainly on improving students' skills in the English language presuming they previously have an advanced proficiency in the Arabic language since it is their L1. Conversely, recent studies in the Saudi context have discovered that students' English proficiency at the university level is below the required level to work either in the translation industry or in any profession related to languages (Alharthi, 2011; AlSaif, 2011; Masrai & Milton, 2012; Rahman, 2011; Shukri, 2014). This low level of English language ability was obvious in various research that scrutinised students' basic receptive and productive skills. One of the studies conducted focused on measuring students' lexical knowledge and its influence on language proficiency (Masrai & Milton, 2012). Other studies have focused on examining the common influential aspects on the learning process such as motivation and attitudes of students towards learning English language, students' learning strategies, and teaching practices (Alseweed, 2009; McMullen, 2009; Moskovsky & Alrabai, 2009). However, there have been calls for more research and analytical studies to identify the problematic linguistic areas in order to improve Saudi students' English proficiency (e.g., Javid et al., 2013; Khan, 2011; Rahman & Alhaisoni, 2013).

This research concentrates on the use of English lexis in translation texts of different genres. Such information about the nature of words and their incorrect use is valuable in deciding on the lexical knowledge needed for professional translators. Thus, one of the main aims of the current research is scrutinising the problematic lexical items in the English language that cause English major students in Saudi universities to translate inefficiently. The next sections will offer a brief clarification about the nature of lexis and lexical knowledge acquisition.

2.1.2 The Nature of Lexis and Lexical Knowledge Acquisition

Knowing a word depends on how much information a speaker can deduce from it. Many language researchers have attempted to approve such a claim in an attempt to explore the appropriate ways to teach L2 lexis (e.g., Allen, 1983; Carter et al.,

1988; Lessard-Clouston, 2013). According to Jack Richards (1976), there are several aspects of knowledge associated with a lexical item. He examined the frequency of words, vocabulary breadth in L1 speakers, collocation, register, word association, and semantic structure including the linguistic, psycholinguistic, and sociolinguistic aspects of lexical knowledge. Finally, Richards listed seven lexical knowledge characteristics that are essential to identify a word including morphology, collocations, word association, semantic aspects, connotations, and lexical use frequency.

In the field of language acquisition, Paul Nation (2001) listed the following aspects of lexical knowledge based on Richards's classification: syntax, collocation, lexical use frequency, compatibility, meaning, concept, word associations, written form and spoken form. He also includes other aspects such as spelling and pronunciation that are significant in assessing the knowledge of a word (see Fig. 2.1). This study is correlated with Nation's classification of word knowledge in the description and classification of the lexical items produced by Saudi L2 learners in their translations.

The acquisition of lexical knowledge is a complicated process. Aspects of lexical knowledge that depend mainly on context (e.g., collocations, semantics, and associations) might carry a lot of information (Nation, 2001). For example, in a certain context, a word can have different semantic features and knowing all these features can reflect the knowledge an individual has of that word. Norbert Schmitt (2010), formulated a scale for each aspect, based on Nation's lexical knowledge assumptions. He explained in detail how learners at different proficiency levels of English progress along this scale. He stated that speech and written forms along with grammar are learnt first. Schmitt (2010) explained that the remaining aspects of lexical knowledge (collocation, register, frequency, and associations) are more difficult to learn, which in return requires lengthy exposure to English to be acquired. These assumptions of lexical knowledge are relevant to this present study as it examines the learner's incorrect assumptions of a word at the level of form and content. Such incorrect assumptions occur when the learner has limited knowledge of a lexical item. Many incorrect assumptions in one aspect of lexical knowledge, for instance semantic lexical errors, may indicate the difficulty of that aspect of knowledge to be learnt.

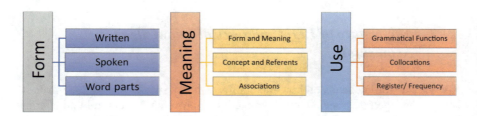

Fig. 2.1 Aspects of lexical knowledge (Based on Nation, 2001)

2.2 The Teaching of Lexis

Learning the English language, like every other language, involves the acquisition of two common linguistic elements: grammar and lexis. In the education setting, the two items take the form of the teaching of language rules and vocabulary teaching. An important aspect of language teaching is also the identification of student errors and teaching students how to avoid these errors. Both grammar and lexis are essential to communication; however, in the field of SLA and EA, research focuses much more on grammar. A significant amount of research has been conducted to explore how learners develop grammatical patterns, common errors and find solutions to prevent grammatical errors.

According to Llach (2011), researchers justify their focus on grammatical aspects, because of the "unstable and unsystematic nature of the lexicon" (p. 70). For most researchers, the lexicon is apparently a group of words that cannot be systematised. Maybe for that reason, less attention has been paid to vocabulary in the teaching and learning of the L2. Usually, grammatical rules are taught explicitly in the L2 classroom and errors are corrected based on these rules, supposing that learners will expand their vocabulary knowledge through the learning process. Nevertheless, since the 1990s, a growing body of literature has encouraged the *lexical approach* which integrates grammar and vocabulary teaching by focusing on the teaching of language in chunks supporting students by providing both content and grammatical context. However, the teaching of lexical chunks and unpacking of errors within these chunks can still lead to the same problem as teaching individual vocabulary items. Incorrect lexical items will always be considered as common errors that should be learnt and remembered if systems for these items are not developed. As well as the content and grammatical contexts already mentioned above, psycholinguistic research systematises words according to their semantic aspects (based on the meaning associated with the word) and formal aspects (based on the word forms) (Aitchison, 2012). Other studies propose that a group of words can be categorised as lexical chunks based on how they occur in a text (Lewis, 1993).

2.2.1 Lexical Chunks

The term lexical chunks has been defined and explained differently in the literature. The various definitions of this language phenomenon show both the significance and the complexity of lexis. Lewis (1993) defined the term lexical chunks as the useful component bits or lexical items produced when continuous text is broken into easy to memorise lexical items. In other words, lexical chunks denote individual morphemes, parts of phrases, and in some instances longer bits of speech stored in the memory and retrieved in the form of pre-assembled language bits. In the English language, for instance, lexical chunks may include such phrases as *take on*, *a fraction of a second*, or *a period of time* among others which comprise pre-fabricated formulaic items that are retained by the speakers of the language and retrieved in combination with other chunks thus aiding the ease with which L1 speakers of the language, in particular, communicate. To Lewis (2002), chunks are essentially the component bits that make up a language. Thus, by learning chunks appropriate for different situations, learners are able to better appreciate the essential patterns of a particular language.

When studying lexical chunks, it is worth noting that lexical phrases are not only associated with the syntactic structure (form), but also with the functional content (meaning) of the attendant phrases. Lexical phrases include both institutionalised sentences and sentence frames, with the former having more readily identifiable pragmatic meaning than the latter. Thus, when analysing continuous text for lexical phrases, one should not only be keen to note the syntactic structure of the whole phrase but also to understand the meaning of the whole phrase. Paying attention to the precise words expressing the pragmatic function of a lexical phrase is the key to the retention of the correct form of a whole phrase and effective chunking. Lewis's definition of lexical chunks is related to this current study, since it aims to classify lexical errors based on their form and content.

2.2.2 Classifications of Lexical Chunks

Lewis (1993) classifies lexical chunks into four different categories: poly-words, collocations, institutionalised expressions, and sentence frames. Poly-words are in essence fixed combinations of lexical items or words and include such phrases as <by the way>, <look up>, or <on the other hand>. Poly-words tend to be relatively short, in that they mostly consist of two or three words; do not have a specific word class; and their meaning varies depending on the words they are made up of. Collocations comprise two co-occurring words. They include such pairs of words as *bread and butter* and *knife and fork*. Collocations tend to be infinitely numerous given the high number of word pairs that go together and can be either free or fixed collocations. Akin to individual words, however, collocations are neither pragmatically identifiable nor pragmatically tied and hence they are closely connected to the content of what is being expressed as opposed to what is being done. Institutionalised expressions denote multi-word units through which users of language manage certain aspects of their oral interaction. They are pragmatic in nature: a function and character that enable the language user to effectively communicate what they are doing. They include such expressions as *not yet*, *sorry to interrupt*, *can I give you a hand*, *just a moment please*, and *certainly not* among others. Institutionalised expressions are useful for non-native learners in that the repertoire of the associated phrases facilitate efficient processing in both writing and speech. Sentence frames are chunks utilised in writing rather than in oral interactions and include such expressions as *my opinion is that* (Qader, 2016).

The classification by Lewis (1993) is important in that it incorporates types of chunks that have a direct relationship with both oral and written forms of the language. The classification can thus be used in studies concerned with both writing and speaking. The classification is also significant in that it complements that by Nattinger and DeCarrico (1992) which classifies lexical chunks into sentence builders, phrasal constraints, institutionalised expressions, and poly-words (Qader, 2016). These linguistic categories are important for the current study since it aims to identify the characteristics of lexical errors; however, this study aims to extend the classification system of lexical chunks to include other categories of lexical items.

2.2.3 Approaches to Teaching Lexical Chunks

There are several teaching approaches that apply lexical chunks to L2 teaching. Michael Lewis's pedagogical chunking approach is the most popular and influential one in L2 teaching. The approach rests on the premise that vocabulary is redundantly stored in the memory as both individual morphemes and parts of phrases and in some cases longer chunks of speech that have been memorised (Lewis, 1993). Lewis thus posited this has momentous implications for vocabulary learning in that if L2 learners were taught how to break up continuous text of the language they are learning in a useful manner and then memorise the appropriate lexical items of the L2, they would not only be able to store the chunks, but also efficiently process them as they communicate or write in the new language. Thus, by enhancing the awareness of the L2 learners on the lexical units that make up a text written in the L2, the learners will be able to have an extensive repertoire of whole phrases in their precise words effectively empowering them to identify their patterns in any text and thus memorise and retrieve them with ease whenever needed. Pedagogical chunking is thus not only integral to language learning but also to teaching of vocabulary as it helps L2 learners to create lexical phrases that are more effective by chunking unfamiliar material in meaningful ways. Pedagogical chunking training will probably ensure teachers increasingly use awareness raising tasks to enhance the capacity of their L2 learners to identify multi-word chunks or items effectively developing their proficiency in the L2 vocabulary.

As part of the current research goals, an analysis of lexical errors produced by Saudi learners of English will be conducted to raise English language instructors' awareness of the common lexical errors made by their learners. The study's results will in turn help them to apply more effective teaching techniques or develop more suitable strategies to address their learners' needs and weaknesses, which, consequently, can improve their language learning outcomes.

The following section deals with language learners' errors with respect to lexis. First, it explains what is meant by *lexical errors* and provides a critical overview of language errors in general. Then, it presents the common approaches used to examine language errors.

2.3 Lexical Errors

A language error, in general, refers to an unacceptable form of language whether in spoken or written form. The occurrence of language errors could be attributed to the learner's incomplete knowledge of the L2 which may reflect his/her level of competence systematically (Crystal, 2008). According to Carl James (2013), language errors usually occur when there is "no intention to commit one" (p. 77). The deliberate incorrect choice of a lexical item is referred to as a deviation in language use rather than an error. For corpus data, it could be problematic, because the only way to identify and describe errors is through the written text and it is difficult to decide if the deviation occurs deliberately or not.

James (2013) defined the notion of error as slips that are easily identified, mistakes that can be self-corrected once pointed out, errors that cannot be self-corrected, and solecisms which refer to the breaches of language rules. EA is primarily concerned with errors and mistakes. It is problematic for corpus data to distinguish between mistakes and errors, because it is difficult to know how the learner thinks when he/she uses the language. Consequently, all unacceptable forms of the L2 in this present study can only be categorised as *errors* since it deals with corpus texts.

Lexical errors appear to be a pervasive feature of L2 learners' spoken and written production. These errors usually occur at multiple linguistic levels, mainly formal and semantic levels. A wide body of language research has been conducted to explore learners' language errors since errors can explain how L2 learners learn and acquire the L2. In particular, lexical errors have received less attention due to the complicated system of lexis. As Llach (2011) pointed out, researchers justify their focus on grammatical aspects of learners' language, because of the "unstable and unsystematic nature of the lexicon" (p. 70).

Llach (2011, p. 71) defined the concept *lexical error* as "the deviations in the learner's production of the L2 norm with regards to the use in production and reception of lexical items." It is not an easy task to decide what a lexical error is or what a grammatical error is since the distinction between them is sometimes confusing. Some linguists consider lexical errors as purely grammatical, while others interpret lexical errors as formal errors, content errors, or errors of classes (Llach, 2011). Lexical errors are defined differently based on what they really mean in a certain study. According to Llach (2011, p. 74), "wrong lexical choice, errors in the lexical choice, lexical deviancies, vocabulary errors, incongruencies in lexical gridding, semantic deviation, lexical confusions, synforms, lexical deficiencies, lexical disruptions, lexical approximations and lexical simplification" can all represent the notion of lexical errors. Despite the disagreement among researchers on what constitutes a lexical error and how it should be classified, lexical errors occur due to causes that can be analysed, explained, and categorised.

> Lexical errors are not accidental or random, but respond to systematic causes that can be accounted for in the analysis of the language sample. In fact, most authors attempt at finding these causes and, thus, at better explaining the lexical errors encountered. Lexical errors are liable to be explained, and therefore, classified. (Llach, 2011, p. 74)

EA studies are always interested in defining lexical errors within their scope of the analysis, forming a classification system of errors and then revealing the reasons behind the errors found in the data used. According to Llach (2011), the type of data used in a study can determine the definition and role of lexical errors, and taxonomies are created for categorising lexical errors based on the data. A lexical error in the current study is an incorrect choice of an L2 lexical item whether in form or in content.

The following section provides a critical overview of language errors in the field of language acquisition.

2.3.1 A Critical Overview of Language Errors

Language errors are by and large viewed as a manifestation of an ineffective fragment of a language. According to James (2013), committing a language error and, in particular, errors in writing and/or speaking constitutes the hallmark of the uniqueness of human beings and can at best be regarded "as an unsuccessful bit of language" (p. 1). Language errors have thus been perceived as a *part and parcel* of the efforts by humans to learn and acquire a new language. Other scholars, among them Norrish (1983), perceived language errors as a systematic deviation informed by unsuccessful learning of language and hence consistent incorrect use of its lexical items. Richards (2003) characterised language errors as an indication of incomplete learning of language as indicated by the significant and imperfect usage of the L2 word items. There seems to be a consensus between the past and present perceptions of language errors that linguistic errors are a function of incomplete language learning as manifested in the ineffective usage of the language. For this project, language errors are perceived as a systematic deviation in language forms owing to various factors such as the learner's L1, the nature of L2 writing, and the learning context.

Current research views learner language errors as an indication of the failure to properly master the L2. According to Muftah and Rafik-Galea (2013), learner language errors show not only what the L2 students have not commanded but also the aspects of the L2 they are yet to internalise. The lexical errors committed by learners can be (rightly) regarded as a sign that they are yet to properly master and internalise the lexical items of the L2 and hence their inadequate lexical knowledge and the related errors they commit. Learners' language errors and the analysis of errors thus offer the best avenue for gauging the definite proficiency levels of the students in an L2.

2.3.2 Approaches to Examine Language Errors

There are several theories for examining language errors. Interlanguage theory, Contrastive Analysis hypothesis, and EA hypothesis are the three commonly used approaches in the field of SLA to examine learners' language errors. In the following section, these approaches are critically interpreted and their strengths and weaknesses are explored on the basis of the current literature available.

2.3.2.1 Interlanguage Approach

In the field of L2 acquisition, a new language learning approach was developed in 1969. Any language from the perspective of this new trend has been perceived as a vigorous world with its own structure, features, syntax, and lexis. This new approach was called "Interlanguage" (Selinker, 1972). The interlanguage theory was the first systematic attempt to clarify the L2 learning process from a nativist perspective, and was first proposed by Selinker between 1969 and 1972. It is defined as "a system that has a structurally intermediate status between the native and target languages" (Brown, 2007, p. 225). It is the transitional language that L2 learners may encounter while learning the L2. Selinker (1972, p. 214) indicated that: "The existence of a separate linguistic system based on the observable output which results from a learner's attempted production of a TL norm. This linguistic system we will call 'interlanguage' (IL)."

Selinker refers to the notion of *interlanguage* as a linguistic tool, which was created by the L2 learner to use the L2. It was employed by the language learners to interact with their learning environment despite the correctness of their language production. However, the language used by those learners was considered as a natural language with its own rules which was comprehended among its users. Selinker (1972) believed that studying L2 learner language production can help to understand the strategies and processes that trigger the learner's language behaviour. Therefore, the interlanguage approach, based on Selinker point of view, is the result of several cognitive processes that are triggered in the human brain. These language behaviours are activated while learning any language after the age of puberty. Selinker (1972) identified five psycholinguistic processes underlying the interlanguage system:

1. Language transfer: fossilised linguistic features that occurred in the interlanguage system owing to L1 transfer phenomena;
2. Transfer of training: fossilisation due to certain linguistic features found in the instruction while learning the L2;
3. L2 learning strategies: fossilisation due to some approach adopted by the learner while learning the L2 material;
4. Communication strategies: fossilisation due to the learner's identifiable approach to communicate with the L2 native speakers; and
5. Overgeneralisation of L2 linguistic features: fossilisation due to the use of the L2 rules and its semantic features where it is not required.

2.3 Lexical Errors

The above processes are illustrated in Fig. 2.2.

Gass and Selinker (2008) stated that learners' interlanguage might have some rules that match the L2 rules, but in some respects the rules could be different. These learners' rules, assumptions, or hypotheses might occur due to several reasons, such as the learner's L1, innate language knowledge, L2 experience, and creative hypotheses. The previous research has noticed inconsistency in some learners' interlanguage because of the increased exposure to the L2 environment. Hence, an increased experience and involvement in the L2 would make the learner's interlanguage more complex.

The interlanguage approach for examining learner language errors is based on the premise that upon struggling with a new language, an independent and active learning mind devises its own generalisations regarding the language. The approach thus deems language errors committed by the learners based on the rules of the L2 to be correct based on the rules of the interlanguage the learners invent and deem as the interim and suitably practicable substitute (Frith, 1978). The interlanguage theory thus regards language errors as a key aspect of the L2 learning process, diminishing the need for emphasis on error-free usage of the new language among the learners (Al-khresheh, 2015). The interlanguage approach perceives language errors committed by learners as a product of this process and hence regards any attempts to penalise the related errors as counterproductive as it impedes the capacity of the learners to arrange their growth in learning the new language in the relevant manner.

Among the strengths of the interlanguage approach to learner language errors, assessment is the fact that it provides a framework for comparing the structures of the learner's L1 and L2 in the process of being learnt. A comparison of the structure of the L1 and the structure of the L2 of the learners is essential in shedding light to the cause and origin of the language errors committed by learners (Tarone, 2018). When examining lexical errors among students for instance, the approach would be critical in helping to understand how the different types of lexical errors committed by learners come about and the best ways of guiding the language learning process

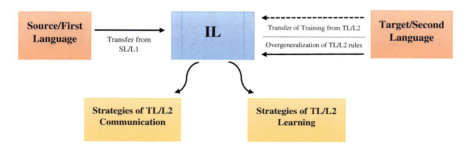

Fig. 2.2 Fossilisation-determining processes (Adapted from Krzeszowski, 1977)

to minimise or even eliminate the errors. By facilitating comparison between the structures of the L1 and L2, the approach would also be useful in identifying the psycholinguistic processes responsible for shaping interlanguage in the course of language learning, among them learning strategies, communication strategies, training transfer, overgeneralisation, and L1 transfer. This would not only be useful in helping to better understand the related language errors but also how to best mitigate them to facilitate successful language learning. In addition, the fact that the interlanguage approach focuses on the language competence can help in predicting the proficiency and language learning trajectory of the learner. According to Mahmood and Murad (2018), the psychological competence of the learner in the L2 is an indispensable indicator of their knowledge in an L2. Underlying assumptions on the L1 of the learner influence their process of learning the L2 and hence the more similar the L1 and L2 of the learner are, the faster they gain competence in the L2.

A major shortcoming of the interlanguage approach for examining learner language errors is its claim that all interlanguages fossilise. Fossilisation as a phenomenon in language learning has been a major source of controversy among interlanguage scholars with regard to its inevitability and origins (Tarone, 2018). Some scholars such as Moreno (2016) argued fossilisation is not inevitable and is a function of sociolinguistic forces, while others such as Scovel (1988) and Selinker (1972) stated fossilisation is inevitable and it's a function of neurolinguistic forces. The argument put forth by the latter counterproductively regards language learning as a finite process while the position of the former group of scholars attests to the continuous and almost infinite nature of L2 learning. In other words, interlanguage fossilisation cannot be limited to cerebral lateralisation but is rather an open process, and attainment of interlanguage fossilisation by a learner is not explicit. This is corroborated by Corder (1967) who affirmed that interlanguage development among learners of an L2 takes place through a series of consecutive stages at the end of which one cannot definitively declare learning of the language has ceased. Another weakness associated with interlanguage fossilisation is its hypothesis that interlanguage study related data should only be limited to the L2 usage in meaningful communication. Frith (1978) asserted that the claim is counterproductive to language learning as it advocates for disregard of language errors committed by learning during communication that is not deemed meaningful. This opens up the possibility of language learners becoming accustomed to using syntactic, morphological, and phonological features of the L2 in ways that vary from the applicable L2 rules. The outcome will be a situation where language learners continue committing certain significant language errors even after years of exposure to and instruction in the L2.

2.3.2.2 Contrastive Analysis Approach

Pedagogically, the contrastive analysis approach is closely linked with structuralism and behaviourism and hence mostly regarded as a structural-behavioural linguistics theory (Mahmood & Murad, 2018). According to Xia (2014), a key

2.3 Lexical Errors

presumption of the contrastive analysis approach is the claim that language learning is a function of habit formation and imitation of the L2's verbal patterns. The theory also holds that L2 learning becomes more complex where the verbal patterns of the L2 are absent in L1 or vary from those of the L1. As can be deduced from the foregoing perspective, the approach is thus an essential part of structural linguistics.

As its name suggests, the contrastive analysis theory provides an approach for comparison of languages with a view to establishing possible errors, thus helping to determine what is worth learning and what is not worth learning during L2 learning. This is affirmed by Johansson (2008) who argued that the comparative capacity of the approach offers a definitive way of discovering potential errors likely to be committed by learners in an L2 learning situation which ultimately helps isolate language learning areas that ought to be focused on. Therefore, the application of the contrastive analysis approach not only facilitates a better understanding of the ways in which the L1 and the L2 writing systems vary from one to another but also enhanced awareness of the potential L2 learner errors that could emanate from the differences. Variously put, the comparative capacity of the approach enables L2 teachers to better anticipate errors likely to be committed by their L2 learners, effectively allowing them the opportunity to reorient their pedagogical practice and activities for enhanced language learning outcomes.

One of the key strengths of the contrastive analysis approach is its capacity to help predict L2 learners' errors in particular language learning situations. Wardhaugh (1970) argued that there exist two versions of the approach with the strong version being able to predict L2 errors among learners and the weak version only predicting L1 language errors manifested in the usage of the L2. In spite of the discrepancy between the predictive ability of the two versions of the theory, the contrastive analysis approach capacity to describe language use patterns that could aid or impede language learning in the future is undisputed. This is echoed by Ipek (2009) who suggested systematic comparison of the L2 and its culture with the L1 of the learner and its culture may help predict and explain the linguistic patterns that could either assist or hinder learning of the new language. Comparing languages is beneficial in that it will help to describe the differences and similarities between the native and learned languages, helping to forecast potential problematic areas. The predictive ability of the approach thus has the potential to enable language teachers to prepare more focused and current pedagogical materials and classroom activities effectively supporting more efficient learning of the L2 by directly addressing the pre-identified areas of difficulty. The approach will also enable language teachers to concentrate their pedagogy on the L2 learning difficulties inducing linguistic patterns to enhance the familiarity of the learners with them and instil in them linguistic behaviours then preclude transfer of error-producing native culture and linguistics to the L2. This premise by the contrastive analytical approach is also advantageous in that it has helped enrich the area of L2 acquisition and applied linguistics in general by laying a foundation for analytic procedures and pedagogical practice that have been successfully applied to translation and other relevant fields of language learning.

The contrastive analysis approach is not free from its share of shortcomings. Mahmood and Murad (2018) speak out about the supposed lack of objectivity and consistency in the procedures put forth by the approach. This is demonstrated by its failure to apply the same standards in its description of the L2 and the L1. Several scholars (e.g., Chastain, 1976; Corder, 1974) felt the inconsistency and subjectivity of the contrastive analysis procedures rendered the outcomes of the approach unreliable. Subsequent empirical research such as that conducted by Whitman (1970) affirmed the unreliability of the results of the contrastive analysis procedures by demonstrating the unfounded nature of the predictions reached through the application of the approach. Another weakness of the approach is its tendency to treat areas of learning difficulty as origins of language errors, disregarding the propensity of learners to be more conscious of the problematic areas and to specially focus on excelling in them, precluding their chances of committing the related errors. The approach also tends to treat L1 influence as the only source of language errors committed by L2 learners. The view disregards intralingual sources of language errors among other common influences (Kaweera, 2013). The perspective that the more varied the culture and the language of an L2 learner is from their L1 the higher the number of language errors the learner is likely to make is erroneous. Mahmood and Murad (2018) have posited studies demonstrating the unreliable nature of error prediction hence proving the claim by the approach to be invalid.

2.3.2.3 Error Analysis Approach

The premise of the EA approach is anchored on the presumed dominance of cognitive psychology. This shift in the psychological framework underscores the reality that educators have switched their orientation, as Corder (1967) indicates, from teaching to learning. The EA theory explains language errors committed by L2 learners based on their sources before analysing and remedying them. Unlike the contrastive analysis approach, the EA approach does not treat L1 as the sole cause of the errors committed by L2 learnings but rather endeavours to evaluate other potential contributing causes. According to Mahmood and Murad (2018), the approach casts the EA theory as a response to the shortcomings of the contrastive analysis theory particularly given that it is associated with structuralism and behaviourism and its hypotheses are based on the principles of the contrastive approach. Compared to contrastive analysis, however, the scope of EA is wider given the fact that the approach assesses psychological and linguistic factors while the former only concerns itself with the linguistic aspects. This is explicitly substantiated by Ellis and Barhkuizen's (2005) view that EA as an approach can be used to evaluate errors committed in writing and speech by L2 learners. Therefore, while the contrastive analysis approach concerns itself with the pedagogical materials based on a comparison of L2 and L1, EA focuses on the L2 performance as demonstrated in the writing and speech of the learner.

2.3 Lexical Errors

From the perspective of language learning and teaching, EA is essentially an approach through which unacceptable forms of L2 produced by a learner are identified and classified systematically based on the applicable linguistic procedures and tenets. By providing a technique for recognising, grouping, and methodically understanding the L2 errors committed by learners, the EA approach helps language teachers to discern the assumptions and strategies learners employ during the L2 learning process besides enabling them to examine the L2 proficiency levels of their students.

Key among the strengths of the EA approach is its ability to reorient the focus of applied linguistics from forecasting errors associated with L2 learning to evaluation of L2 errors. As asserted by Corder (1967) and reiterated by Mahmood and Murad (2018), EA concerns itself with the assessment of L2 errors with a view to understanding their causes and how they can be corrected. The approach provides a model for detecting, analysing, and locating problem areas for systematic linguistic errors made by L2 learners, techniques that effectively provide applied linguists with a solid basis for establishing the best pedagogical approaches for addressing the errors during L2 learning. Another strength of the EA approach is its treatment of language performance as the best indicator of the competence of the learner in L2. Corder (1967) posited performance as manifested in the L2 writing and speaking abilities of an L2 learner as the tangible evidence of the appropriate and correct usage of the L2 linguistic systems and categories. The perspective offered by the EA approach allows for the assessment of the grammatical and lexical appropriateness of the utterances and writings produced by an L2 learner which can enable language teachers to gauge the L2 knowledge and competence levels of their learners based on how appropriately and correctly they are able to use the applicable L2 systems and categories based on their performance of the L2. The EA approach is also lauded for its ability to offer feedback to language instructors. According to Mahmood and Murad (2018), the feedback obtained through the approach allows teachers to re-evaluate the efficacy of the designs of their syllabuses and the appropriateness of the teaching time allocated for each learning area. Through the EA approach language teachers are able to continually review and reorient their teaching materials and pedagogical techniques and approaches for more successful learning of the L2.

The EA approach, unavoidably, has its shortcomings. A key drawback of the approach is its use of terminologies that are inconsistent in its efforts to explain language errors. The use of such terminologies as systematic error and unsystematic error which denote language competence related errors and language performance errors respectively tend to be confusing due to the thin line between the two (Corder, 1967; Mahmood & Murad, 2018). Regardless of the applicable terminology, language errors essentially denote gaps in the L2 knowledge of the learner and often manifest in their performance of the language as reflected in the forms of the L2 they produce. Another downside of the approach is its tendency to restrict its focus on the errors that L2 learners commit while disregarding instances where they correctly use the L2 (Mahmood & Murad, 2018; Young, 2000). The skewed outlook has the disadvantage of making learners of a foreign language feel like the forms of the L2 they produce are always riddled with errors which could discourage their future performance and hence be counterproductive to the L2 process learning in the long run. As much as the approach endeavours to assess, classify, and correct errors, its focus should be reoriented to allow for acknowledgement of and building on instances of fluent, appropriate, and correct usage of the L2 for the purpose of motivating and encouraging the learner in the learning process. However, focusing on errors is not entirely counterproductive as it draws attention to the learner language errors and the questions of why they occur, makes teachers more aware of the errors committed, and lays a foundation for learners to self-correct (Krashen, 1994). The approach is also faulted for its inability to discern instances where L2 learners employ the avoidance strategy to evade using or dealing with L2 structures and features they find complicated (Young, 2000). This is due to the tendency of the approach to only focus on detecting, assessing, and addressing the errors committed resulting in instances where certain features of the L2 ought to have been applicable being missed.

Error Analysis Procedures

In EA studies, there are some steps as suggested by Corder (1974) for conducting an analysis of language errors. Below is a brief explanation of each of these procedures of EA and how they are perceived by the current research.

The First Step: Collection of a Language Sample

Language sample collection commences with first choosing the appropriate sample and then deciding on the appropriate technique for collecting the sample. According to Keller (2010), there are three kinds of samples, namely: the massive sample, where a number of L2 use samples are drawn from a huge population of learners; the specific sample, where a single language use sample is drawn from a small population of learners; and the incidental sample, where a single sample is drawn from an individual L2 learner. Al-Khresheh (2016) argues that collection of a learner language sample that is well-defined is pegged on how well the different factors that influence errors among L2 learners are put into consideration. These factors include the L1, level of education and language learning experience of the learner, and the L2 content, genre, and medium involved (Al-Khresheh, 2016; Amiri & Puteh, 2017).

The Second Step: Identification of Errors

This step entails scrutiny of the various learner language samples collected to detect and determine instances of L2 use that are inappropriate and incorrect. In written instances of learner language performance, the forms of sentences and words produced by an L2 learner are checked and compared with the corresponding correct and appropriate words and sentences in the L2. This helps identify erroneous forms of words and sentences produced by the learners as well as instances where the preferred forms of the same have not been used leading to inappropriate L2 usage. According to Ellis (2008), identification of errors is not as straightforward as it may sound since some *supposed* errors may be an accidental slip or any other type of deviant form and not necessary a language error. A good grasp of what constitutes mistakes and errors and of the distinction between the two is thus critical for accurate identification of language errors.

The Third Step: Description of Errors

This step entails accounting for all the identified errors and classifying them into the respective types. According to Ellis (1997), errors may be classified based on whether they are grammatical or lexical and then into the respective subtypes or by examining the forms of the L2 produced and then categorising the errors based on how they vary from correct performance of the learner language. Explanation and classification of language errors is essential in diagnosing the learning difficulties being experienced by the learners in different phases of the learning process besides helping to discern how the error patterns evolve as time passes by. Al-Khresheh (2016) states that description of errors allows for a vivid explanation of L2 errors, how frequently they occur or are committed, and development of groups and subgroups of errors from which a complete taxonomy for the applicable learner language errors can be derived.

The Fourth Step: Explanation of Errors

The focus of this step is to explain and clarify the reasons as to why the detected language errors occur or are committed. As elucidated by Mahmood and Murad (2018), language errors committed by learners are considerably predictable and systematic. Consequently, language errors do not occur haphazardly and hence it is possible to explain why they arise. Ellis (1997) stated that language learners have the tendency to construct rules that are different from the L2 which causes them to systematically commit the identified errors. Ellis argued not all errors are systematic in that some tend to be universal. Therefore, when explaining errors, it is critical to clarify whether an error is universal, that is affecting many learners in particular stage of language learning, systematic, or prevalent only among learners whose L1 has an identical linguistic property.

The Final Step: Evaluation of Errors

This step entails assessment of the gravity of the identified L2 errors committed by learners. The goal of this phase of EA is to facilitate a deeper understanding of the L2 errors and their effects on language learning by the learner to establish a basis for developing mechanisms through which the learner can be assisted and supported to learn the L2. Ellis (1997) regarded some language errors to be graver than others, especially given their potential to inhibit the intelligibility and comprehensibility of verbal and written forms of the L2 produced by the learner. In this respect, error evaluation is a vital phase of EA in that it helps to categorise learner errors that are more serious, thereby allowing language instructors to concentrate their pedagogical efforts on addressing these errors.

Implications of Error Analysis

In the field of language teaching, EA findings have significant pedagogical implications for both teachers and syllabus designers. In the classroom setting, EA can be very useful in developing remedial measures, preparing appropriate teaching materials, and making insightful suggestions about the strategies employed by language learners. As pointed out by Corder (1967, p. 167), EA provides teachers with information about the learner's progress in language learning and what remains for them to learn. Being aware of the learner's progress, the teacher can use different teaching practices according to their students' needs. Additionally, EA can work as a feedback tool for language teachers since it reflects the efficacy level of the teaching techniques used and the language gaps that need more consideration. Above all, language errors can be addressed efficiently when their sources are identified (Brown, 2007).

The results and information gained from EA are valuable for syllabus designers as well. EA studies provide useful details of the language difficulties encountered by learners and their weaknesses at a specific language learning level. Furthermore, it confirms what language items need more attention in syllabus design and how they can be presented in an effective way. Brown (2007) highlighted the contribution of EA and studying language errors to the understanding of the language learning process, which can enhance teaching practices and the learning outcomes.

2.4 Sources of Language Errors

Errors are derived from two main sources: interlingual and intralingual influence, according to J.C. Richards (2015). For this project, the sources of lexical errors are one of the essential aspects which will be investigated and will be discussed in the following sections.

2.4.1 Interlingual Influence

Interlingual influence refers to forms of the L2 produced by the learner that are reflective of the form and structure of their L1 (Richards, 2015). Al-Khresheh (2016) asserted interlingual errors are a function of the effect of the mother

2.4 Sources of Language Errors

tongue or the L1 of the learner. Schachter and Celce-Murcia (1977) went further and explained that interlingual errors are caused by the effect of the L1 on the L2 production, particularly in areas where the L1 of the learner differs with the L2. Language errors originating from interlingual influence are thus a function of the negative transfer of certain L1 linguistic forms and structures to the production of the L2. Al-Khresheh (2016) attributed the negative transfer to application of L1 pattern rules to the L2 leading to errors. This form of interlingual interference impacts negatively on L2 learning and hence the need for language teachers to understand how the L1 of the learner affects their L2 production.

Research has demonstrated the impact of interlingual interference on written forms of the L2. Mahmoud (2005) and Al-Khresheh (2016) contended interlingual interference affects the writing process in the L2. Another study by Lim (2010) echoes these findings and terms interlingual interference as a major cause of the L2 acquisition difficulties experienced by learners. Given that a large proportion of errors are caused by interlingual influence, the negative transfer of the L1 comprises a complex concept that can only be comprehended from the perspective of cognitive models of language learning as opposed to the behavioural ones (Ellis, 1997). Interlingual errors produced by learners of an L2 occur due to the processes that inform incorrect transfer of linguistic structures and rule patterns of the L1 to the L2.

Interlingual influences of the negative L1 transfer notwithstanding, there is a consensus among scholars that the use of the L1 when learning L2 is unavoidable. Al-Nofaie (2010) contended learners of a foreign language tend to use their L1 in the process of learning the new language. Al-Khresheh (2016) argued that what matters is whether the use of the L1 to learn L2 is negative or positive. Negative use of the L1 to learn the L2 leads to negative transfer of L1 structures in the production of the L2, hence the occurrence of interlingual errors. The use of L1 in learning L2 should thus be positive to avert the incidence of the related errors.

2.4.2 Intralingual Influence

Intralingual influence denotes items and forms produced by an L2 learner that are reflective of the generalisations the learner has constructed due to the incomplete knowledge of and limited familiarity with the L2. According to Richards (2015), as some learners learn the L2, they tend to derive rules underpinning the L2 forms and structures they are exposed to; the outcome of which often leads to the development of hypotheses regarding the structure of the L2 that can neither be traced back to the L1 of the learner nor to the L2. The hypotheses developed by an L2 learner about the L2 manifested in the form of, as Ellis (1997) stated, learner constructed L2 rules that vary from those of the L1, effectively laying the foundation for the systematic errors commonly committed by the learner. Intralingual sources of language errors thus lead to the development of a consistent pattern of usage of certain L2 structures and forms that are different from both the L1 and L2 of the learner and hence the errors. Richards (2015) contended systematic intralingual errors mostly entail semantic errors, incomplete application of the L2 by the learner, and the tendency to ignore rule restrictions and overgeneralisation. These manifestations of intralingual influence depict the learning difficulties encountered by L2 learners in learning and internalising L2 rules presumed to be low level or basic.

Intralingual interference is also a significant linguistic factor that could hinder the process of L2 acquisition in that it can be informed by transfer resulting from varying applications of general learning strategies akin to those used in acquiring the L1. Corder (1967) posited learners of an L2 tend to adopt the strategies used to acquire the L1 in the acquisition of the L2. This is corroborated by Al-Khresheh (2016) in his assertion that negative transfer or interferences may inform intralingual errors where learners of an L2 apply the general learning strategies they used to acquire their L1 in their acquisition of the L2. The negative interference of the application of the L1 learning strategies to the L2 acquisition has the potential to inform intralingual errors despite the learning sequence of the two languages not being similar. Al-Khresheh (2016) stated that some intralingual errors are a reflection of certain general characteristics of L1 acquisition. Richards (2015) argued intralingual errors tend to be reflective of universal attributes of learning language rules, namely, false concepts hypotheses, incomplete rule application, rule restriction disregard, and overgeneralisation. Intralingual errors are therefore a manifestation of general features of the acquisition of language rules and hence the resultant language errors resemble those committed by native speakers of the L2.

2.4.3 Interlingual Errors or Intralingual Errors

One of the common research topics in the field of SLA is investigating the role of interlingual influence on the process of L2 learning. The L1 role was emphasised since the 1950s and the formulation of the contrastive analysis theory. Contrastive analysis, as mentioned earlier, stated that a systematic comparison between the L1 and L2 can explain the differences between the two languages. L2 learners may encounter learning difficulties as a result of the different linguistic elements that exist between the L1 and L2. Lado (1957) referred to the contrastive analysis hypothesis as "those elements which are similar to the learner's L1 will be simple for him, and those elements that are different will be difficult" (p. 45). In other words, in cases of similarity between L1 and L2, transfer of L1 habits could occur which in this situation is called positive transfer. In other cases, where L1 and L2 are different, negative transfer (L1 structure does not exist in L2) might occur. However, Simensen (1998) stated that L1 cannot always account for L2 learners' mistakes and a large number of errors could not be anticipated by contrastive analysis.

The increasing evidence against contrastive analysis theory and the limited ways of examining the sources of language errors has led to the formulation of

EA to study interlingual and intralingual errors in more depth. In the past two decades, intralingual influence has been examined in different contexts and now it is widely acknowledged as an influential factor of L2 errors. However, the contradiction between *interlingual* versus *intralingual* influences is still confusing to some extent. Ellis (2008) claimed that "a large number…of the errors that learners produce are intralingual in origin rather than transfer," but later he stated that "the proportion of transfer and interlingual errors varies in accordance with the task used to elicit samples of learner language" (p. 55).

The difference between interlingual and intralingual influences is not as precise and straightforward as reported above. Errors can be a result of different sources. As an example, Hasselgren (1993) conducted a study on the incorrect lexical choice of Norwegian learners of English. It was necessary for her to create a category which covered cases where both L1 and L2 tended to be one source of the occurrence of a specific error (Hasselgren, 1993).

Some researchers are sceptical of categorising the sources of L2 errors, because of the possible different sources, and because it is impossible to be certain about the learners' real intention when producing the errors in free writing. Classifying the sources to errors may rely mainly on the researcher's judgement (Flick, 1979, as cited in Ellis, 1994). Nonetheless, one of the main goals of this research is to discover the potential sources of lexical errors evident in the L2 learners' language products.

Since the current study focuses on examining the L2 products of Arab learners of English, particularly in the appropriate use of English lexis, the following section presents an overview of the Arabic language characteristics focusing on Arabic lexical features that are different from English, which may have a negative influence on the learning process of L2 learners.

2.5 A Brief Overview of Arabic Lexis

Like any other language, Arabic, which is essentially a Semitic language, has its own and unique lexicon (Haywood & Nahmad, 1965; Salim, 2013). In other words, the vocabulary and collection of words that make the Arabic lexis is distinctive. This, however, should not be construed to mean that the identifying features and morphological processes of the Arabic lexis do not bear some resemblance with those of the other major languages (Ryding, 2005). Far from it, the English and Arabic languages generally follow common word formation, derivative and morphological processes with each lexical system having its own set of productive patterns and rules for language use. In noun-formation processes as conversion, blending, compounding, affixation, and borrowing among others, the two lexical systems are parallel (Haywood & Nahmad, 1965; Ibrahim, 2010). However, significant commonalities and disparities abound in relation to applicability of the aforementioned processes on words formation.

2.5.1 Characteristics of Arabic Lexis

Arabic lexis demonstrates elegant and rigorous logic. According to Yushmanove (1961, as cited in Salim, 2013), the Arabic language has unique features for established rules of word formation. The Arabic lexis, like the lexis of most of the other Semitic languages, is based on a fundamental but largely trilateral consonantal root; in plain terms, this means that most of the lexical items in the Arabic lexical system comprise of three consonants. As a result, word formation or derivation entails insertion of vowels and, at times, supplementary consonants to create actual words whose basic consonantal root depicts various word patterns (Salim, 2013). As such, variation in the vowel alternation and incorporation of infixes, suffixes, and prefixes in the basic consonantal root that make up Arabic words thus tend to lead to alterations in the meanings of the words. Arabic lexis is also characterised by extensive use of prefixes, suffixes, and infixes which not only help to vary the meaning of the tri-consonantal base but also to generate new forms and patterns of words (Ibrahim, 2010).

2.5.2 Similarities Between the Arabic and English Lexical Systems

Similarities between the Arabic and English lexical systems abound. In the English and Arabic languages, several pronouns are used in rhematic clause or sentence to denote the same object, only one pronominal tie is considered, the number of instances the pronoun recurs notwithstanding. In addition, the vocabularies of both English and Arabic languages have equivalent deictics and definite articles such as <those>, <these>, <that>, and <this> for the former and *tilka, ha:Dihi, Dalika,* and *ha:da* for the latter (Williams, 1989). Additionally, in both English and Arabic lexis, words assume somewhat similar morphological processes including affixation where suffixes and prefixes are affixed to the root word to vary its meaning (Ibrahim, 2010). For instance, in English various formative morphemes as depicted in such words as *in*-competent, *dis*-like, and girl-*ish* are recurrently added to the roots, while in the Arabic lexis affixation is evident in such words as *darasa, darasa-t,* and *daras-tu* where a prefix or suffix is added to the roots or a section of the root (Salim, 2013). Generally put, both English and Arabic lexical systems follow somewhat similar noun-formation processes and word derivation patterns and rules as depicted in their use of acronyms, conversion, diminutives, borrowing, onomatopoeia, blending, compounding, and affixation (Ibrahim, 2010). Another key similarity between English and Arabic lexis is the class maintaining nature of their prefixes and the class-changing nature of their suffixes. In both lexical systems, all noun prefixes tend to maintain the class of the words formed and at the same time modify the meaning of the root while all suffixes tend to be class-changing given their ability to form adjectives,

2.5 A Brief Overview of Arabic Lexis

verbs, and nouns from the root (Ibrahim, 2010; Salim, 2013). Moreover, the number of classes of words in both Arabic and English lexical systems is equal, hence the somewhat similar derivational effects of the prefixes and suffixes in the two languages.

2.5.3 Differences Between the Arabic and English Lexical Systems

While in the Arabic, lexical system definiteness is conveyed before every adjective and noun in each nominal group, in English lexis, definiteness is stated in one instance in a nominal group. It is worth noting, however, that Arabic lexis only allows one signifier of definiteness to be considered as a pronominal tie in every nominal. For instance, in such a nominal group as *al bayt al kabi:r* 'big house,' the indicator of definiteness in the nominal considered will be only one 'al' as opposed to both. Also, in the Arabic lexical system, definiteness is not always expressed prior to every adjective or noun especially if the adjectives or nouns comprise the possessed element in إضافة *idafa* 'annexation' construction or construct as Williams (1989) stated.

Second, while Arabic lexis with regard to stem structure adopts the three consonantal roots, essentially C1C2C3, the English lexis is based on simple, derived, secondary, and compound stem structures (Salim, 2013). Third, while affixation is the most common morphological process in both English and Arabic lexis, the use of infixes where formative morphemes are inserted in the root is commonly found in the Arabic but only applies to the English vocabulary in the use of expletives and curse words.

In addition, English and Arabic lexis differ in terms of word formation or derivation. While both lexical systems produce nouns or new words following either the derivation or inflectional approaches, word formation in Arabic lexis assumes the form, pattern, and root concepts where a purely consonantal root is used to express different word patterns and vowels, and at times extra consonants, added to the root to create the definite form of a noun; whereas in English lexis, new words are produced by the use of numerous and varied elements of derivational and inflectional affixes including such suffixes and prefixes as *-s, -er, -ly, -ir, -ness, -ment, -dis, -ship*, and *-hood* among others as depicted in cap-*s*, lean-*er*, man-*ly*, *ir*-revocable, pale-*ness*, deploy-*ment*, *dis*-locate, relation-*ship*, and man-*hood* respectively (Ibrahim, 2010; Salim, 2013). While English lexis generally has and follows regular rules for word formation, Arabic lexis incorporates somewhat irregular rules of noun derivation.

Personal pronouns in Arabic are more complicated compared to those in English lexis. According to Salim (2013), personal pronouns in the Arabic lexical system are categorised into independent and dependent pronouns; 12 independent pronouns are further classified as singular, dual, or plural while English lexis

38   2 Literature Review

has 8 personal pronouns that are distinguished based on case, gender, and number. Finally, with regard to demonstrative pronouns, the Arabic lexical system differentiates in terms of number and gender while the English system distinguishes between close-by and far-off objects as opposed to differentiating on bases of gender (Salim, 2013).

The preceding disparities between the English and Arabic lexical systems provide a crucial platform for understanding issues likely to confront Arabic students learning English as a second or foreign language. The analysis of errors will offer valuable insight to English as Foreign Language (EFL) instructors on how they can support language learning among their students as well as counteract related linguistic challenges.

Since the current study focuses on lexis, the following section will provide a review of previous EA studies that investigate L2 learners' errors in relation to lexis.

2.6   EA Studies on L2 Learners' Lexical Errors

Writing through translation is a complicated process and a very challenging skill, particularly for non-L1 language learners as it requires different language skills that language learners need to master in order to write and translate efficiently, such as planning, organising, orthography, and above all accurate lexical choice (Awadalbari, 2015; Khalifa, 2015; Llach, 2011).

There has been growing research interest in the analysis of lexical errors made by L2 learners in their written production. Lexis is an essential component of a language and it is vital to L2 learning. According to Laufer (1986, p. 69), "no language acquisition, whether first, second, or foreign; child, or adult, can take place without the acquisition of lexis." Lexis is considered one of the major problematic language areas that confront learners while learning an L2, and due to their weak vocabulary knowledge, they are unable to communicate their thoughts as clearly as they would like to. According to Al-Kufaishi (1988), limited vocabulary has a negative influence on learners' productive skills. Zimmerman (1997) also asserted that lexis presents a serious linguistic difficulty to many language learners. The production of lexical errors which leads to humorous meanings or causes incomprehensibility is described as language mutilation (Larik, 1983).

Lexical errors, generally, have received less coverage in scientific writing than grammar errors, even though vocabulary is a crucial part of a learner's knowledge of a language (Llach, 2011). Even less research has been carried out with respect to lexical errors in a written language (Hemchua & Schmitt, 2006). There is a lack of consistent rules in the area: the lexical system and its elements are much less capable of a generalisation than, for example, morphology or syntax. Consequently, the errors in this area are less generalisable as well. Apart from that, they often depend on context, which makes them even more challenging to generalise. The overlap of the areas of grammatical and lexical studies (for example, the

2.6 EA Studies on L2 Learners' Lexical Errors

issue of grammatical words) has also been a complicating factor. As a result, the analysis of lexical errors in written production, such as translated texts, remains underdeveloped, which invites further research in this area.

Studying lexical errors in ESL/EFL contexts is essential for different reasons. First, according to Lennon (1991) and Webber (1993), lexical errors are the most prevalent kind of errors in English. They are more serious than other linguistic errors, such as, phonological, morphological, and syntactic errors (Johanson, 1978). They have a negative influence on the quality of academic writing (Engber, 1995; Llach, 2007) and L1 speakers of the language consider them as "irritating" errors (Santos, 1988, p. 69). Second, inappropriate lexical choice could fail to convey the intended meaning in certain communicative settings, particularly in translating from one language to another (Awadalbari, 2015; Khalifa, 2015). Carter (1998) stated that incorrect lexical choice might be less tolerated outside the school setting than syntax errors.

Hemchua and Schmitt (2006) who explored lexical errors in the Thai context, and Llach who explored the same issue in the Spanish context, noted that lexical errors are pervasive and serious, but they are still under-researched. This appears to also be the case in the Saudi context where no study to date has conducted a systematic and comprehensive analysis of lexical errors in translated English texts by English majors at the university level. The analysis of lexical errors in the written translations could facilitate the understanding of theoretical implications in ESL/EFL learning and vocabulary acquisition (Belz, 2004; Hunston & Francis, 2000). It is also useful for students' progression and development and educationist in course and material design (Chapelle, 2004; Krishnamurthy & Kosem, 2007).

In the field of EA, it is obvious that research engaging a complete taxonomy of lexical error categories in an EFL context is rare. Most recent research conducted on Saudi English learners to identify the common types of lexical errors relied on limited classification systems and categorised only a small number of error types. Therefore, the most significant types of lexical errors do not feature such analyses in detail, if at all. However, there are a few exceptions, (e.g., Shalaby et al., 2009). The limitations in error categories limit the number of errors that could be identified. According to Hemchua and Schmitt (2006), the overlap between error categories is problematic in the field of EA. Therefore, a more comprehensive classification framework can contribute to more accurate identification and description of error types.

Lexical errors have commonly been categorised according to formal and semantic perspectives. A formal classification of lexical errors was proposed by James (2013), whereby he divided it into three categories: misselection, misformation, and distortion errors. As for the semantic classification, the author highlighted two categories of semantic errors: confusion of sense relations and collocation errors. He further included 17 subcategories as a part of the two main classifications (a summary can be found in Table 2.1).

The interest in lexical error taxonomy for this current research originates from the need to find the characteristics of the errors made by Saudi learners of English. In this regard, one of the main purposes of this research is to present a detailed

Table 2.1 James's (2013) lexical error taxonomy

I. Formal errors
1. *Formal misselection*
1.1. Suffix type
1.2. Prefix type
1.3. Vowel-based type
1.4. Consonant-based type
2. *Misformations*
2.1. Borrowing (L1 words)
2.2. Coinage (inventing based on L1)
2.3. Calque (Translation from L1)
3. *Distortions*
3.1. Omission
3.2. Overinclusion
3.3. Misselection
3.4. Misordering
3.5. Blending
II. Semantic errors
1. *Confusion of sense relations*
1.1. General term for specific one
1.2. Overtly specific term
1.3. Inappropriate co-hyponyms
1.4. Near synonyms
2. *Collocation errors*

classification of lexical errors that occur in the written translations produced by university English majors. In addition, it aims to identify the different types of lexical errors and their significant sources to create strategies and guidelines which can help in teaching English vocabulary efficiently and improving students' writing and translation skills. Finally, it is possible that the analysis of error types and their sources could help in developing the current taxonomies of lexical errors.

The following two sections discuss some of the research that has been concerned with the analysis of lexical errors in EFL/ESL contexts as well as in the Saudi context. Focusing on the categorisation of lexical errors in the previous literature will provide deep insights into the weaknesses and strengths of the taxonomies used in different contexts (Llach, 2005).

2.6.1 A Review of Previous Studies Investigating Lexical Errors in EFL/ESL Contexts

Several studies on lexical errors have been conducted on EFL/ESL learners from diverse L1 backgrounds using different English language samples, though most of these studies tend to use a limited classification system to categorise the different types of lexical errors common among EFL/ESL learners. The studies also tend to

2.6 EA Studies on L2 Learners' Lexical Errors

base their analysis only on free writing data, effectively leading to a deficit in studies that focus on lexical errors in translation products.

This section will review some of these recent studies, illustrate their classification systems, and summarise their findings. The significance of implementing a comprehensive classification system in the investigation of lexical errors in EFL/ESL contexts for purposes of facilitating an in-depth analysis and better understanding of the nature and causes of the errors will be emphasised. To achieve this, the first subsection focuses on previous studies investigating lexical errors in non-Arab EFL/ESL contexts (see Table 2.2) while the second subsection explores studies assessing lexical errors in Arab EFL/ESL contexts and, in particular, the Saudi context (see Table 2.3).

2.6.1.1 Studies Examining Lexical Errors in Non-Arab EFL/ESL Contexts

The first study investigating lexical errors in a non-Arab EFL/ESL context is the study conducted by Llach (2011) on fourth grade Spanish EFL learners. In the study, Llach analysed written composition texts produced by the learners and used a classification system in which she categorised the emerging lexical errors into four main groups, that is, coinage, borrowing, spelling, and calque (literal translation) errors. Although the study found a significant relationship between the proficiency levels of the EFL learners and the frequency of lexical errors in their written texts, the limited nature of the classification system used in the study skewed the analysis of lexical errors in this EFL context towards misformation errors effectively leading to neglect of the different types of equally important misselection and distortion errors.

Another example of a very limited taxonomy is the study of Akande et al. (2006) by which they analysed the lexical errors of 225 final year Nigerian students at the technical college. Based on the results of a multiple-choice test and an essay writing exercise, the researchers found that their students' lexical errors were related to only three categories: mistakes resulting from overgeneralisation of rules, wrong analogy, and wrong spelling. Despite the failure in providing a comprehensive detailed taxonomy, the researchers suggested that English teachers in the institution should shape their English teaching techniques to develop the lexical knowledge and competence of their learners.

Roberts et al. (2002) also investigated lexical errors in the Italian EFL/ESL context in their study of lexical and syntactical errors committed by native Italian speakers learning EFL. They analysed the translated products produced by the Italian EFL learners for lexical errors which they classified into four major categories, that is, the use of general words, false cognates, omission, and selection errors. The classification system used for the linguistic errors, however, fails to clearly distinguish the different categories of lexical errors identified in the translated sentences. The findings of the study indicated a strong correlation between the linguistic abilities of the EFL learners and the age at which they acquire the L2, as well as, their frequency of use of the L1.

Table 2.2 Summary of major findings of previous studies on the written production of non-Arab EFL learners

Study	Participants	Language-sampling method	Major findings
Llach (2011)	283 fourth grade Spanish EFL learners	Written composition texts	• Llach developed four main categories of lexical errors: spelling, borrowing, coinage, and calque (literal translation) • She stated that spelling errors were the most frequent type of errors in her learners' writings • She found a strong relationship between the proficiency level of the students and the number of lexical errors in their compositions • Her classification has neglected the semantic part which played a significant role in labelling new categories of errors in the previous studies
Akande et al. (2006)	225 final year Nigerian technical college	A multiple-choice test and an essay writing exercise	• The researchers found that their students' lexical errors are related to only three categories: mistakes resulting from overgeneralisation of rules, wrong analogy, and wrong spelling • The researchers suggested that English teachers in the institution should shape their English teaching techniques to develop the lexical knowledge and competence of their learners
Roberts et al. (2002)	72 native Italian speakers	Translation texts (30 sentences)	• The researchers identified a number of lexical errors (overgeneralisation, i.e., use of general words, false cognates, omission, selection errors) into which the different translation errors committed by the participants were classified • They affirm omission errors comprised the most frequent type of lexical errors committed • The study established a significant relationship between the level of the linguistic proficiency of the learners and the age of acquisition of the L2 and their L1 use • Although their classification considered both the syntactic and semantic aspects, it did not comprehensively address the lexical errors thus leading to categorisation of omission errors as a separate class of linguistic errors

(continued)

Table 2.2 (continued)

Study	Participants	Language-sampling method	Major findings
Picot (2017)	20 Greek EFL students		• Picot created four categories of lexical errors (Suffix type, calque, i.e., translation errors, semantic word selection, near synonyms) • Picot established some error types are more common and that lexical errors tend to be unevenly distributed across the error-type continuum • Found the list of rules for classification of lexical errors put forth by Hemchua and Schmitt (2006) to be incomprehensive and some rules unclear which makes error classification problematic • Picot declares the Hemchua and Schmitt framework to be 'fit for purpose' despite the glaring shortcomings he outlines
Hemchua and Schmitt (2006)	20 third-year Thai undergraduate students		• Hemchua and Schmitt developed five categories of lexical errors (near synonyms, preposition partners, suffix type, calque/translation, and verbosity) • They opine the various lexical errors are potentially problematic for ESL/EFL students in different contexts • Its inadequacies notwithstanding, the lexical error analysis framework provides a comprehensive and holistic model for investigating and classifying linguistic errors
Ander and Yıldırım (2010)	53 Turkish EFL students from Anadolu University	4 to 5 paragraph compositions	• Seven categories of lexical errors have been created (wrong word choice, literal translation, omission/incompletion, misspelling, redundancy, collocation, and word formation errors) • Wrong word choice errors are the most common and comprise the most deviant lexical items • Imply elementary level non-Arab EFL learners also commit numerous omissions and misspelling due to their limited knowledge of the L2 lexis • Cites the tendency by the Turkish EFL learners to avoid complex sentences, phrases, or words in their writings as the reason for the few word formation and collocation errors • While the classification framework used facilitates the identification, categorisation, and analysis of the lexical errors, it ignores other types of errors effectively precluding its ability for in-depth and comprehensive analysis of different lexical errors and their causes

Table 2.3 Summary of major findings of previous studies on the written production of Arab EFL learners in the Saudi context

Study	Participants	Language-sampling method	Major findings
Shalaby et al. (2009)	96 university-level Saudi students at Taibah University learning English as a part of requirements of the preparatory year	Written composition texts	• Errors have been categorised into formal errors including misselection, misformations (borrowing and coinage), spelling errors (impeding comprehension, inappropriate meaning and L1 transfer), and semantic errors including confusion of sense relation (general term for specific one, overly specific terms, inappropriate hyponymy, near synonyms, translation from L1, binary terms, inappropriate meaning, and distortion of meaning), collocation errors, and stylistic errors (verbosity, misuse of compounds, and circumlocution) • Semantic errors were found to be more frequent than formal errors • L1 played a major role in the occurrence of errors
Ridha (2012)	80 Iraqi EFL university students	English writing samples	• The research only employed one category in lexical errors identification, that is, semantic errors • The findings indicate that most of the students' errors are a result of L1 transfer
Zughoul (1991)	Arab students at Yarmouk University in Jordan	Written composition texts	• Zughoul presented a categorisation of 13 lexical errors, but it was mainly based on two approaches of classification: L2 oriented and L1 oriented. He explained that synonymity was the most frequent type of errors made among his participants. According to the results of his analysis, L1 interference was an influential factor in word choice which led some of his EFL subjects to have errors related to synonymity, derivativeness, calque, and idiomaticity. However, from Hemchua, Schmitt, and Llach's perspective, more classification of errors could be provided

(continued)

Table 2.3 (continued)

Study	Participants	Language-sampling method	Major findings
Nuruzzaman et al. (2018)	90 Saudi non-English major/foundational EFL learners	Writing sample paragraphs from final exam papers	• Errors are categorised into four major groups (grammatical, lexical, semantic, and mechanics) • A coding system is further used to classify lexical errors into seven subcategories (noun, pronoun, verb, preposition, adverb, article, and word form) • Grammatical errors were the most frequent (occurring 47 times, i.e., 7.9%) followed by lexical errors (35 times or 5.93%) • The classification system is somewhat comprehensive in that it classifies the errors into four major categories and their subcategories thus offering a basis for in-depth analysis of the errors and what informs them
Ahamed and Othman (2019)	2018/19 3rd level EFL students from King Khalid University, Art and Science College	Descriptive written essays	• Developed six major categories of lexical errors (word formation, distortion, paraphrasing, redundancy, literal translation, and word choice errors) • Stated lexical errors are a function of inadequate vocabulary knowledge and mother tongue interference • The classification system is simplistic in that it overlooks semantic and other errors and hence its incapability of facilitating in-depth analysis and holistic understanding of the effects, nature, and sources of lexical errors

Picot (2017) analysed lexical errors committed by EFL learners based on the study conducted by Hemchua and Schmitt (2006) on Thai students. Following the Hemchua and Schmitt (2006) framework, he analysed the compositions written by Greek EFL learners. Picot found the frequency and distribution of lexical errors committed by the Greek students remarkably similar to those committed by Thai learners in the Hemchua and Schmitt study. Owing to the use of Hemchua and Schmitt's holistic and comprehensive framework for lexical error analysis, Picot (2017) was able to distinguish between the different formal and semantic errors and to further categorise the errors into four of the five most frequent subgroups of errors found in the original study. While the study demonstrated the capacity of the framework to reveal common lexical issues among diverse EFL learners with diverse L1 when applied to varied nationalities and ESL/EFL contexts, it highlighted the incomprehensive nature of the list of different error types put forth by Hemchua and Schmitt and the likelihood to assign lexical errors to more than one category.

Ander and Yıldırım (2010) examined the compositions of elementary level Turkish EFL students with a view to identifying and classifying the lexical errors they committed. Ander and Yıldırım determined the number of identified errors and grouped them into seven major categories. They found wrong word choice errors to be the most common besides many omission and misspelling errors. The classification framework was integral in helping to identify, group, and analyse the lexical errors which in turn led to the revelation that the L2 proficiency level of the students was the major impediment to their ability to write complete sentences, spell correctly, and make correct lexical choices.

2.6.1.2 Studies Examining Lexical Errors in Arab EFL/ESL Contexts and in Particular in KSA

A number of studies have been conducted on lexical errors in the written language of Arab ESL/EFL learners. Some studies focused on a particular aspect of lexical error, or mainly used a limited taxonomy in errors classification. Ridha (2012) for example, conducted an EA on Iraqi EFL university students, but only employed one category in lexical errors identification, that is, semantic errors. The use of a limited categorisation for describing the learners' lexical errors is unsuitable because it can result in unclear parameters and random classifications due to the complexity of lexis (Hemchua & Schmitt, 2006).

Zughoul (1991) examined the writings of Arab students at Yarmouk University in Jordan and employed an exhaustive taxonomy of lexical errors. He stated that a detailed classification of EFL university students' writings appears to be useful for a better understanding of interlanguage and for giving insights into the strategies used by language learners for lexical choice. Zughoul presented a categorisation of 13 lexical errors, but it was mainly based on two approaches of classification: L2 oriented and L1 oriented. He explained that synonymity was the most frequent type of error made among his participants. According to the results of his analysis,

2.6 EA Studies on L2 Learners' Lexical Errors

L1 interference was an influential factor in word choice which led some of his EFL subjects to have errors related to synonymity, derivativeness, calque, and idiomaticity. However, from Hemchua, Schmitt, and Llach's perspective, more classification of errors could be provided.

In the Saudi context, Nuruzzaman et al. (2018) comparatively assessed writing errors committed by non-English major Saudi foundational EFL learners in different faculties. They found orthography, semantics, lexis, and grammar to be the four major categories of linguistic errors common among the students. Nuruzzaman et al. used a coding system to classify the different types of errors into four main categories before further identifying subcategories for each type of the linguistic errors for the analysis. The study found a strong correlation between the linguistic errors committed by the EFL learners and the degree course pursued by the students, with those in the engineering college committing the highest number of errors and those in the faculty of medicine the lowest.

Shalaby et al. (2009) analysed lexical errors prevalent in the written compositions of Saudi ESL university students and noted the need to modify and expand the current scarce categories of lexical errors. To this end, Shalaby et al. modified Hemchua and Schmitt's (2006) framework and formed a comprehensive taxonomy for explaining lexical errors common among Saudi ESL learners. The new classification system had two major types of lexical errors—semantic and formal errors—with the former having three main categories with a further 13 subcategories, and the latter three main categories with further eight subcategories, which effectively gave rise to 21 subgroups of lexical errors. Application of the expanded classification system helped to identify a high number of lexical errors (718 or 39.55%) and an even higher number of semantic errors (60.45%). However, their classification needs to be re-examined for further analysis using different language samples. Examining lexical errors in different language products, such as translation products, may show different results and consequently new categories related to formal and semantic types could be identified. Furthermore, their analysis of the sources of lexical errors was not discussed in-depth which calls for more investigations to have a better understanding of the nature of errors.

Ahamed and Othman (2019) explored lexical errors and their impact on the written proficiency of the Saudi ESL learners. The classification system adopted in the study categorises lexical errors into six major groups including word formation, distortion, paraphrasing, redundancy, literal translation, and word choice errors. The study attributed lexical errors common in essays written by Saudi EFL students to limited vocabulary knowledge and mother tongue interference. The classification system adopted by Ahamed and Othman ignores semantic and other common types of lexical errors and could thus undermine efforts to understand the effects, nature, and sources of such errors.

To date, no study has been published that has employed a comprehensive list of lexical error categories on the translation texts of university English majors in KSA. The lexical error classification framework for the current research, therefore, will be mainly drawn from previously developed lexical error taxonomies. These are discussed thoroughly in the Methodology Chapter (Chap. 3).

2.7 Summary of the Identified Gaps in the Literature

This chapter has critically reviewed the theoretical and empirical literature on lexical errors in the written production of ESL/EFL learners. First, it presented the significance of lexis and the relationship of lexical knowledge to successful communication. The theoretical background to language errors and the major approaches to studying learner errors, followed by a review of previous EA studies on lexical errors made by L2 learners were discussed. Second, the chapter discussed pedagogical issues of teaching lexis, lexical chunks, in addition to the classification of lexical chunks and the teaching approaches of lexical chunks. Third, the chapter presented a detailed explanation of the notion of lexical errors with a general critical review of language errors as well as the common approaches and theories to examine language errors. Then, the common sources of language errors and how interlingual and intralingual influences play a major role in the occurrence of errors were illustrated. Finally, the chapter concluded with a review of previous EA studies focusing on the lexical errors of L2 learners.

The critical literature review on lexical errors presented in this chapter reveals the significance of learners' errors to understand the language learning process and to find out what areas of lexis are more problematic to learners at different stages of their language learning. It also emphasises the important contribution of the EA approach in the field of SLA research as a means to study learners' lexical errors in terms of their different linguistic categories and potential sources. The literature demonstrates that the EA approach has been commonly used in the field of SLA research. Previous EA studies on L2 learners' lexical errors have yielded different results in terms of error types, frequency, and sources. For instance, previous studies adopt different taxonomies to categorise errors. Some studies use a broad or very limited taxonomy, while others use a more detailed taxonomy (see Ahamed & Othman, 2019; Akande et al., 2006; Al-Jabri, 1998; Ander & Yıldırım, 2010; Nuruzzaman et al., 2018; Picot, 2017; Ridha, 2012; Roberts et al., 2002; Sheshsha, 1993). James's (2013) lexical error taxonomy, which is based on form- and content-oriented classification, has been used in many EA studies for lexical error categorisation purposes.

The review of SLA literature in relation to English learners with Arabic as the first language indicates that their L1 cannot contribute much to the learning process of their English because of the different lexical system between Arabic and English. Previous studies on English learners' written production in the Arab context reveal that learners encounter serious difficulties with regard to lexis. Generally, lexical errors due to formal misselection, approximation, assumed synonymity, and sense relation have been shown to be among the most frequent errors made by Arab learners of English, with some differences in frequency among those learners from different Arab contexts. In addition, previous studies reveal variations in results regarding lexical errors sources. Lexical errors made by Arab learners of English have been attributed to both interlingual and intralingual influences as the main sources of errors.

The review of the literature relating to Saudi English learners reveals a number of gaps in the literature in relation to the Saudi context. First, Saudi English major students at the university level have received little attention until recently and, to best of the researcher's knowledge, no study was found that examines lexical errors made in English major students' written translated production. However, most of the current studies centre on grammatical errors and little attention has been paid to lexical errors. There is a lack of studies that provide an in-depth analysis of lexical errors made by Saudi English major students at the university level which can provide more insight into their writing and translation skills. Furthermore, previous studies on written errors of Saudi English major students also have some limitations regarding description and explanation of lexical errors. With few exceptions, previous studies use a limited taxonomy which does not help to provide accurate and precise in-depth analysis of lexical errors. For instance, most of the studies examining lexical errors adopt only one taxonomy with limited categorisation, either the linguistic category taxonomy (focus on phonology, orthography, morphology, syntax, semantics, and pragmatics) or the origin of influence taxonomy (focus on the sources of errors). A better understanding of the nature of lexical errors can be gained when a combination of both taxonomies are used, as a miscellaneous taxonomy, which can offer a more comprehensive description of lexical errors (James, 2013; Llach, 2011). EA research emphasises that a comprehensive taxonomy is very useful to have a better understanding of learners' errors and the strategies employed (Hemchua & Schmitt, 2006; Llach, 2011). Even though previous studies reveal that interlingual influence is the main cause of lexical errors made by Saudi learners of English, they do not offer sufficient explanations for each type of lexical error, which could reveal which specific lexical features of Arabic contribute to the occurrence of lexical errors.

Based on the aforementioned gaps in research, there is a need for further research in the Saudi context to provide more insight into the problematic lexis encountered by Saudi English major students while writing through translation at their university study. Therefore, this study intends to fill the gaps in the literature in relation to Saudi English major students and contribute to the existing body of knowledge by providing an in-depth analysis of the lexical errors in their written translation products.

The following chapter presents the research design and methodology employed in this study.

References

Ahamed, F. E., & Othman, H. M. (2019). Analysis and assessment of lexical errors committed by Saudi EFL University students in descriptive essay writing (A Case study of College of Science & Arts-Tanumah, King Khalid University). *International Journal of English Language and Linguistics Research, 7*(6), 1–26.

Aitchison, J. (2012). *Words in the mind: An introduction to the mental lexicon*. Wiley.

Akande, A. T., Adedeji, E. O., & Okanlawon, B. O. (2006). Lexical errors in the English of technical college students in Osun State of Nigeria. *Nordic Journal of African Studies, 15*(1), 71–89.

Alharthi, K. (2011). *The impact of writing strategies on the written product of EFL Saudi male students at King Abdul-Aziz University* [Unpublished PhD thesis, Newcastle University].

Al-Jabri, S. M. H. (1998). *An analysis of lexical errors in written English of Saudi college freshman female students* [Unpublished master's thesis, Girls College of Education].

Al-Khresheh, M. H. (2015). A review study of interlanguage theory. *International Journal of Applied Linguistics and English Literature, 4*(3), 123–131.

Al-Khresheh, M. H. (2016). A Review study of error analysis theory. *International Journal of Humanities and Social Science Research, 2,* 49–59.

Al-Kufaishi, A. (1988). A vocabulary building program is a necessity not a luxury. *English Teaching Forum, 26*(2), 42–44.

Allen, V. F. (1983). *Techniques in teaching vocabulary.* Oxford University Press.

Al-Nofaie, H. (2010). The attitudes of teachers and students towards using Arabic in EFL classrooms in Saudi public schools—A case study. *Novitas Royal (research on Youth and Language), 4*(1), 64–95.

AlSaif, A. (2011). *Investigating vocabulary input and explaining vocabulary uptake among EFL learners in Saudi Arabia* [Unpublished PhD thesis, Swansea University].

Alseweed, M. (2009). Attitudes of Saudi secondary school level students towards learning of English as a foreign language. *Journal of Arabic and Human Sciences, 2*(1), 9–22.

Amiri, F., & Puteh, M. (2017). Error analysis in academic writing: A case of international postgraduate students in Malaysia. *Advances in Language and Literary Studies, 8*(4), 141–145.

Ander, S., & Yıldırım, Ö. (2010). Lexical errors in elementary level EFL learners' compositions. *Procedia—Social and Behavioral Sciences, 2*(2), 5299–5303.

Awadalbari, M. (2015). Translation as an aid to enhance students' writing skills at university level. *SUST Journal of Humanities, 16*(4), 241–252.

Baker, M. (2011). *In other words: A coursebook on translation* (2nd ed.). Routledge.

Barcroft, J. (2004). Second language vocabulary acquisition: A lexical input processing approach. *Foreign Language Annals, 37*(2), 200–208.

Belz, J. A. (2004). Learner corpus analysis and the development of foreign language proficiency. *System, 32,* 577–591.

Brown, H. D. (2007). *Principles of language learning and teaching* (5th ed.). Pearson Longman.

Carter, R. (1998). *Vocabulary: Applied linguistics perspectives* (2nd ed.). Routledge.

Carter, R., McCarthy, M., Channell, J., & McCarthy, M. (1988). *Vocabulary and language teaching* (pp. 68–75). Longman.

Chapelle, C. A. (2004). Technology and second language learning: Expanding methods and agendas. *System, 32,* 593–601.

Chastain, K. (1976). *Developing second-language skills: Theory to practice.* Rand McNally College Pub.

Corder, S. P. (1967). The significance of learner's errors. *International Review of Applied Linguistics, 5*(4), 161–170.

Corder, S. P. (1974). *Error analysis.* In J. P. B. Allen & S. P. Corder (Eds.), *Techniques in applied linguistics (The Edinburgh course in applied linguistics: 3)* (pp. 122–154). Oxford University Press (Language and Language Learning).

Crystal, D. (2008). *A dictionary of linguistics and phonetics.* Blackwell Publishing.

Ellis, N. C. (1994). Implicit and explicit language learning. *Implicit and Explicit Learning of Languages, 27*(2), 79–114.

Ellis, R. (1997). *Second language acquisition.* Oxford University Press.

Ellis, R. (2008). *The study of second language acquisition.* Oxford University Press.

Ellis, R., & Barkhuizen, G. (2005). *Analyzing learner language.* Oxford University Press.

Engber, C. A. (1995). The relation of lexical proficiency to the quality of ESL compositions. *Journal of Second Language Writing, 4*(2), 139–155.

Eszenyi, R. (2016). The modern translator's profile. In I. Horvath (Ed.), *The modern translator and interpreter.* Eotvos University Press.

Frith, M. B. (1978). Interlanguage theory: Implications for the classroom. *McGill Journal of Education/Revue des sciences de l'éducation de McGill, 13*(002), 155–165. Retrieved December 1, 2020, from https://mje.mcgill.ca/article/view/7202

References

Gass, S., & Selinker, L. (2008). *Second language acquisition: An introductory course* (3rd ed.). Routledge.

Hasselgren, A. (1993). *Right words, wrong words and different words: An investigation into the lexical coping of Norwegian advanced learners of English* [Unpublished "hovedfag" thesis, University of Bergen].

Hatim, B. (2001). *Teaching and researching translation*. Pearson Education.

Hatim, B., & Mason, I. (2005). *The translator as communicator*. Routledge.

Haywood, J. A., & Nahmad, H. M. (1965). *A new Arabic grammar of the written language*. Lund Humphries.

Hemchua, S., & Schmitt, N. (2006). An analysis of lexical errors in the English compositions of Thai learners. *Prospect, 21*, 3–25.

Huckin, T., & Coady, J. (1999). Incidental vocabulary acquisition in a second language: A review. *Studies in Second Language Acquisition, 21*(2), 181–193.

Hunston, S., & Francis, G. (2000). *Pattern grammar: A corpus-driven approach to the lexical grammar of English*. John Benjamins.

Ibrahim, A. I. (2010). Noun formation in standard English and modern standard Arabic: A Contrastive Study. *Journal of Language Teaching and Research, 1*(5), 614–623.

Ipek, H. (2009). Comparing and contrasting first and second language acquisition: Implications for Language Teachers. *English Language Teaching, 2*(2), 155–163.

James, C. (2013). *Errors in language learning and use: Exploring error analysis*. Routledge.

Javid, C. Z., Farooq, M. U., & Umer, M. (2013). An investigation of Saudi EFL learners' writing problems: A case study along gender-lines. *Kashmir Journal of Language Research, 16*(1), 179.

Johanson, S. (1978). The uses of Error analysis and Contrastive analysis. *English Language Teaching, 29*(3), 246–253.

Johansson, S. (2008). *Contrastive analysis and learner language: A corpus-based approach*. University of Oslo.

Kaweera, C. (2013). Writing error: A review of interlingual and intralingual interference in EFL context. *English Language Teaching, 6*(7), 9–18.

Keller, T. (2010). *Error analysis in SLA. An investigation of errors made by Polish learners of English*. TUB.

Khalifa, M. (2015). Problem in translating English and Arabic languages' structure: A case study of EFL Saudi students in Shaqra University. *European Journal of English Language and Literature Studies, 3*(4), 22–34.

Khan, I. (2011). Role of applied linguistics in the teaching of English in Saudi Arabia. *International Journal of English Linguistics, 1*(1), 105. Retrieved June 20, 2018 from https://ssrn.com/abstract=2857575

Krashen, S. D. (1994). Self-correction and the monitor: Percent of errors corrected of those attempted vs percent corrected of all errors made. *System, 22*(1), 59–62.

Krishnamurthy, R., & Kosem, I. (2007). Issues in creating a corpus for EAP pedagogy and research. *Journal of English for Academic Purposes, 6*(4), 356–373.

Krzeszowski, T. P. (1977). Contrastive analysis in a new dimension. *Papers and Studies in Contrastive Linguistics Poznan, 6*, 5–15.

Lado, R. (1957). *Linguistics across cultures*. Michigan U.P.

Larik, K. (1983). English as an international language. *English Language Teaching, 21*(2), 15–18.

Laufer, B. (1986). Possible changes in attitude towards vocabulary acquisition research. *International Review of Applied Linguistics, 24*(1), 69–75.

Lennon, P. (1991). Error: Some problems of definition, identification, and discussion. *Applied Linguistics, 12*(2), 180–196.

Lessard-Clouston, M. (2013). *Teaching vocabulary*. TESOL International Association. 1925 Ballenger Avenue Suite 550, Alexandria, VA 22314.

Lewis, M. (1993). *The lexical approach*. Language Teaching Publication.

Lewis, M. (2002). *The lexical approach: The state of ELT and a way forward*. Heinle.

Lim, J. M.-H. (2010). Interference in the acquisition of the present perfect continuous: Implications of a grammaticality judgment test. *The Open Applied Linguistics Journal, 3*(1), 24–37.

Llach, M. P. A. (2005). A critical review of the terminology and taxonomies used in the literature on lexical errors. *Journal of English and American Studies, 31*(1), 11–24.

Llach, M. P. A. (2007). Lexical errors as writing quality predictors. *Studia Linguistica, 61*(1), 1–19.

Llach, M. P. A. (2011). *Lexical errors and accuracy in foreign language writing*. Multilingual Matters.

Mahmood, A. H., & Murad, I. M. (2018). Approaching the language of the second language learner: Interlanguage and the models before. *English Language Teaching, 11*(10), 95–108.

Mahmoud, A. (2005). Collocation errors made by Arab learners of English. *Asian EFL Journal, 5*(2), 117–126.

Masrai, A., & Milton, J. (2012). The vocabulary knowledge of university students in Saudi Arabia. *Perspectives (TESOL Arabia), 19*(3), 13–19.

McMullen, M. (2009). Using language learning strategies to improve the writing skills of Saudi EFL students: Will it really work? *System, 37*(3), 418–433.

Meara, P. (1980). Vocabulary acquisition: A neglected aspect of language learning. *Language Teaching and Linguistics: Abstracts, 13*(4), 221–246.

Milton, J. (2009). *Measuring second language vocabulary acquisition*. Multilingual Matters.

Moreno, L. (2016). *Channeling Charlie: Suprasegmental pronunciation in a second language learner's performance of others' voices* (MA Qualifying Paper), University of Minnesota.

Moskovsky, C., & Alrabai, F. (2009). Intrinsic motivation in Saudi learners of English as a foreign language. *The Open Applied Linguistics Journal, 2*(1), 1–10.

Muftah, M., & Rafik-Galea, S. (2013). Error analysis of present simple tense in the interlanguage of adult Arab English language learners. *English Language Teaching, 6*(2), 146–154.

Munday, J. (2012). *Introducing translation studies: Theories and applications*. Routledge.

Nation, I. S. P. (2001). *Learning vocabulary in another language*. Cambridge University Press.

Nation, I. S. P. (2006). How large a vocabulary is needed for reading and listening? *Canadian Modern Language Review, 63*(1), 59–82.

Nation, I. S. P. (2011). Research into practice: Vocabulary. *Language Teaching, 44*(4), 529–539.

Nattinger, J. R., & DeCarrico, J. S. (1992). *Lexical phrases and language teaching*. Oxford University Press.

Nida, E., & Taber, C. (2003/1969). *The Theory and practice of translation*. Brill.

Norrish, J. (1983). *Language learners and their errors*. Macmillan Press.

Nunan, D. (1991). *Language teaching methodology: A Textbook for teacher*. Prentice Hall.

Nuruzzaman, M., Islam, A. B., & Shuchi, I. J. (2018). An analysis of errors committed by Saudi non-English major students in the English paragraph writing: A study of comparisons. *Advances in Language and Literary Studies, 9*(1), 31–39.

Picot, A. (2017). Lessons in lexical error analysis. Revisiting Hemchua and Schmitt (2006); An analysis of the lexical errors in the compositions of Greek learners. *International Journal of English Language Teaching, 5*(4), 40–59.

Qader, H. B. (2016). The effect of lexical chunks on Kurdish EFL learners' writing skill. *Education, 6*(4), 101–106.

Rahman, M. M. (2011). English language teaching (ELT) in Saudi Arabia: A study of learners' needs analysis with special reference to community college, Najran University. *Language in India, 11*(4), 367–461.

Rahman, M., & Alhaisoni, E. (2013). Teaching English in Saudi Arabia: Prospective and challenges. *Academic Research International, 4*(1), 112–118.

Ramos, R., & Dario, F. (2015). Incidental vocabulary learning in second language acquisition: A literature review. *Profile Issues in Teachers Professional Development, 17*(1), 157–166.

Richards, J. (1976). The role of vocabulary teaching. *TESOL Quarterly, 10*(1), 77–89.

Richards, J. (2003). *Dictionary of language teaching and applied linguistics* (3rd ed.). Longman.

References

Richards, J. C. (2015). *Error analysis: Perspectives on second language acquisition*. Routledge.

Ridha, N. S. (2012). The effect of EFL learners' mother tongue on their writings in English: An error analysis study. *Journal of the College of Arts, University of Basrah, 60*, 22–45.

Roberts, P. M., MacKay, I. R., & Flege, J. E. (2002). Lexical and syntactic errors in translation by Italian/English bilinguals. *Brain and Cognition, 48*(2–3), 513–516. https://doi.org/10.1006/brcg.2001.1408

Robinson, D. (2004). *Becoming a translator: An introduction to the theory and practice of translation*. Routledge.

Ryding, K. C. (2005). *A reference of grammar of modern standard Arabic*. Cambridge University Press.

Salim, J. A. (2013). A Contrastive study of English-Arabic noun morphology. *International Journal of English Linguistics, 3*(3), 122–132.

Santos, T. (1988). Professors' reactions to the academic writing of nonnative-speaker students. *TESOL Quarterly, 22*, 69–90.

Schachter, J., & Celce-Murcia, M. (1977). Some reservations concerning error analysis. *TESOL Quarterly, 11*(4), 440–451.

Schmitt, N. (1999). The relation between TOEFL vocabulary items and meaning, association, 325 collocation, and word-class knowledge. *Language Testing, 16*, 189–216.

Schmitt, N. (2000). *Vocabulary in language teaching*. Cambridge University Press.

Schmitt, N. (2008). Instructed second language vocabulary learning. *Language Teaching Research, 12*(3), 329–363.

Schmitt, N. (2010). *Researching vocabulary: A vocabulary research manual*. Palgrave Macmillan.

Scovel, T. (1988). *A time to speak*. Heinle.

Selinker, L. (1972). Interlanguage. *International Review of Applied Linguistics, 10*(3), 209–231.

Shalaby, A. N., Yahya, N., & El-Komi, M. (2009). Analysis of lexical errors in Saudi college students' compositions. *Journal of the Saudi Association of Languages and Translation, 2*(3), 65–93.

Sheshsha, J. A. (1993). Lexical error analysis in learning English as a foreign language. *Social Science Research Series, 24*, 5–30.

Shukri, N. A. (2014). Second language writing and culture: Issues and challenges from the Saudi learners' perspective. *Arab World English Journal, 5*(3), 190–207.

Simensen, A. M. (1998). *Teaching a foreign language*. Fagbokforlaget Vigmostad & Bjorke AS.

Tarone, E. (2018). Interlanguage. *The Encyclopedia of Applied Linguistics*, 1–7. https://doi.org/10.1002/9781405198431.wbeal0561.pub2

Wardhaugh, R. (1970). The contrastive analysis hypothesis. *TESOL Quarterly, 4*(2), 123–130.

Webber, P. (1993). Writing medical articles: A discussion of common errors made by L2 authors and some particular features of discourse. *UNESCO-ALSED LSP Newsletter, 15*(2), 38–49.

Whitman, R. L. (1970). Contrastive analysis: Problems and procedures. *Language Learning, 20*(2), 191–197.

Wilkins, D. A. (1972). *Linguistics in language teaching*. Edward Arnold.

Williams, M. P. (1989). *A comparison of the textual structures of Arabic and English written texts a study in the comparative orality* [Doctor of Philosophy thesis, University of Leeds].

Xia, Y. (2014). Language theories and language—From traditional grammar to functionalism. *Journal of Language Teaching and Research, 5*(3), 559–565.

Young, R. (2000). Error analysis: Avoidance (Based on Schachter, J. (1974). An error in error analysis. *Language Learning, 24* (205–214). Retrieved March 11, 2021, from https://dept.english.wisc.edu/rfyoung/333/avoidance.ho.pdf

Zimmerman, C. (1997). Do reading and interactive vocabulary instruction make a difference? *TESOL Quarterly, 31*(1), 121–140.

Zughoul, M. (1991). Lexical choice: Towards writing problematic word lists. *International Review of Applied Linguistics, 29*(2), 45–60.

Chapter 3
Research Design and Methodology

3.1 Introduction

The current research used an error analysis (EA) approach to scrutinise the distributional patterns of lexical errors from a quantitative perspective. The main objective was to provide an indepth analysis and identify the possible reasons behind the lexical errors made by Saudi English major students. To have a better understanding of the characteristics of students' lexical errors, a taxonomy for lexical errors to be outlined in this chapter was used to define the different patterns based on the number of instances lexical errors take place in formal and semantic categories. The data collected for this study was a corpus of written translations by Saudi English major students at the university level. The corpus was cross-sectional data, since it represented one group in a fixed time.

This chapter presents a full description of the research design and methodology used for the study's analysis. It discusses the methods and data collected, provides information about the setting and the population sample, and presents the issues related to the ethics of this study. Furthermore, the chapter illustrates the steps and procedures involved in the data analysis. At the end, a summary is presented.

3.2 Theoretical Framework

3.2.1 Error Analysis

In the field of second language acquisition (SLA), many theories have evolved to try to explain the linguistic features in learners' language production. The current study adopted EA as an essential tool to examine how the L2 is learnt or acquired (Ellis, 2008). In the 1970s, Pit Corder developed this conception of EA and it has

---

© The Author(s), under exclusive license to Springer Nature Singapore Pte Ltd. 2022
Y. Alenazi, *Exploring Lexical Inaccuracy in Arabic-English Translation*,
New Frontiers in Translation Studies, https://doi.org/10.1007/978-981-19-6390-2_3

been further developed and commonly used by most SLA researchers as a useful approach that has significantly contributed to SLA research.

From a pedagogical perspective, EA is a practical tool to examine, identify, and explain L2 learners' errors because of its effectiveness in locating the L2 learners' errors and their sources. According to Jiang (2009), EA is useful as "a means to empower L2 teachers in that their error feedback can be made more effective and more beneficial to L2 learners" (p. 116). EA can also assist language teachers in understanding the potential causes of L2 errors and find the most effective pedagogical solutions to treat these errors. James (2013) stated that an EA approach serves two main purposes: it identifies the gaps in L2 learners' knowledge and examines the way learners compensate for these gaps.

This study followed the five steps in the EA approach as originally suggested by Corder (1974) and acknowledged mostly by SLA researchers (e.g., Ellis, 2008; Gass & Selinker, 2008; James, 2013). These five steps are summarised as follows:

1. *Collection of a language sample*

In this step, the collection of a sample of learner language data was undertaken over a period of time and compared.

2. *Identification of errors*

Once the language sample was collected, errors were identified by comparing the learner's language production with the L2.

3. *Description of errors*

In this step, the analysis of the language sample involved a detailed description of the identified errors.

4. *Explanation of errors*

The analysis of the language sample procedures involved explanation of the identified errors which focus on finding the potential sources of errors. Once the errors were identified, they were re-examined and further analysed according to their likely causes. As stated by Ellis and Barkhuizen (2005) "explaining errors involves determining their sources in order to account for why they were made" (p. 62). Therefore, possible linguistic explanations for the identified errors in each category were provided based on the evidence from the types of errors that occur (see Sect. "Explanation of Lexical Errors").

5. *Evaluation of errors*

This step is concerned with the readers' comprehension and reaction to errors. L1 and non-L1 speakers use different standards in their evaluation. Therefore, errors may be judged differently taking into consideration the context of errors (Ellis, 2008). However, the step of the evaluation of errors "has generally been handled as a separate issue" in previous EA studies (Ellis, 1994, p. 48). Therefore, this step was not included in the current analysis since it was beyond the scope of the study and there is no scale to evaluate the errors identified.

3.3 Conceptual Framework

A wide range of research endeavoured to agree on an EA tool (taxonomy) to be implemented for the analysis of lexical errors. Llach (2011) overviewed a number of taxonomies that apply the qualitative, quantitative, and EA approaches. She presented several classification criteria considered in the categorization of lexical errors, including formal/semantic distinction, descriptive criterion, psycholinguistic criterion, origin of influence criterion, linguistic criterion, word-class criterion, product-/process-oriented taxonomies, and miscellaneous criteria (see Table 3.1 for details).

It is not always an easy task to systematise taxonomies into these criteria, because some of them might be based on more than one categorisation criterion (Llach, 2011). The following section discusses in detail the taxonomy chosen for this study.

Table 3.1 Lexical error taxonomies and their classification criterion

Classification Criterion	Characteristics
Formal/Semantic distinction	Lexical errors are categorised based on their formal or semantic associations
Descriptive criterion	This criterion is descriptive in nature and centres only on the surface form of the errors neglecting their sources
Psycholinguistic criterion	This criterion classifies lexical errors according to their sources, describing their mental processes how these errors originate
Origin of influence criterion	This criterion classifies lexical errors according to three origins: interlingual factors, intralingual factors, and teaching-induced errors
Linguistic/Grammatical criterion	This categorisation of lexical errors is based on the linguistic level (phonology, orthography, morphology, syntax, semantics, and pragmatics) at which the error occurs
Word-class criterion	This criterion discriminates between lexical error categories based on the word class, such as nouns, verbs, adjectives, etc
Product-/process-oriented taxonomies	According to Llach (2011), "Taxonomies of lexical errors can also be classified according to their focus. Therefore, we distinguish process-oriented taxonomies from product-oriented taxonomies. The only difference between these two types is whether they take the psycholinguistic processes that generate the lexical error as the centre of their typology, for example transfer and overgeneralisation, or whether they prefer to depart from the product of that process, the lexical error itself, to establish the taxonomy" (p. 86)
Miscellaneous criteria	The miscellaneous taxonomies merge different classifications systems in order to create a comprehensive taxonomy that gathers many error types

58

Based on the nature of this study and the type of data collected, miscellaneous classification was established in order to create a comprehensive taxonomy able to describe various types of lexical errors (see Sect. "Categorisation of Lexical Errors"). According to Llach (2011), lexical error taxonomies are usually developed for an EA study according to the type of data collected, not vice versa. Hence, it is difficult to adopt lexical error taxonomies designed to analyse language errors of specific data sets (spoken, written, language tests, essays, reports, or translations) that are collected form L2 learners of different L1 backgrounds (Llach, 2011). Based on Llach's perspective and the objectives of this research, it is important to use a taxonomy of lexical errors developed to analyse language samples from Arabic L1 speakers. Shalaby et al. (2009), established a comprehensive classification for Arabic learners of English that includes multiple linguistic categories with respect to lexis. The taxonomy that is based on the formal and semantic distinction of errors was adopted by the researcher for the purpose of the analysis. Thus, the following section will discuss Shalaby et al.'s taxonomy briefly.

3.3.1 Shalaby Et Al.'s Lexical Error Taxonomy

Shalaby et al.'s (2009) taxonomy originated from the investigation of various taxonomies already established by many researchers (e.g., Hemchua & Schmitt, 2006; James, 2013; Llach, 2005; Zughoul, 1991). The lexical error classification is based on the distinction between form and content. Hemchua and Schmitt's taxonomy comprises 24 types of lexical errors distributed across two main categories: formal errors which includes misselection, misformation, and distortion errors; semantic errors which includes confusion of sense relations, collocation errors, connotative errors, and stylistic errors. Their taxonomy, according to Llach (2011), is "an exhaustive classification that allows for fine-grained analysis of the different lexical errors found" (p. 77). Shalaby et al. (2009) adopted Hemchua and Schmitt's classification system because of its inclusive nature to establish the foundation of their study on lexical errors, modifying and refining the adopted taxonomy while analysing their own data. This taxonomy is divided into two main types of errors: formal and semantic. The formal type comprised three groups of eight subcategories, while the semantic type included four categories of 13 subcategories. Their taxonomy, therefore, incorporated 21 subcategories of lexical errors (see Fig. 3.1). With regard to the sources of lexical errors, the current study followed Richards' (2015) classification of errors according to their potential causes as interlingual or intralingual (see Sect. "Explanation of Lexical Errors").

3.4 Research Design

3.4.1 Quantitative Analysis

As appropriate to the nature of this study, a quantitative approach was used. McEnery and Wilson (2001) stated that quantitative analysis provides a detailed description of the identified errors and helps in allocating the distributional

3.4 Research Design

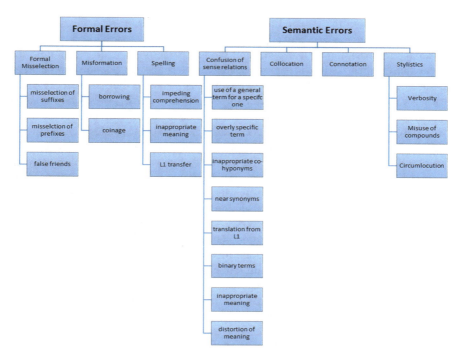

Fig. 3.1 Taxonomy of lexical errors (Based on Shalaby et al., 2009)

patterns of the identified errors. Therefore, to analyse the lexical errors identified in the study, the errors were examined from a quantitative perspective to describe them and reveal their sources. Additionally, their frequency percentage was calculated through the use of statistics. The use of quantitative analysis can provide researchers with both depth and breadth of insight into the data (Mcenery & Wilson, 2001). Such an approach of analysis has been commonly used in EA studies (e.g., Hemchua & Schmitt, 2006; Mariko, 2007; Shalaby et al., 2009).

3.4.2 The Data and Participants

3.4.2.1 Translation Data

In EA studies, there are two main types of written language samples: translation texts and free production texts (Mahan, 2013). Written translations are texts provided to the L2 learners in their L1 (e.g., Arabic) to be translated to their L2 (e.g., English). Translation data as a language sample is very useful to examine the language products of L2 learners as it can tell the reader how the learner conveys the

L1 lexical items in the L2, and accordingly how the learner recognises the relationship between the L1 and L2 words. Translated texts provide a significant advantage in providing a clear picture of the L2 learner's intended meaning to the researcher (Mahan, 2013). It is much easier to determine the relationship between L1 and L2 vocabulary if the intended meaning is available. For instance, if an L2 learner wrote *global* as a translation for the Arabic word عالمي *alami* meaning "global", it is easy to see how the learner has selected the correct equivalent L2 word based on the source text and its context. Having access to the intended meaning is very useful for the language errors analyst, since it is easy to identify the errors source by looking at how the L2 learner "perceives the relationship between L1 and L2 words" (Mahan, 2013, p. 46). However, translation texts have some drawbacks. First, considering the L1 words, the L2 learner may have never learned or used the word provided in the translation task in both their L1 and L2. Second, in a translation task L2 learners are required to use specific words that best fit the L1 text and its context. Moreover, sometimes translations are the result of individual interpretation between an L2 lexical item and an L1 lexical item, and not how the L1 lexical item is conveyed in different contexts.

Free production texts (free writing) can provide valuable language data, since written compositions yield information about learners' language performance. Free production texts are considered to be one of the best sources to obtain written samples of relatively spontaneous language produced by learners for the purpose of EA. However, according to Karina Mahan (2013) there are disadvantages of using free production texts for an EA study, such as:

1. It is difficult to track the learner's intended meaning, and context is the only way to understand the nature of errors. Therefore, identifying errors depends more on the researcher interpretation;
2. In free writing, L2 learners may avoid the use of L2 words that they do not know, because they are not bound to use certain L2 words as in translation tasks; and
3. Information gathered on individual errors in free production tasks is not sufficient, since the learners can choose the words they know. Consequently, the chances of having different types of errors in all learners' writings are small.

While Shalaby et al. (2009) used free production texts, this study draws on translation texts. Shalaby et al.'s research is the only work that has tried to provide a comprehensive list of lexical errors of Saudi non-English major students at the university level. The focus of the present project is to examine the lexical errors made in Saudi English major students' translation texts. It is expected that insights garnered from using different data type (translation texts) will facilitate the understanding of theoretical implications in ESL/EFL learning, translation practice, and vocabulary acquisition. In addition, as pointed out by Elmahdi (2016) and Khalifa (2015), even though English major students in Saudi universities are expected to be professional translators and English teachers upon graduation, they still make lexical errors while writing through translation. Therefore, conducting EA research in this academic discipline will benefit Saudi students by improving their English learning experience, leading to greater academic success. In short, by analysing translation texts produced by this group of students, the study extends the growing body of knowledge concerning lexical errors in Saudi English learners' written products.

3.4.2.2 Cross-Sectional Corpus Data

Corpus data is a large collection of spoken or written texts upon which a linguistic analysis is based. Corpus data provides grammarians, lexicographers, and other interested linguists with better descriptions of a language (Mcenery & Wilson, 2001). The main purpose of corpus data is to determine how a specific sound, word, or syntactic structure in a language is used (Crystal, 1992). For this study, a text corpus was used as a cross-sectional data (a data collected from a population at a particular point in time). These corpora are set at a specific time and do not demonstrate the learners' development over a time period. This type of data is easy to access and helps to conduct an investigation at a specific point in time. However, such data cannot explain the participants' progress over an extended period of time. According to Ellis (2008), snap shot language samples are a "static view of second language acquisition" (p. 61). Since longitudinal language samples for Saudi English major students were not available, the study made use of cross-sectional data for the purpose of the analysis.

3.4.2.3 Setting of the Study

The study was conducted at the English Language and Translation department at one of the Kingdom of Saudi Arabia's public universities. This department offers a four-year undergraduate programme, which is divided mainly into two stages, including the preparatory year stage and the advanced stage (the second, third, and fourth years). In the preparatory year stage, students will have the opportunity to develop and practise their English language skills through a comprehensive English curriculum during two academic semesters. On the other hand, the advanced stage offers a variety of courses in the field of literature, linguistics, writing, and translation. The main objectives of the translation courses are to familiarise English major students with the basic principles of translation, improve their basic linguistic skills, and enrich their vocabulary knowledge of both the L1 and the L2.

The following two sections provide details about the participants of the study and their corpus texts.

3.4.2.4 The Participants of the Study

The study targeted the whole population of Saudi English major students who were enrolled in the English programme at one of Saudi Arabia's public universities at the time of the study (2019). The total number of participants at that time was about 150 students across different university year levels.

All participants were enrolled in different courses of translation as a core requirement of the English programme. They were all Arabic L1 speakers in their 2nd, 3rd, and 4th year of their university study. The age factor was already controlled because normally all undergraduate students at the university belong to the same age group of 18 to 25 years old based on their current year level of study. They all finished secondary school before enrolling in university. They studied English as a foreign language at school for about seven years. The data for the study were collected from male students only, due to cultural consensus. In the Saudi context, male and female students are separated at different campuses and it is not permitted for a male researcher to have access to the female's campus or vice versa for a female researcher.

3.4.2.5 Participants' Corpus

This study analysed a corpus of 105 translation texts written in English by Saudi English major students. A large sample size is useful to increase the likelihood of discovery and increase the level of precision the study requires to provide a clear picture of the data for analysis (DePaulo, 2000). At the university, students across their three-year English degree receive English instruction in different language areas: linguistics, writing, literature, and translation. The primary objective of the translation courses is to improve the learners' translation and writing skills in different genres and discipline areas such as literature, journalism, policy, economy, law, marketing, science, medicine, and education. The students in the translation courses are instructed to practise translating literary and non-literary texts from Arabic to English. As part of the translation courses requirements, English major students are given translation assignments to be achieved in-class as part of their training. The students are mainly asked to translate Arabic texts to English texts and vice versa. As the semester consists of 14 weeks, after the first seven weeks, students have a mid-term examination and after 14 weeks they sit their final examination. In both exams, students are required to complete the translation tasks without using reference materials such as dictionaries. For the mid-term and final exams, students are asked to translate different literary and non-literary texts from Arabic to English. Therefore, the corpus texts collected for the current study were mainly responses to the translation courses' mid-term and final exams.

3.4.3 Data Collection Procedure

Before collecting the translation data, Ethics Approval to conduct the study was obtained from the Human Research Ethics Committee of the researcher's institution. In addition to the Ethics Approval, a formal Saudi university approval was obtained and a formal consent process was carried out to obtain access to the university and its students, from both the Provost of the school and the Head of Department. The permission and information sheet provided by the researcher was sent via email by the Department Secretary to all students studying for an English major. After the mid-term and final examinations completed as part of the students' translation course requirements, the Departmental Secretary extracted the examination papers of those students who had provided consent and photocopied these before returning the originals.

To ensure privacy and confidentiality and in line with the institution human ethics permission, the data were only accessed by the researcher. The researcher coded the scripts with the class code and number, and scanned the texts removing all identifiable information a week after collecting the papers. The students' personal details were cropped from the papers during the process of scanning the papers. The full pack then was returned to the Departmental Secretary in the order received. The scanned papers and electronic data were stored in the researcher's personal password protected computer. In accordance with the researcher's institution code for the responsible conduct of research, data will be securely stored for five years in the researcher's secure office at his institution as well as in secure storage in the researcher's personal password protected computer. The results did not identify the participants in any way. Only de-identified and aggregated data were utilised for the project.

3.4.4 Ethical Considerations

It is essential that any research project should not cause harm to any party. Also, the research should not be influenced by the interest of any parties (McBurney & White, 2007). All the research ethics, the information demands, consent, free choice, and privacy were taken into consideration in the study in order to obtain the Ethics Approval from the Human Research Ethics Committee.

Since the data were collected from a public university in KSA, a formal university approval was obtained and a formal consent process was carried out. In addition, permission and consent forms from the department were obtained in order to use the corpus data of its students. All English major students enrolled in translation courses across the three-year English Language and translation degree were invited to participate in the study. Only students who had completed the consent form had their translation texts included in the study and these were de-identified and provided with a code.

Participants were clearly informed in an email sent by the Department Administrative Officer that their participation was entirely their own decision. The researcher explained to student participants that their participation or non-participation would not affect their standing or progression in the course or the programme and no student would be disadvantaged regardless of their choice. The students completed the permission form electronically. Staff from the Department of English Language and Translation at the university were informed that their students' participation in the study was voluntary and that participation/non-participation would not affect their grades. The researcher obtained the pack of student texts for each translation class from the Department and matched permission forms with the completed electronic consent forms. Teachers were not aware of which students had provided consent and which had not. Participants were capable of giving consent of their participation in the study as they were all over 18 years and, as English major students, had a suitable level of English to understand the consent information.

As mentioned earlier, in order to maintain privacy and anonymity, translation texts with consent forms attached were de-identified and then scanned and only the de-identified texts were used for research analysis. The original texts were returned to the teachers involved. The researcher only viewed the de-identified texts. All information remained confidential to the researcher and his supervisors, and no participant was identifiable in any reports of the research beyond their institution and class level.

3.4.5 The Validity and Reliability of the Data

To ensure validity and reliability of the data collected, it was necessary to collect the translation samples from the participants using their translation course exam papers, instead of using homework tasks or take-home examinations. Home translation tasks may not be valid, because the data could be affected in terms of the learner language accuracy. In other words, students may get assistance from others or use the Internet as a reference source.

Regarding the data analysis, lexical errors were identified by the researcher and reviewed by two English lecturers to ensure accuracy in lexical errors' identification based on the taxonomy designed for the study. They checked the errors' list and their classifications and subclassifications and the sources of these errors to assure that there was no biased judgement. Moreover, the researcher sought the advice of academic experts in statistics. This was conducted because the statistical analysis was useful to organise the collected data in charts, graphs, and tables by converting the raw data into numbers, percentages, and parameters that provided the research with a summary of the results needed to answer the research questions (Brown & Rodgers, 2002).

3.4.6 Corpus Data Analysis Procedures

The corpus data were analysed considering the lexical errors made in multiple linguistic categories. The number of texts comprising the corpus data, that is, 105 translation texts, allows for an indepth analysis of the texts. They were analysed following the key procedures in EA approach: identification, description, and explanation of errors. The analysis procedures followed in each stage are explained in detail below.

3.4.6.1 Identification of Lexical Errors (Error Count)

After collecting the written translations, they were read carefully to identify lexical errors. Since there are different definitions of language error that are suggested by different researchers, it is important to agree on what constitutes an error in a specific study in order to identify errors. Choosing a working definition of errors is useful for the purpose of analysis which "allows for delimitation of the topic of study" (Llach, 2011, p. 75). Therefore, a working definition for "lexical error" was chosen for the purpose of this study to correct errors and analyse them. According to Llach (2011), "a [lexical error] is a deviation in form and/or meaning of a target-language lexical word" (p. 75). Based on the working definition adopted, lexical errors (either a word, or two words, such as: collocations, or whole phrases and sentences, such as: stylistic errors) were identified, regardless of other writing skills such as organisation and cohesion.

Lexical errors were identified by the researcher in consultation with an L1 Arabic speaker and an L1 English speaker both holding a higher degree in linguistics and with English second/foreign language teaching experience to ensure accuracy in lexical errors' identification. In the analysis, all lexical errors included were discussed and agreed upon. To facilitate the next stage of the analysis of the corpus data, all the identified lexical errors were entered into Excel worksheets organised according to their linguistic categories (formal and semantic).

Figure 3.2 presents a full-screen interface of a Microsoft Excel Spreadsheet where the corpus with the translations of 105 students is presented. On the main screen, all the participants' translations are listed in the order of the university year level, from Year 2 to Year 4. When selecting each column and using the function of "Filter" then "Auto Filter" from the Data menu, the user of the corpus can sort all the translations by year, sentence, or the error category and count the total number of each type of error. The table in Microsoft Excel includes 6 columns: (1) sentence number, (2) lexical error, (3) text genre, (4) error subcategory, (5) error main category, and (6) year level, as shown in Fig. 3.2.

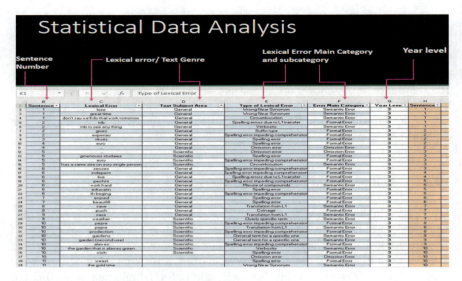

Fig. 3.2 Microsoft excel spreadsheet of errors categorisation

3.4.6.2 Description of Lexical Errors

The second stage of the corpus data analysis involved a description of the identified lexical errors. Description of errors includes a linguistic categorisation of errors based on a taxonomy designed particularly for this study. As mentioned earlier, many EA studies develop error classification systems to describe the language samples collected systematically (Llach, 2011). Description of lexical errors, consequently, includes two stages—categorisation of lexical errors and statistical analysis—which are explained in detail below.

Categorisation of Lexical Errors

The categorisation of lexical errors stage involved the process of comparing the learners' incorrect lexical items with the categorisation of lexical errors under certain lexical error taxonomy. As appropriate to the nature of this study and its objectives, the study developed a comprehensive taxonomy drawn mainly from the taxonomy proposed by Shalaby et al. (2009) which is based on the distinction between form and content. As new lexical error categories occurred from the data, some categories were added by the researcher to the taxonomy as appropriate to fit all the lexical error types identified in the data (see Table 3.2 for details). The categorisation of lexical errors in this study was done by the researcher in consultation with an L1 Arabic speaker and an L1 English speaker to ensure accuracy in lexical error classification. The lexical error taxonomy created for this study are explained below in detail.

3 Research Design and Methodology 67

Table 3.2 Taxonomy of lexical errors with coding scheme for analysis purposes

Formal Lexical Errors	(FE)	Semantic Lexical Errors	(SE)
Misselection	(FM)	**Confusion of Sense Relations**	(CSR)
The Suffix Type	(ST)	General Term for a Specific One	(GTS)
The Prefix Type	(PT)	Overly Specific Term	(OST)
False Friends	(FF)	Inappropriate Co-Hyponyms	(ICH)
Misformations	(M)	Wrong Near Synonym	(WNS)
Analogy	(A)	Translation From L1	(TL1)
Borrowing	(B)	Binary Terms	(BT)
Coinage	(C)	Inappropriate Meaning	(IM)
Distortions	(D)	Distortion of Meaning	(DM)
Errors Impeding Comprehension	(SEIC)	**Collocation Errors**	(CE)
Errors Resulting in Inappropriate Meaning	(SEIM)	**Connotation Errors**	(CNE)
L1 Transfer Errors	(SEL1)	**Stylistic Errors**	(STY)
Capitalisation Errors	(SEC)	Verbosity	(SV)
Addition Errors	(SEA)	Misuse of Compounds	(SMC)
Omission Errors	(SEO)	Circumlocution	(SC)
Substitution Errors	(SES)	**Incompletion Errors**	(IE)
Transposition Errors	(SET)		
Grapheme Substitution Errors	(SEGS)		
Word Segmentation Errors	(SEWS)		
Unique Spelling Errors	(SEU)		

A. **FORMAL ERRORS**

Formal errors are categorised into three types: (1) misselection errors; (2) misformation errors; and (3) distortions. The subtypes and examples of each type are as follows:

1. **Misselection Errors**

In this category, lexical errors are subcategorised into 3 subtypes:

1.1. Suffix errors.

Lexis in this subcategory have different suffixes of the same word base (for example, *break breakable*, *polite politeness*).

1.2. Prefix errors.

Lexis in this subcategory have different prefixes of the same word base (for example, *order reorder*, *correct incorrect*).

1.3. False friends.

This subcategory refers to lexis in two languages that are similar in form and maybe in pronunciation, but are different in meaning (for instance, the English word *see* and the German word *See* meaning "lake").

2. **Misformation errors**
   In this category, some lexis used do not exist in the L2. Misformation errors are classified into three types as follows:

2.1. Analogy.

   This subcategory refers to the formation of a lexical item that is similar to another lexical item in form. According to Zughoul (1991, p. 52), language learners sometimes coin new words based on "existing paradigms" of another word as in *eyeche for eyestrain based on other word forms such as headache.

2.2. Borrowing.
   In this subcategory, L1 words are used in the L2 context (for example, "Girls use *kuhul to look beautiful." In Arabic kuhul means "eye-liner"). According to Hemchua and Schmitt (2006), the source of errors in this category is traced back to the learner's L1 which are also referred to as interlingual errors.

2.3. Coinage.
   This subcategory refers to the tendency of inventing a word that does not exist in the L2.

3. **Distortions**
   In this category, lexical items also do not exist in the L2. However, the errors are the result of misspelling which is subdivided into 11 subcategories. The categorisation of spelling errors resulted from the investigation of different EA studies conducted by other researchers (e.g., Ahmed, 2017; Al-Jarf, 2010; Cook, 2014; Shalaby et al., 2009). Additional subcategories have been added to the current taxonomy because they seemed to be particularly recurrent features of learner spelling. The spelling errors in this study were subcategorised as follows:

3.1. "Spelling errors impeding comprehension: a lexical item in the source text is translated into another lexical item that does not exist in the L2 and is incomprehensible to readers. In this category, the lexical item written is partially or completely a coined word (for example, *asch *each* or *geun *gain*).

3.2. Spelling errors resulting in inappropriate meaning (for example, *pest *best*).

3.3. L1 transfer errors, that is, the transfer of the L1 phonological rules into English accounts for the occurrence of misspelled words (for example, L1 Arabic speakers tend to produce misspelled words such as *bopular *popular*, because the phoneme /p/ does not exist in the phonological system of the Arabic language).

3.4. Spelling errors due to addition of a letter (for example, *everry *every* or *kingdome *kingdom*).

3.5. Spelling errors due to omission of a letter (for example, *geat *great* or *importnt *important*).

3.6. Spelling errors due to substitution of one letter for another (for example, *citicen *citizen* or *fawrard *forward*).

3.7. Spelling errors due to transposition of two neighbouring letters (for example, *recieve *receive* or *lucky *lucky*).

3.8. Spelling errors due to grapheme substitution. In this category, more than two letters are substituted for the usual form based on the sounds associated with individual letters, for example, *knoldg *knowledge*.

3.9. Spelling errors due to segmentation. The L2 lexical items are either divided by a space or an unnecessary space is added between lexical items, such as *black board *blackboard* and *shortsighted *shortsighted*.

3.10. Spelling errors due to capitalisation of a letter (necessary or unnecessary capitalisation), for example *john for *John* or *I Have time for *I have time*.

3.11. Unique spelling errors (multiple errors): in this category, more than one type of spelling error is identified" (Alenazi et al., 2021, p. 11).

B. SEMANTIC ERRORS

Semantic lexical errors are categorised into five main types which are further subcategorised into serval subtypes as follows:

1. **Confusion of sense relations**

   Aitchison (2012) indicated that lexemes are stored in people's minds based on each item's semantic relations. Accordingly, the confusion of sense relations' category based on Shalaby et al. (2009) involves "8 subcategories: the use of a general term for a specific one; overly specific terms, inappropriate co-hyponyms, near synonyms, translation from L1, binary terms, inappropriate meaning and distortion of meaning" (p. 73). These subcategories are discussed below in detail.

1.1. A general lexical item is used where a specific term is required. That is using a hypernym for a hyponym. According to Hemchua and Schmitt (2006), the meaning is underspecified in this category (for example, *modern equipment for *appliances*).

1.2. Using an overly specific lexical item (a hyponym for a hypernym). For instance, * biologists *scientists*.

1.3. Inappropriate use of co-hyponyms, such as (*silver *gold*).

1.4. Incorrect use of near synonyms, for example, *exercise *practice*.

1.5. Direct translation from L1. In this subcategory, each L1 word is translated into an equivalent word in the L2.

1.6. Binary terms. In lexical semantics, a binary system is a pair of related words or concepts that are opposite in meaning (for example, *big: small, long: short, buy: sell*).

1.7. Words with inappropriate meaning. In this subcategory, L2 lexical items are semantically inappropriate (for example, *join *combine* two elements).

1.8. Distortion of meaning.

In this subcategory, lexis are used in a way that deviates from its standard meaning in a negative manner (for example, People are *addict *attracted* to Dubai)

2. **Collocation errors**

Collocations are lexical items that often occur together. Misuse of collocations sound inappropriate to L1 speakers. For example, *<u>protect time</u> save time*

3. **Connotation errors**

Connotation refers to the different implied positive/negative associations that most lexis naturally have. Connotation errors usually occur when a learner means something else by using a certain word, something that might be initially hidden. For example, "There are over 1000 *vagrants (negative) *homeless* (positive) in the city."

4. **Stylistic errors**

Based on Shalaby et al.'s taxonomy, the stylistic error category has three subcategories:

4.1. Verbosity, which is a term that is used in this taxonomy to indicate that a construction in a language contains more words than is necessary for communication;

4.2. Misuse of compounds. A compound word is a combination of two or more words to convey one meaning that is not clearly conveyed by separated words; and

4.3. Circumlocution which refers to the use of many words where fewer would do, particularly in a deliberate attempt to be vague or evasive. According to Zughoul (1991), errors of this category use a paraphrase strategy to convey the intended meaning of the source text, instead of providing the exact lexical item.

5. **Incompletion errors**

In this category, necessary lexical item/s in a particular context is/are omitted, which results in an incomplete sentence. This type of error has a negative influence on the semantic aspect of the L2 since the intended meaning of the source text is not fully conveyed owing to the omission of significant words while translating. This category has been added to the taxonomy as appropriate to the nature of the data this study is dealing with. Previous studies did not use this error category because they were analysing free written texts. In analysing free written texts, the research does not have direct access to the student's intended meaning, while in translation the intended meaning is available through the source text.

Statistical Data Analysis

Statistics have always been a necessary measure for language researchers in many respects. They provide more accurate, meaningful, and reliable analysis of a phenomena's frequency (Allen, 2017). In order to determine the relationship between major categories /subcategories of lexical errors and the total number of errors

3.4 Research Design 71

among all categories, a frequency percentage for each main linguistic category and subcategory (formal/semantic) was calculated.

To facilitate the analysis, SPSS software was used to describe and categorise and determine the frequency percentage of the distributional patterns of lexical errors in the corpus data. The frequencies procedure in this software was useful to the researcher in producing detailed summary measures for the different categories in the form of frequency tables, bar charts, and pie charts. Table 3.2 shows the error-coding scheme that was created for this part of the analysis. The percentage frequency distributions for formal/semantic lexical errors (major categories/subcategories) were calculated.

3.4.6.3 Explanation of Lexical Errors

The final stage of the analysis of the corpus data procedures involved explanation of the identified lexical errors. This stage is concerned with the possible sources of lexical errors. The identified lexical errors were re-examined and further analysed according to their likely causes which are due to either interlingual or intralingual influence. According to Ellis and Barkhuizen (2005), "explaining errors involves determining their sources in order to account for why they were made" (p. 62). Therefore, the potential sources for the identified lexical errors in each category are provided based on the evidence from the types of lexical errors that occurred. Lexical errors that originate from the influence of the learners' L1 were categorised as interlingual errors. If L2 learners produce language errors in their L2 that are related to their L1, then they are referred to as interlingual errors (Richards, 2015). On the other hand, lexical errors that are not attributed to the linguistic structure of the learners' L1, but as a result of the learners' lacking knowledge of the L2, are classified as intralingual errors. Consequently, adopting Richards's classification of language error causes, lexical errors in the current study were divided into these two factors.

More details about the description and explanation of lexical errors are presented in Chaps. 4 and 5.

3.5 Summary and Conclusion

This chapter reviewed the research design and methodology employed in the study. First, the research design was presented and its rationale was discussed. A detailed description of the corpus data was provided, in addition to the description of the participants, data collection, and analysis procedures.

The study adopted an EA approach to examine the lexical errors distributed in the translation texts of Saudi English major students at the university level. For this study, a corpus of translation texts was used as cross-sectional data (a data collected from a population at a particular point in time). These corpora were set at a specific time and do not demonstrate the learners' development over a time period. The use of the corpus data helps to conduct an EA investigation of a written language at a specific point in time.

The corpus data (translation texts) were analysed following the main steps of EA procedures: identification, description, and explanation of errors. At the identification stage, all lexical errors were identified and entered into Excel worksheets organised according to their linguistic categories. The description of errors stage involved both categorisation of lexical errors and statistical analysis (frequency percentage of lexical error distribution). The final stage of the analysis of the corpus data procedures involved an explanation of the identified lexical errors to reveal their main sources. In summary, this chapter dealt with the overall theoretical and methodological approaches applied in this research to achieve the target research questions. In the following two chapters, Chap. 4: *Formal lexical error analysis* and Chap. 5: *Semantic lexical error analysis* the results of the study are presented.

References

Ahmed, I. A. (2017). Different types of spelling errors made by Kurdish EFL learners and their potential causes. *International Journal of Kurdish Studies, 3*(2), 93–110. https://doi.org/10.21600/ijoks.334146

Aitchison, J. (2012). *Words in the mind: An introduction to the mental lexicon*. John Wiley & Sons Inc.

Alenazi, Y., Chen, S., Picard, M., & Hunt, J. W. (2021). Corpus-focused analysis of spelling errors in Saudi learners' English translations. *International TESOL Journal, 16*(7), 4–24.

Al-Jarf, R. (2010). Spelling error corpora in EFL. *Sino-US English Teaching, 7*(1), 6–15. https://www.researchgate.net/publication/267834979

Allen, M. (Ed.). (2017). *The sage encyclopedia of communication research methods*. Sage Publications.

Brown, J. D., & Rodgers, T. S. (2002). *Doing second language research: An introduction to the theory and practice of second language research for graduate/master's students in TESOL and applied linguistics, and others*. Oxford University Press.

Cook, V. J. (2014). *The English writing system*. Routledge.

Corder, S. P. (1974). *Error analysis*. In J. P. B. Allen & S. P. Corder (Eds.) *Techniques in applied linguistics (the Edinburgh course in applied linguistics: 3)* (pp 122–154). Oxford University Press (Language and Language Learning).

Crystal, D. (1992). *An encyclopaedic dictionary of language and languages*. Blackwell.

DePaulo, P. (2000). *Sample size for qualitative research: The risk of missing something important*. Quirk's Marketing Research Review.

Ellis, N. C. (1994). Implicit and explicit language learning. *Implicit and explicit learning of languages*, 79–114.

Ellis, R. (2008). *The study of second language acquisition*. Oxford University Press.

Ellis, R., & Barkhuizen, G. (2005). *Analyzing learner language*. Oxford University Press.

Elmahdi, O. E. H. (2016). Translation problems faced by Saudi EFL learners at university level. *English Literature and Language Review, 2*(7), 74–81.

Gass, S., & Selinker, L. (2008). *Second language acquisition: An introductory course* (3rd ed.). Routledge.

References

Hemchua, S., & Schmitt, N. (2006). An analysis of lexical errors in the English compositions of Thai learners. *Prospect, 21*, 3–25.

James, C. (2013). *Errors in language learning and use: Exploring error analysis.* Routledge.

Jiang, W. (2009). *Acquisition of word order in Chinese a foreign language.* Mouton de Gruyter.

Khalifa, M. (2015). Problem in translating English and Arabic languages' structure: A case study of EFL Saudi students in Shaqra University. *European Journal of English Language and Literature Studies, 3*(4), 22–34.

Llach, M. P. A. (2005). The relationship of lexical error and their types to the quality of ESL compositions: An empirical study. *Porta Linguarum, 3*(1), 45–57.

Llach, M. P. A. (2011). *Lexical errors and accuracy in foreign language writing.* Multilingual Matters.

Mahan, K. R. (2013). *Lexical errors in Norwegian intermediate and advanced learners of English* [Unpublished Master's thesis]. University of Oslo.

Mariko, A. (2007). Grammatical errors across proficiency levels in L2 spoken and written English. *The Economic Journal of Takasaki City University of Economics, 49*(3,4), 117–129.

McBurney, D. H., & White, T. L. (2007). *Research methods* (7th ed.). Thomson Wadsworth.

Mcenery, T., & Wilson, A. (2001). *Corpus linguistics* (2nd ed.). Edinburgh University Press.

Richards, J. C. (2015). *Error analysis: Perspectives on second language acquisition.* Routledge.

Shalaby, A. N., Yahya, N., & El-Komi, M. (2009). Analysis of lexical errors in Saudi college students' compositions. *Journal of the Saudi Association of Languages and Translation, 2*(3), 65–93.

Zughoul, M. (1991). Lexical choice: Towards writing problematic word lists. *International Review of Applied Linguistics, 29*(2), 45–60.

Chapter 4
Formal Lexical Error Analysis

4.1 Introduction

As Chap. 3: *Methodology* provided a detailed description of the research design and methodology employed, this chapter examines the results and discussion of formal lexical error analysis of the collected corpus data in relation to the aims and questions of the research and its interpretations. Due to the comprehensive nature of the taxonomy used in the study, the results and discussion of each main category of the lexical errors are presented in separate chapters (Chap. 4: *Formal Lexical Error Analysis* and Chap. 5: *Semantic lexical error analysis*). This chapter consists of two main sections. The first Sect. (4.1) presents a description of the formal lexical errors identified. It provides a linguistic description of the formal lexical errors made in the translation texts, along with detailed statistical analysis. The second Sect. (4.2) presents a discussion of formal lexical errors. It focuses on explaining the potential sources of formal lexical errors made by Saudi English major students. It also provides a comparison between the previous studies conducted by many scholars (Ander & Yıldırım, 2010; Carrió-Pastor & Mestre, 2014; Hemchua & Schmitt, 2006; Huaqing, 2009; Llach, 2011; Meara & English, 1987; Rezai & Davarpanah, 2019; Saud, 2018; Shalaby et al., 2009; Zimmerman, 1987) and the current study's results.

4.2 Quantitative Analysis and Description of Formal Lexical Errors

As has been mentioned in Chap. 3: *Methodology*, the data was a corpus of translation texts of 105 Saudi English major students at the university level. The classification of formal lexical errors employed is an extension and innovation of

---

© The Author(s), under exclusive license to Springer Nature Singapore Pte Ltd. 2022
Y. Alenazi, *Exploring Lexical Inaccuracy in Arabic-English Translation*,
New Frontiers in Translation Studies, https://doi.org/10.1007/978-981-19-6390-2_4

previous taxonomies of lexical errors made by other researchers (e.g., Hemchua & Schmitt, 2006; James, 2013; Shalaby et al., 2009). The framework of the formal lexical error classification system is summarised in Fig. 4.1.

In the following section, all types of formal lexical errors are examined, statistically analysed and described in detail. After all the formal lexical errors are identified, they are classified under three main types: (1) misselection errors, (2) misformation errors, and (3) distortion errors. Misselection was subdivided into suffix errors, prefix errors, and false friends. Misformation includes analogy, borrowing, and coinage, whereas distortion includes various types of spelling errors within the L2 lexical items, errors impeding comprehension, errors resulting in inappropriate meaning, L1 transfer, addition, omission, substitution, transposition, word segmentation, capitalisation, and unique spelling errors.

All types of formal lexical errors are provided with examples and are discussed. In each subheading demonstrating one main type or subcategory of formal lexical errors, the total number of errors and the frequency percentage of errors made by the Saudi English major students are put in tables and all examples shown are inappropriate translations from the students.

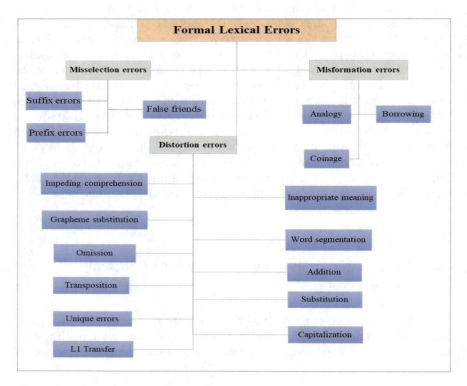

Fig. 4.1 Formal lexical error classification

4.2 Quantitative Analysis and Description of Formal Lexical Errors

4.2.1 Formal Lexical Errors

Even though the students were studying English as their major, a significant number of lexical errors were identified. The two largest categories of errors with very similar number of errors were formal and semantic errors. In this section, only formal errors are discussed.

As shown in Table 4.1, the corpus of translation texts comprised 12,284 individual words. The average text length per student was 116 words, with each student contributing to just under 1% of the total corpus. Of all the words in the corpus, 511 (4.15%) words were identified as formal lexical errors. Each student's contribution contained approximately 4.8% erroneous formal lexical items. Theses formal lexical errors had been classified into three main types and subdivided into 17 subtypes, and the frequency of each type and subtype had been presented. Some formal lexical error types were common; others were relatively infrequent. This indicates that certain lexical error types appear to be particularly problematic for the students while writing through translation in English (see Fig. 4.2 for the percentage distribution of the main categories of formal lexical errors).

Table 4.1 Length of the corpus texts and number of formal lexical errors

1. Total texts	105
2. Total English words	12,284
3. Mean length per text	116
4. Total formal lexical errors	511
5. Mean number of formal lexical errors	5

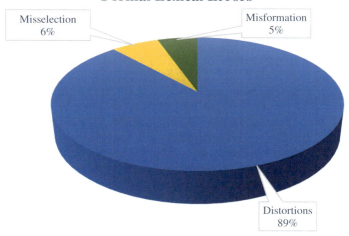

Fig. 4.2 Types of formal lexical error overall percentage

Table 4.2 Types of formal lexical errors and their frequency percentage distribution

Error code	Type of errors	Number of errors	Frequency percentage
FM	Misselection errors	32	6.3
M	Misformation errors	27	5.3
D	Distortion errors	452	88.5
Total		511	100

Table 4.3 Misselection error subtypes frequency percentage

Error code	Type of misselection errors	Number of errors	Frequency percentage
PT	Prefix errors	1	0.2
ST	Suffix errors	31	6.1
Total		32	–
Total formal lexical errors		511	100

In the corpus data analysed, distortion errors in Saudi English major students' translation texts were more pervasive than other types of formal lexical errors. Thus, new subcategories were added to the lexical error taxonomy developed by Shalaby et al. (2009) for comprehensive and accurate analysis: addition, omission, substitution, transposition, grapheme substitution, word segmentation, capitalisation errors, errors impeding comprehension, errors resulting in inappropriate meaning, errors owing to L1 transfer, and unique (miscellaneous type) errors. In Shalaby et al.'s study, misselection errors were more frequent than misformation and distortion errors. However, in the current study, distortion errors occurred with the highest frequency, 452 times (89%) followed by misselection errors, 32 errors (6%), and misformation errors occurring 27 times, with the proportion of (5%) (see Table 4.2).

4.2.1.1 Misselection Errors

Suffix misselection was the most frequent type of lexical errors in this subcategory, occurring 31 times out of the total of 511 formal lexical errors, at the rate of 6% of all formal lexical errors. The subtype prefix misselection occurred only once in the 105 translation texts analysed in the word *indiscovered *undiscovered*, and no incorrect choice of words was found in the use of false friends.

As shown in Table 4.3, of the misselection errors, suffix errors were the most common in comparison with the other subtypes in this category, occurring 31 times out of a total of 32 misselection errors, 6% of the formal lexical errors, and 3% of the total number of lexical errors. The inappropriate choice of suffixes reveals the students' insufficient lexical knowledge of the morphological structure of English vocabulary and indicates the need for direct teaching of derivational morphology.

4.2 Quantitative Analysis and Description of Formal Lexical Errors

The findings showed that suffixation, rather than prefixation, caused most difficulty for the students. The following examples cited from the corpus demonstrate the issue: in the examples, the asterisk * represents the error, and *italics* indicates the corrected word:

1. *Eat and *drink *Eating and drinking* all day is bad for health.
2. Development *journalist *journalism*.
3. People have *difference *different* skills …
4. *Tourist *Tourism* is an important source of national income in Egypt.
5. Bad habits *obstruction *obstruct* our way to progress.

Some suffix errors consist of similar lexical forms of the same word class (e.g., *Tourist *Tourism* is an important source of national income in Egypt) and the incorrect use of a specific word class (e.g., Bad habits *obstruction *obstruct* our way to progress). It was found that most suffix errors were owing to the incorrect choice of a specific word class, whereas only few errors occurred as a result of similar forms of misperception. It appears that the students encountered more difficulties in choosing the correct derivative form of a certain lexical item than the use of similar lexical forms of the same class. One possible reason for the occurrence of such errors is due to the students' limited morphological and syntactical knowledge of the L2.

4.2.1.2 Misformation Errors

The most frequent type of error in this subcategory was that of coinage. This error occurred 25 times out of the total of 511 formal lexical errors, at the rate of 5% of all formal lexical errors. The subtype borrowing occurred only twice in the 105 translation texts we analysed, and no incorrect choice of words was identified under the subtype analogy (see Table 4.4).

In the 105 translation texts analysed, only two instances of borrowing from the source text that is written in Arabic (the students' L1) were found. This could be related to the students' awareness of the negative influence of lexical borrowing while translating to the L2. If English lectures put emphasis on the appropriate translation strategies and the consequence of using lexical borrowing as an incorrect translation strategy, this could also help in minimising the number of this type

Table 4.4 Misformation error frequency percentage

Error code	Type of misformation error	Number of errors	Frequency percentage
B	Borrowing	2	0.4
C	Coinage	25	4.9
Total		27	–
Total formal lexical errors		511	100

of error. The examples of borrowing from L1 source text are illustrated in the following (the first script presented is a Romanisation of the Arabic text):

1. *tabdhul almamlakat alearabiat alsaeudiat kl aljuhud almumkinat liasud alsalam   fa   mintaqat   alshrq   al'awsat*
تبذل المملكة العربية السعودية كل الجهود الممكنة ليسود السلام فى منطقة الشرق الأوسط

'Saudi Arabia is making every possible effort to spread *the slam *peace* in the Middle East.'

2. *min jid wajad wamin zara'a hasad* من جد وجد ومن زرع حصد
'Who *jid *works hard* will get great benefits.'

One likely explanation for the production of such errors is that the students could not find a suitable word in their English lexicon; thus, they relied on their L1 lexicon to fill the L2 lexical knowledge gap.

As for coinage errors, most of the coined words were incomprehensible, and the intended meaning could not be understood without returning to the source text. The following examples below have been corrected syntactically and orthographically except for the coinage error for the purpose of clarity:

3. *tueadu alsiyaha min 'ahami masadir aldakhl alqawmaa fa misr*
تعد السياحة من أهم مصادر الدخل القومى فى مصر

'*The coinsc is an important source of income in Egypt.'

4. *tabdhul alhukumat qusaraa jahdiha litawfir altaeam likuli muatin*
تبذل الحكومة قصارى جهدها لتوفير الطعام لكل مواطن

'The government does all there *atteiaed to provide food to all civilians.'

Producing such errors while translating is attributed to the limited lexical knowledge of the learner. These two coined words *the coinsc and *atteiaed are not related phonologically or morphologically to either the L1 or L2 lexical systems. However, based on the original source texts, the coined word *the coinsc is an incorrect word for the L1 word *alsiyaha* 'tourism' and the coined word *atteiaied is an incorrect word for the L1 word *jahdiha* 'effort.' This type of error shows the total lack of such words in the student's lexical knowledge of the L2 which led the student to invent odd words.

4.2.1.3 Distortion Errors

In this category, the lexical items identified do not exist in the L2. However, the errors occurred as a result of misspelling which are subdivided into 11 subcategories as mentioned earlier. The categorisation of distortion errors (misspellings) resulted from the investigation of different published taxonomies (e.g., Ahmed, 2017; Al-Jarf, 2010; Cook, 2014; Shalaby et al., 2009). Additional subcategories have been added to the current classification because they seemed to be particularly recurrent features of learner misspellings.

In the analysed 105 corpus texts, Saudi English major students yielded 452 distortion errors. The average number of spelling mistakes made by each individual was

4.2 Quantitative Analysis and Description of Formal Lexical Errors

4.1%. The 452 distortion errors have been classified into eleven subcategories and the frequency of each type has been presented. Some types of distortion errors were common; others were relatively infrequent (see Table 4.5). This indicates that certain error types appear to be particularly problematic for the students when they attempt to translate in the English language. The distortion error subcategories are presented in order of their frequency in the next section in detail with examples from the data.

1. Capitalisation errors

Table 11 demonstrates that the most common type of distortion errors made by the students was capitalisation spelling errors (29%). In the 105 translation texts analysed, 129 instances of capitalisation errors were found. This type of error is made by students when translating through either a lack of capitalisation or unnecessary capitalisation of letters of words. The students in this research made many errors of this type. Uncapitalising the initial letter of proper nouns and words at the beginning of sentences while translating in the L2 was pervasive among the students, such as *arabia for *Arabia* or *middle east for *Middle East* or capitalising a letter in the middle of a sentence. This type of error is attributed to the different writing systems between Saudi English major students' L1 and English. Capitalisation is not used in the Arabic writing system due to the nature of Arabic alphabets which explains why English learners in this study produce such errors. Examples of this type of distortion error are illustrated in Table 4.6.

2. Omission errors

The next subcategory in frequency was spelling errors by omission (19%) which were prevalent in the students' translation products occurring 86 times. Omission errors include omitting a consonant or a vowel within the L2 word. In the students'

Table 4.5 Percentage frequency distribution of distortion error subcategories

Error code	Type of distortion error	Number of error	Frequency percentage
SEA	Addition	34	7.5
SEC	Capitalisation	129	28.5
SEGS	Grapheme substitution	12	2.7
SEIC	Errors impeding comprehension	38	8.4
SEIM	Errors resulting in inappropriate meaning	3	0.7
SEL1	Errors due to L1 transfer	7	1.5
SEO	Omission	86	19.0
SES	Substitution	70	15.5
SET	Transposition	15	3.3
SEU	Unique spelling errors	41	9.1
SEWS	Word segmentation	17	3.8
Total		452	–
Total Formal lexical errors		511	100

4 Formal Lexical Error Analysis

Table 4.6 Types of capitalisation errors in the translation texts

Sound category	Capitalisation	Misspelled word	Correct form	Error
Consonant (C)	Required	*saudi	*Saudi*	<s>
Consonant (C)	Unrequired	Many *Life forms …	… *life*…	<L>
Consonant (C)	Required	*we …	*We* …	<w>
Consonant (C)	Required	… *west …	… *West* …	<w>
Consonant (C)	Required	*there are …	*There* are …	<t>

Table 4.7 Types of omission errors in the translation texts

Sound category	Type of omission	Misspelled word	Correct form	Error
Silent letter (V/C)	V omission	*lif	*life*	<e> omitted
Consonant (C)	C omission	*midde	*middle*	<l> omitted
Silent letter (V/C)	V omission	*incom	*income*	<e> omitted
Silent letter (V/C)	C omission	*shoud	*should*	<l> omitted

Table 4.8 Types of substitution errors in the translation texts

Sound category	Type of error	Misspelled word	Correct form	Error
Vowel (V)	V substitution by V	*mast	*must*	<u> substituted by <a>
Vowel (V)	V substitution by V	*pirson	*person*	<e> substituted by <i>
Vowel (V)	V substitution by V	*enjoe	*enjoy*	<y> substituted by <e>
Vowel (V)	V substitution by V	*warking	*working*	<o> substituted by <a>

translation texts, "omission of the silent letters in the L2 lexical items was also common" (Alenazi et al., 2021, p. 14). Examples of spelling omission errors are presented in Table 4.7.

Furthermore, some omission errors occurred where the end consonant in a word should be doubled when a certain suffix is added to it, but it has not been doubled, such as in *mentaly for *mentally*, *stoped for *stopped,* and *runing instead of *running*. Such errors are possibly related to the student's limited orthographic knowledge of the L2.

3. Substitution errors

This was followed by substitution errors with a frequency percentage of (15.5%). This type of distortion was quite common among the students taking place 70 times in their translation text. The students tend to substitute English letters (vowels or consonants) with other letters. A possible explanation for such errors is related to the students' pronunciation of the L2 lexical items. Most of the substitution instances in the students' translation occurred when attempting to use English vowels. Examples of this subcategory are listed below in Table 4.8:

"The substitutions of the English consonants /b/ for /p/ and /v/ for /f/ are classified as a separate type of distortion error (L1 transfer errors) in this study" (Alenazi et al., 2021, p. 15) (see subsection 10).

4.2 Quantitative Analysis and Description of Formal Lexical Errors

4. Impeding comprehension errors

In this subcategory, the students made 38 errors with the proportion of (8.4%) of the total distortion errors. These errors were very difficult to comprehend without returning to the source text. Table 4.9 shows a few examples of the misspellings under this category; the correct form of the listed lexical items has been extracted directly from the source text:

From the examples illustrated, "the lexical items in the source text were translated into other lexical items that do not exist in the L2, and as a consequence, they are incomprehensible" (Alenazi et al., 2021, p. 15). The L2 lexical items written were partially or completely a coined word. The potential cause for this type of spelling error could be related to the students' limited phonological, morphological, and orthographical knowledge of the L2.

5. Addition errors

This subcategory of distortions occurred 34 times in which the student added an extra letter in the L2 lexical item. The addition of vowels or consonants in an English word could be traced back to the way that word is articulated. According to Othman (2018), English is not a phonetic language like Arabic. Therefore, some Arab learners of English write an English word based on how it is pronounced which is an incorrect writing technique. They usually apply the same writing strategy when they write in Arabic, which causes them to have spelling mistakes due to the addition of extra letters. Examples of such errors are presented in Table 4.10. Some additional errors could be related the student's limited orthographic knowledge of the L2 in words such as *careing *caring* and *saveing *saving*.

6. Unique errors

Unique errors occurred 41 times in the students' written texts with a frequency percentage (9%) of the total distortion errors. In this subcategory, several types of errors were identified within the L2 lexical item. Table 4.11 shows the misspelled words as examples of this error. These errors can be attributed to the students' lack of the L2 orthographical and morphological knowledge.

7. Word segmentation errors

Word segmentation errors occurred 17 times with the proportion of (4%). Errors made in this category could also be traced back to the students' L1 writing system and its interference with the L2 (see Sect. 4.3 for detail). Examples of space inaccuracy of the students' writings are illustrated in Table 4.12.

Table 4.9 Types of impeding comprehension errors in the translation texts

Sound category	Type of error	Misspelled word	Correct form	Error
Vowel (V)	N/A	*geun	*gain*	<e>, <u>
Vowel (V)	N/A	*xet	*exist*	<e>, <i>, <s>
Consonant (C) Vowel (V)	N/A	*habbite	*hobby*	<a>, <i>, <t>, <e>
Consonant (C) Vowel (V)	N/A	*terest	*tourism*	<e>, <e>, <t>
Consonant (C) Vowel (V)	N/A	*asch	*each*	<a>, <s>

Table 4.10 Types of addition errors in the translation texts

Sound category	Type of error	Misspelled word	Correct form	Error
Consonant (C)	C addition	*off	*of*	<f> added
Vowel (V)	V addition	*tickeet	*ticket*	<e> added
Consonant (C)	C addition	*beatch	*beach*	<t> added
Vowel (V)	V addition	*maiking	*making*	<i> added
Vowel (V)	V addition	*huoman	*human*	<o> added

Table 4.11 Types of unique errors in the translation texts

Sound category	Type of error	Misspelled word	Correct form	Error
Consonant (C) Vowel (V)	V substitution, CV transposition	*navre	*never*	<e> substituted by <a>, <r> & <e> transposed
Vowel (V)	V addition, V omission	*coollct	*Collect*	<o> added, <e> omitted
Consonant (C) Vowel (V)	C substitution, C omission	*hopies	*hobbies*	<b> substituted by <p>, <b> omitted
Vowel (V)	V substitution, V substitution	*midacally	*medically*	<e> substituted by <i>, <i> substituted by <a>
Vowel (V)	V addition, V omission	*beitwen	*between*	<i> added, <e> omitted

Table 4.12 Types of word segmentation errors in the translation texts

Sound category	Type of error	Misspelled word	Correct form	Error
N/A	Word space required	*alot	*a lot*	N/A
N/A	Word space unrequired	*with out	*without*	N/A
N/A	Word space required	*donot	*do not*	N/A
N/A	Word space required	*onearth	*on earth*	N/A
N/A	Word space unrequired	*every thing	*everything*	N/A

In the English language writing system, a normal word space is necessary between two separate lexical items and it is not required with the use of some compound words. In contrast, space is not always required at the lexical level in the Arabic language writing system. Usually, segmentation occurs at the level of the sentence which causes some Saudi students to have such errors while writing in English.

8. Transposition errors

Transposition errors were the next highest subcategory of distortions after word segmentation with the percentage (3%) of the total number of errors. The students made 12 errors reversing two neighbouring letters in the L2 lexical item (see Table 4.13 for examples). Cook (2014) identified similar errors in his study and attributed them to the students' incomplete knowledge of the L2 lexical items correct forms.

4.2 Quantitative Analysis and Description of Formal Lexical Errors 85

Table 4.13 Types of transposition errors in the translation texts

Sound category	Type of error	Misspelled word	Correct form	Error
Consonant (C) Vowel (V)	CV transposition	*monye	*money*	<y>, <e> reversed
Consonant (C) Vowel (V)	CV transposition	*pepole	*people*	<e>, <o> reversed
Vowel (V)	VV transposition	*thier	*their*	<i>, <e> reversed
Vowel (V)	VV transposition	*abuot	*about*	<u>, <o> reversed
Vowel (V)	VV transposition	*langauge	*language*	<a>, <u> reversed

Table 4.14 Types of grapheme substitution errors in the translation texts

Sound category	Type of error	Misspelled word	Correct form	Error
Consonant (C) Vowel (V)	CV substitution by CC	*pachent	*patient*	<ti> substituted by <ch>
Consonant (C) Vowel (V)	C omission, V omission, V omission	*knoldg	*knowledge*	<w> omitted, <e> omitted, <e> omitted
Vowel (V)	VV substitution by V	*becose	*because*	<au> substituted by <o>
Consonant (C) Vowel (V)	V omission, V substitution by V, CV substitution by C	*expirians	*experience*	<e> omitted, <e> substituted by <a>, <ce> substituted by <s>
Vowel (V)	V substitution by VV	*beard	*bird*	<i> substituted by <ea>

9. Grapheme substitution errors

Similar to the previous subcategory, grapheme substitution errors occurred 12 times with the proportion of (3%). Examples of errors in this subcategory are illustrated in Table 4.14. These errors could be related to the students' mispronunciation of the L2 words. Another possible reason is the difference between Arabic and English phoneme-graphemes correspondence rules. "According to Watson (2002), Arabic letters are written based on how they are pronounced" which explains "the occurrence of this type of misspelling in the students' English writing because the latter has more complex spelling rules" (Alenazi et al., 2021, p. 21). In the English language, a phoneme can be symbolised by several graphemes, such as /ʃ/ can be found in words like *shoot, patient, sure, and social,* while in Arabic /ʃ/ coincides with one letter which is ش.

10. L1 transfer errors

Distortion errors due to the transfer of the L1 phonetic features to the L2 lexical item were infrequent in comparison with the previous subcategories. There are 12 instances of this type of spelling error. Examples from the students' texts are shown in Table 4.15. The students in this subcategory produced misspelled words such as *bopular *popular* and *falue *value* due to the lack of voicing contrasts

Table 4.15 Types of L1 transfer errors in the translation texts

Sound category	Type of error	Misspelled word	Correct form	Error
Consonant (C)	C substitution	*stambs	*stamps*	<p> substituted by <b>
Consonant (C)	C substitution	*facation	*vacation*	<v> substituted by <f>
Consonant (C)	C substitution	*hapit	*habit*	<b> substituted by <p>
Consonant (C)	C substitution	*imbortant	*important*	<p> substituted by <b>

Table 4.16 Types of inappropriate meaning errors in the translation texts

Sound category	Type of error	Misspelled word	Correct form	Error
Vowel (V)	V substituted by V, V addition	*rude*	*road*	<oa> substituted by <u>, <e> added
Vowel (V)	V omission	*pace*	*peace*	<e> omitted

between bilabial stops and labio-dental fricatives in the students' L1. In the Arabic language, the phonemes /p/ and /b/ and /f/ and /v/ are allophonic variants, while they are considered four separate phonemes in English.

11. Inappropriate meaning errors

Distortion errors resulting in an inappropriate meaning were infrequent in the students' translation texts. However, a couple of instances took place when translating an L1 word to the English language. This type of error (see Table 4.16) could also be attributed to the student's incomplete knowledge of the L2 orthographic and morphological rules.

4.3 Discussion and Explanation of Formal Lexical Errors

This section provides a detailed discussion and explanation of the possible sources of the formal lexical errors made by Saudi English major students in their translation products. In error analysis studies, language errors are usually classified as either interlingual errors or intralingual errors (James, 2013; Richards, 2015). Subsequently, the potential sources of formal lexical errors in this study were classified according to these two sources which were further subdivided into two groups related to the subtypes of formal lexical errors and their possible causes. Formal lexical error subcategories related to the two sources (interlingual and intralingual) are summarised in Fig. 4.3.

The first group includes interlingual errors (borrowing errors, L1 transfer errors, capitalisation errors, word segmentation errors). In this group, the different writing systems between Saudi English major students' L1 (Arabic) and English have led

4.3 Discussion and Explanation of Formal Lexical Errors

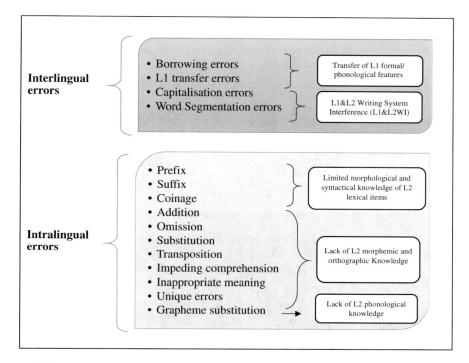

Fig. 4.3 Sources of formal lexical errors

them to make distortion errors such as capitalisation errors and word segmentation errors. In addition, transferring the form of L1 lexical items and its phonological features to the L2 played a role in the occurrence of some formal lexical errors.

The second group includes the intralingual errors in which the students made some formal lexical errors because of their unfamiliarity of the L2 morphemic and orthographic rules such as omission errors, substitution errors, transposition errors, addition errors, unique errors, impeding comprehension errors, and errors resulting in inappropriate meaning. Some intralingual errors are made owing to the lack of L2 phonological knowledge such as grapheme spelling errors, and other errors are related to the leaners' incomplete syntactical and morphological knowledge of the L2 lexical items, such as prefix, suffix, and coinage errors.

As illustrated in Fig. 4.4, more than half of the formal lexical errors occurred were due to intralingual influence (69.65%); that is, the lack of L2 morphemic, orthographic knowledge (LL2MOK) (56.16%), limited morphological and syntactical knowledge of L2 lexical items (LL2SMK) (11.15%), and lack of L2 phonological knowledge (LL2PK) (2.3%) significantly influenced the lexical items used in the translated texts. Interlingual influence (30.35%), on the other hand, made up a considerable percentage of the total formal lexical errors due to interference between the students' L1 and the L2 writing systems (L1/L2WI) (28.60%) and the transfer of L1 phonological system (L1PST) (1.75%).

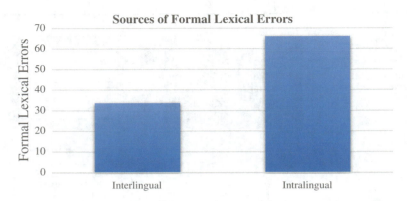

Fig. 4.4 Percentage distribution of formal lexical errors based on their possible sources

Table 4.17 demonstrates in detail the total percentage and frequency distribution of formal lexical errors in relation to their potential causes.

4.3.1 Analysis of Interlingual Errors

As illustrated in Table 4.17, four formal lexical errors fall under the interlingual errors category. These include capitalisation errors, word segmentation errors, L1 transfer errors, and borrowing errors. The former two are distortion errors emanating from interference of L1 and L2 writing systems, while the latter two are L1 transfer errors originating from transferring of L1 formal and phonological features. Each of the four subtypes of interlingual errors and their sources is examined in detail below.

4.3.1.1 Analysis of Capitalisation Errors

Capitalisation errors made by Saudi English major students can be largely attributed to differences between the Arabic and English writing systems. Capitalisation is not employed in the Arabic writing system due to the nature of Arabic alphabets. As indicated by foregoing results of the analysis, the difference in the use of capital letters and word space in the English and Arabic writing systems has been a major source of lexical errors for the students by leading to either unnecessary capitalisation or lack of capitalisation of words or letters. The findings corroborate previous research which put capitalisation among the top three writing errors made by Saudi English major students (Alzamil, 2020). While older studies found capitalisation errors accounted for 6.8 per cent (Althobaiti, 2014) of writing errors made by Saudi L2 learners, in this study, the figure is significantly higher at 28.5 per cent, effectively highlighting the gravity of the influence these subtypes of formal lexical errors have on their writing and translation products.

4.3 Discussion and Explanation of Formal Lexical Errors

Table 4.17 Total percentage frequency distribution of formal lexical errors based on their possible causes

Formal lexical error source	Possible Cause	Error Category	No	Total frequency	Percentage	Total %
Interlingual	L1/L2WI	Capitalisation	129	146	28.60	30.35
		Word segmentation	17			
	L1PST	L1 transfer	7	9	1.75	
		Borrowing	2			
Intralingual	L2LMOK	Addition	34	287	56.16	69.65
		Omission	86			
		Substitution	70			
		Transposition	15			
		Inappropriate meaning	3			
		Impeding comprehension	38			
		Unique errors	41			
	LL2SMK	Prefix errors	1	57	11.15	
		Suffix errors	31			
		Coinage	25			
	L2LPK	Grapheme substitution	12	12	2.34	
Total				511	100	100

The prevalence of capitalisation errors among Saudi English major students is problematic in that it significantly affects their ability to accurately write and translate in English. This is particularly serious in that capitalisation is used in every English sentence and for all proper nouns and some pronouns. Such errors could have a negative impact on the image of the translator and his/her profession, particularly for those students who are expected to be professional and competent translators.

Interference of the Arabic language (L1) results in the various forms of capitalisation errors depicted in Table 4.18, thus negatively influencing their writings and translations by giving rise to inaccurate written texts and substandard translation products.

4.3.1.2 Analysis of Word Segmentation Errors

The source of word segmentation errors affecting Saudi English major students can also be attributed to differences in the English and Arabic writing systems. The variation in word space usage in the two languages leads to the transference of the L1 writing system phonological trends to the L2. The ability of a student to acquire L2 spelling and writing skills is dependent on how well they can segment

Table 4.18 Different forms of capitalisation errors

Capitalisation errors	
Failure to capitalise	**Proper nouns**
	Days of the week e.g. *Thursday for *Thursday*
	Names of months e.g. *june for *June*
	Names of places e.g. *saudi arabia for *Saudi Arabia*
	Pronouns
	I e.g. *<u>i was there</u> for *I was there*
	First letter of word in a sentence
	e.g. *<u>he left</u> for *He left*
Unnecessary capitalisation	**Nouns**
	Letter within a word e.g. *cLips for *clips*
	Word in a sentence
	e.g. There are *Many *many* life forms

the L2 words into the appropriate phonological components (Alenazi, 2018). Difficulties faced by Saudi English major students in their efforts to segment English words into their accurate phonological units thus lead to inadequacies witnessed in their English writing and translation skills. The use of unknown words, that is, words not present in the corpus or the dictionary such as derived words, proper names, or abbreviations, could also inform word segmentation errors in the writings and translations made by Saudi English major students.

Examples of word segmentation errors among Saudi English major students are represented in difficulties in breaking or dividing a word into two. In Arabic, while word space is used for the purposes of delimiting a word, usage of space in the English writing system is not as consistent as effectively leading to either space insertion or space omission mistakes, and hence occurrence of word segmentation errors by the L2 learners (Altamimi et al., 2018). It is therefore not uncommon for the students to erroneously insert space within an English word, for instance, write *my self in place of *myself* thus breaking it into two words. There is also the tendency to omit space between two English words, for instance, write *alot in place of *a lot* effectively joining the two words into one word. The inability by Saudi English major students to recognise English words absent in the Arabic lexicon hinders them from accurately undertaking word segmentation, and, by extension, their capacity to write and translate in the L2.

4.3.1.3 Analysis of L1 Transfer Errors

L1 transfer errors are a function of the influence of the primary language on the L2. Previous studies have attributed L1 transfer errors to the L1 effects on a language acquired later in life (Aloglah, 2018). L1 transfer errors witnessed among

4.3 Discussion and Explanation of Formal Lexical Errors

Saudi English major students can thus be rightly attributed to the effect of the Arabic language on the English language they later learn or acquire. While the carryover of phonological and lexical items from Arabic to English may be positive, where features of the previous language facilitate learning of the L2, transfer of various forms of L1 phonological features and lexical items is often negative. This is evidenced by incorrect application of the L1 (Arabic) phonological features and lexical items to the L2 (English), thus leading to writing and translation errors in the text and translated products generated by EFL students.

For Saudi English major students, negative transfer of the features of L1 to L2 hinders successful learning and acquisition of English writing skills. As they learn English, the Saudi English major students already have information and knowledge derived from their L1 Arabic language and hence the tendency to rely on and be influenced by the lexical and phonological items of the native language as they learn the English language. Owing to this reason, features of their L1 are bound to interfere with and influence their understanding of the L2 as well as their ability to accurately write in that language. Divergence and transference from Arabic lexical features are excellent examples of L1 transfer distortion errors common among the students in this study. For instance, the use of *imbortant *important*, *falue *value,* and *sheap *cheap*. In the Arabic language, the phonemes /p/ and /b/, /ʃ/ and / tʃ /, and /f/ and /v/ are allophonic variants. Since the phonemes /p/ and /v/ are not distinguished in the Arabic sound system, Saudi English major students have the tendency to mispronounce these phonemes which leads them to have orthographic errors and as a consequence distorting meaning.

4.3.1.4 Analysis of Borrowing Errors

Borrowing errors emanate from the transfer of L1 formal or phonological features. The findings indicate borrowing errors are not as prevalent as other forms of writing errors common among Saudi English major students. However, previous studies have shown the frequency of borrowing errors to be higher among preparatory year university students (Shalaby et al., 2009). Thus, as students advance in their university studies and major in the English language, their knowledge of the English lexicon improves and hence the reduction in the incidence of this type of formal lexical errors among Saudi English major students. In the current study, the students appear to avoid lexical borrowing in their translation products unlike other learners from different disciplines as in Shalaby et al.'s (2009) study. There is a possibility that English majors are more aware of this phenomenon and its negative influence on the L2 written production due to the extensive instructions they get about the L2 unlike other majors.

The interlingual errors are caused by the limited knowledge of the English lexicon by the Saudi English major students effectively prompting them to compensate for the deficiency by transferring various forms of lexical and phonological features from the L1 to the L2. The amount of borrowing errors in written texts or translations might also be dependent on the nature of the text genre being tackled. In the two different translated texts below, the students inserted Arabic words instead of English words:

1. 'Saudi Arabia is making every possible effort to spread *the slam *peace* in the Middle East.'
2. 'Who *jid *works hard* will get great benefits.'

Such errors made by the students in their translations indicate that they had limited lexical knowledge of the L2, and consequently used borrowing as a strategy to compensate for their lexical gaps. Llach (2011, p. 197) refers to lexical borrowings as "a sign of lack of lexical knowledge" when an L2 learner uses an equivalent L1 word for an unknown word of the L2. This phenomenon is a major issue for the students as it negatively influences the comprehensibility of their translation and writing.

4.3.2 Analysis of Intralingual Errors

From Fig. 4.3, 11 intralingual sources of formal lexical errors made by Saudi English major students were identified. These include prefix, suffix, coinage, addition, omission, substitution, transposition, impeding comprehension, inappropriate meaning, unique errors, and grapheme substitution errors. Intralingual errors comprise errors that arise due to the disjoint between the L1 and the L2. Intralingual sources of the formal lexical errors include partial exposure to L2 which lead to overgeneralisations as reflected by the production of items that hardly reflect the structure of L1 (Seifeddin & Ebedy, 2016).

4.3.2.1 Analysis of Prefix, Suffix, and Coinage Errors

Prefix, suffix, and coinage errors could be attributable to the limited morphological and syntactic knowledge of L2 lexical items among the students. Prefix and suffix errors are a function of misselection, while coinage errors are informed by misformation. As established, suffix errors (e.g., the use of *journalist in place of *journalism* and *difference instead of *different*) tend to be more prevalent than prefix errors denoting the students had significant difficulties selecting the right suffix for words in their translation.

Suffix and prefix errors may also occur due to the tendency to overgeneralise or ignore rules of the L2 and failure to acknowledge the rules have some exceptional cases. Limited knowledge of English morphemes could lead to prefix errors such as the use of *indiscovered in place of *undiscovered*. According to Alenazi (2018), this type of prefix error is also attributed to overgeneralisation of the applicable grammatical rules. Coinage errors such as the use of *coinsc and *atteiaed in place of *tourism* and *effort* in translations respectively could be attributable to inadequate

4.3 Discussion and Explanation of Formal Lexical Errors

knowledge of the English lexicon, the outcome of which is noun misformation as students make up words that neither exist in their L1 nor in their L2 (Alsahafi, 2017). The errors lead to either unclear or total lack of meaning in their translations.

4.3.2.2 Analysis of Addition, Omission, Substitution, Transposition, Impeding Comprehension, Inappropriate Meaning, and Unique Errors

Some distortion errors could be attributable to a lack of L2 morphemic and orthographic knowledge among the Saudi English major students. Addition errors (e.g., *maiking for *making*) and omission errors (e.g., *diffrent for *different*) among Saudi English major students marked by addition or deletion of letters in L2 lexical items could be attributable to differences in L1 and L2 where the phonetic nature of the L1 causes the learners to assume L2 words are written as they are pronounced. In addition, the insertion of inflectional suffixes to some English words requires either retention of the vowel <e> at the end of the word if the suffix starts with a consonant (e.g., complete *completely*) or deletion of the same if the suffix starts with a vowel (e.g., *complete instead of *completing*). Overgeneralisation of this rule or lack of knowledge of the exceptional instances when this rule should not apply also leads to addition errors (such as *completeing instead of *completing*) that could negatively affect the accuracy of the translation. While substitution (e.g., *picnic* written as *piknik) and transposition errors (e.g., *two* written as *tow) are a function of inadequate L2 orthographical knowledge. Similarity in orthographical features has been found to cause confusion and hence errors. Jose (2014) indicates that such errors are attributed to the insufficient orthographic knowledge of the L2. The cognitive errors are a significant problem for the Saudi English major students as the misconception or unawareness of correct spelling of L2 words leads to deviant spellings which further undermines the correctness of their writing and translation.

Errors impeding comprehension such as *geun for *gain* and *asch for *each* and inappropriate meaning errors could also arise if students misconceive or lack knowledge of the spelling or structure of a word or mispronounce it. The errors drastically alter the form of the written L2 words, thus rendering the translation and the writing incomprehensible in the absence of the original L1 text.

4.3.2.3 Analysis of Grapheme Substitution Errors

Grapheme substitution errors are the function of a lack of L2 phonological knowledge among Saudi English major students. According to Cook (2014) and Ahmed (2017), errors occur when the usual form of an L2 word, often more than two letters, is substituted with a matching form of the word based on sound association rules. The variation in L1 and L2 phoneme grapheme association rules significantly contributes to grapheme substitution errors among Saudi English major students where graphemes in such English words as *thought* are substituted with a corresponding phoneme and thus written as *thort.

Differences in the phonetics of the L1 and L2 are also a major cause of grapheme substitution errors. The students tend to mispronounce English words and then inadvertently proceed to write them as they pronounce them thus producing this type of writing error. In their pronunciations for instance, graphemes in such English words as *because* and *experience* are replaced with their corresponding speech sounds and hence incorrectly written as pronounced, that is *becose and *expirians, respectively. The intralingual error is a major problem for Saudi English major students given that it is not only a function of dissimilarity between the English and Arabic languages but also a function of inadequate phonological knowledge of English. This renders the writings and translations of the students significantly prone to spelling mistakes that could cause their intended meanings to be altered or even lost.

4.3.3 Comparison of the Study's Findings with Previous Studies in relation to the Frequency and Sources of Formal Lexical Errors

This study contributes to the literature in relation to lexical errors made by ESL/EFL learners, and Saudi English major students in particular, in their translation products (e.g., Ander & Yildirim, 2010; Carrió-Pastor & Mestre, 2014; Hemchua & Schmitt, 2006; Huaqing, 2009; Llach, 2011; Meara & English, 1987; Shalaby et al., 2009; Zimmerman, 1987). In comparison with previous studies, some similarities and differences were found between the findings and results of previous research and this study. The current study showed that lexical errors were pervasive in Saudi English major students' translation products which hamper the intended meaning of the source text. Consistent with previous studies (e.g., Hemchua & Schmitt, 2006; Rezai & Davarpanah, 2019; Saud, 2018; Shalaby et al., 2009), formal lexical errors were found in this study to be a frequent type of lexical errors in Arab EFL writings. However, Hemchua and Schmitt (2006) concerning Thai EFL learners, Saud (2018), and Shalaby et al. (2009) concerning Saudi EFL learners found that misselection errors were more frequent than distortion and misformation errors. In Rezai and Davarpanah's (2019) study, misformation errors were also reported to be the most common type of formal lexical errors among their Persian EFL students. The findings of the current study on the other hand show that distortion errors are the most frequent type of formal lexical errors in Saudi English majors' translation products as new subcategories of errors were identified. Such differences in the frequency of formal lexical errors might be related to different variables such as the learning context, the type of data elicited, and the lexical error classification system used. The taxonomy of errors employed for the analysis of lexical errors in this study was refined and expanded to include new error categories such as the ones under the distortion errors category. Other factors are related to the students' L1 background and the type of language sample collected. Most of the previous studies conducted in this field have used free essays, written reports, and language tests in different contexts. In contrast, the current research used translation texts as the language sample for the analysis which could be the reason behind the variation in the number and frequency of errors identified. This is also apparent for the semantic lexical error analysis presented in Chap. 5.

Regarding the potential sources of formal lexical errors, this study showed originality because it uses a comprehensive classification of lexical errors. It found that interlingual and intralingual factors have a major role in the occurrence of most formal lexical errors in the Saudi English major students' translation products. The formal lexical errors occurring as a result of the interlingual influence were owing to the interference between the students' L1 and the L2 writing systems and the transfer of the L1 phonological system to the L2. As for the intralingual influence, the Saudi English major students made lexical errors due to a lack of L2 morphemic and orthographic rules and due to a lack of L2 phonological knowledge.

The percentage distribution of intralingual errors was higher than interlingual errors. These results were different from other researchers' studies who found that interlingual errors were the most frequent errors in Saudi English learners' written production in comparison with intralingual errors (e.g., Albalawi, 2016; Mahmoud, 2005; Othman, 2018; Zughoul, 1991). Albalawi (2016) noted that the different orthographic rules between the Arabic and English languages (interlingual errors) are the main source of the distortion errors made by Saudi English learners. In addition, he used a limited classification system of errors in which distortion errors fit under only three categories: omission errors; addition errors; and substitution errors. Othman (2018) also stated in his study that L1 interference is the main reason behind the occurrence of spelling errors in the Saudi students' writings. However, the main sources of Saudi English learners' formal lexical errors in this study were due to their unfamiliarity of L2 orthographic rules such as omission errors, substitution errors, transposition errors, addition errors, unique errors, impeding comprehension errors, and errors resulting in inappropriate meaning. Some intralingual errors are made owing to the lack of L2 phonological knowledge such as grapheme spelling errors, and other errors are related to the leaners' incomplete syntactic and morphological knowledge of the L2 lexical items, such as prefix, suffix, and coinage errors.

4.4 Conclusion

From the analysis of formal lexical errors presented in this chapter, distortion errors were found more prevalent than other types of formal lexical errors with the highest frequency, 452 times followed by misselection errors, 32 errors, and misformation errors occurring 27 times. In addition, the lexical errors witnessed among Saudi English major students are not homogeneous. While the source of the identified formal lexical errors can be traced back to either interlingual or intralingual causes, they are connected to either differences in Arabic and English writing systems or limitations in the morphological, orthographical, phonological, or syntactic knowledge of the students.

The analysis of the different formal lexical errors helps us to understand how the various subtypes of these errors constitute a problem for Saudi English major students and the way they alter the spellings, meanings, and comprehensibility of their writings and translations. While the interference of the L1 writing system and transfer of L1 phonological features account for a significant number of the formal lexical errors, the importance of Arabic in teaching English writing to the L1 native speaking Saudi students cannot be understated.

Next, Chap. 5: *Semantic lexical error analysis* presents the results and discussion of semantic lexical error analysis of the collected corpus texts in relation to the research objectives.

References

Ahmed, I. A. (2017). Different types of spelling errors made by Kurdish EFL learners and their potential causes. *International Journal of Kurdish Studies, 3*(2), 93–110. https://doi.org/10.21600/ijoks.334146

Albalawi, M. J. (2016). The academic writing performance and spelling errors of English as foreign language students at Tabuk University: A case of the introductory year students. *Asian Journal of Social Sciences, Arts and Humanities, 4*(1), 1–8. https://multidisciplinaryjournals.com/ajsah-vol-4-no-1-2016/

Alenazi, O. S. (2018). Spelling difficulties faced by Arab learners of English as a foreign language. *Arab World English Journal, 9*(2), 118–126.

Alenazi, Y., Chen, S., Picard, M., & Hunt, J. W. (2021). Corpus-focused analysis of spelling errors in Saudi learners' English translations. *International TESOL Journal, 16*(7), 4–24.

Al-Jarf, R. (2010). Spelling error corpora in EFL. *Sino-US English Teaching, 7*(1), 6–15. https://www.researchgate.net/publication/267834979

Aloglah, T. M. (2018). Spelling errors among Arab English speakers. *Journal of Language Teaching and Research, 9*(4), 746–753.

Alsahafi, N. A. (2017). *An investigation of written errors made by Saudi EFL foundation year students* [Unpublished PhD Thesis]. The University of New South Wales, Sydney, Australia.

Altamimi, D. A., Rashid, R. A., & Elhassan, Y. M. (2018). A review of spelling errors in Arabic and non-Arabic contexts. *English Language Teaching, 11*(10), 88–94.

Althobaiti, N. (2014). Error correction in EFL writing: The case of Saudi Arabia, Taif University. *Journal of Modern Education Review, 4*(12), 1038–1053.

Alzamil, A. (2020). An investigation of writing errors made by Saudi English-major students. *International Journal of English Linguistics, 10*(2). https://doi.org/10.5539/ijel.v10n2p92

Ander, S., & Yıldırım, Ö. (2010). Lexical errors in elementary level EFL learners' compositions. *Procedia - Social and Behavioral Sciences, 2*(2), 5299–5303.

Carrió-Pastor, M. L., & Mestre, E. M. M. (2014). Motivation in second language acquisition. *Procedia-Social and Behavioral Sciences, 116*, 240–244.

Cook, V. J. (2014). *The English writing system*. Routledge.

Hemchua, S., & Schmitt, N. (2006). An analysis of lexical errors in the English compositions of Thai learners. *Prospect, 21*, 3–25.

Huaqing, H. (2009). An analysis of lexical errors in non-English majors' writing: A corpus based study [J]. *Foreign Language World, 3*.

References

James, C. (2013). *Errors in language learning and use: Exploring error analysis*. Routledge.

Jose, F. T. (2014). Orthographic errors committed by Sophomore students: A linguistic analysis. *Mediterranean Journal of Social Sciences, 5*(23), 2439–2443.

Llach, M. P. A. (2011). *Lexical errors and accuracy in foreign language writing*. Multilingual Matters

Mahmoud, A. (2005). Collocation errors made by Arab learners of English. *Asian EFL Journal, 5*(2), 117–126.

Meara, P., & English, F. (1987). *Lexical errors and learners' dictionaries*. Birkbeck College.

Othman, A. Kh. A. (2018). An investigation of the most common spelling errors in English writing committed by English-major male students: At the University of Tabuk. *Journal of Education and Practice, 9*(1), 17–22. https://www.iiste.org/Journals/index.php/JEP/article/view/40733

Rezai, M. J., & Davarpanah, F. (2019). The study of formal and semantic errors of lexis by Persian EFL learners. *International Journal of Cognitive and Language Sciences, 13*(1), 41–47.

Richards, J. C. (2015). *Error analysis: Perspectives on second language acquisition*. Routledge.

Saud, W. I. (2018). Lexical errors of third year undergraduate students. *English Language Teaching, 11*(11), 161–168.

Seifeddin, A. H., & Ebedy, H. G. (2016). The effects of the frequency of lexical errors on the quality of EFL learners' writing through email communication. *Journal of Research in Curriculum Instruction and Educational Technology, 2*(3), 67–93.

Shalaby, A. N., Yahya, N., & El-Komi, M. (2009). Analysis of lexical errors in Saudi college students' compositions. *Journal of the Saudi Association of Languages and Translation, 2*(3), 65–93.

Watson, J. (2002). *The phonology and morphology of Arabic*. Oxford University.

Zimmerman, R. (1987). Form-orientated and content-orientated lexical errors in L2 learners. *International Review of Applied Linguistics., 25*(1), 55–67.

Zughoul, M. (1991). Lexical choice: Towards writing problematic word lists. *International Review of Applied Linguistics, 29*(2), 45–60.

Chapter 5
Semantic Lexical Error Analysis

5.1 Introduction

The importance of lexis in written translation and how formal lexical errors could affect the quality and clarity of the Saudi English major students' translation products was detailed in Chap. 4: *Formal Lexical Error Analysis*. The formal lexical errors identified were categorised into 17 subtypes and, based on a taxonomy developed specifically for this study, a quantitative analysis was implemented. The chapter provided a detailed explanation of the possible sources of the identified formal lexical errors. The findings indicated that inadequate knowledge of the L2 phonological, morphological, and orthographical aspects and the difference between the linguistic systems of the target and home languages accounted for the occurrence of these lexical errors.

Due to the comprehensive nature of the taxonomy used in the study, this current chapter presents only the results of semantic lexical error analysis of the translation texts with respect to the aims and questions of the research. This chapter is presented in three main sections. Section 5.1 presents a description of the semantic lexical errors identified. It provides a linguistic description of the semantic lexical errors made in the translation texts, along with detailed statistical analysis. Section 5.2 presents a discussion of semantic lexical errors. It focuses on explaining the potential sources of semantic errors made by the students. The chapter ends (Sect. 5.3) with a comparison between the previous studies and the current study's results.

5.2 Quantitative Analysis and Description of Semantic Lexical Errors

As has been mentioned in Chap. 3: *Research Design and Methodology*, the data was a corpus of translation texts of 105 English majors at the university level. The classification of semantic lexical errors was based on the investigation of previous

---

© The Author(s), under exclusive license to Springer Nature Singapore Pte Ltd. 2022
Y. Alenazi, *Exploring Lexical Inaccuracy in Arabic-English Translation*,
New Frontiers in Translation Studies, https://doi.org/10.1007/978-981-19-6390-2_5

error analysis studies (e.g., Hemchua & Schmitt, 2006; James, 2013; Shalaby et al., 2009) and further developed for the purpose of this research and the type of data collected. The framework of the semantic lexical error classification system is summarised in Fig. 5.1.

In the following section, all types of semantic lexical errors are examined, analysed, and described in detail. After all the semantic lexical errors are identified, they are classified under five main types: (1) confusion of sense relations errors; (2) collocation errors; (3) connotation errors; (4) stylistic errors; and (5) incompletion errors. Confusion of sense relations errors include: the use of a hypernym for a hyponym (general term for specific one), overly specific terms, inappropriate co-hyponyms, wrong near synonyms, direct translation from L1, binary terms, words with inappropriate meaning, and words distorting meaning. Stylistic errors comprise: circumlocution errors; verbosity errors; and misuse of compounds.

All types of semantic lexical errors are provided with examples and are discussed. In each subheading demonstrating one main type or subcategory of semantic lexical errors, the total number of errors and the frequency percentage of errors made by the students are put in tables and all examples presented are incorrect translations from the students.

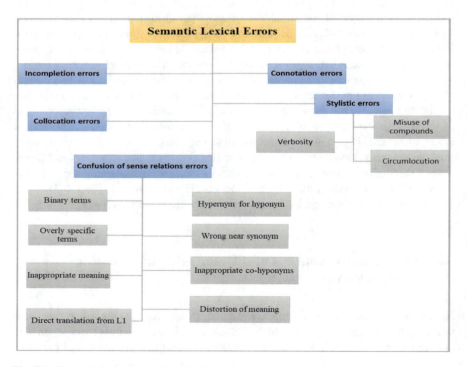

Fig. 5.1 Semantic lexical error classification

5.2 Quantitative Analysis and Description of Semantic Lexical Errors

5.2.1 Semantic Lexical Errors

The written translations by the students yielded 524 semantic lexical errors. The average number of semantic errors made in each translated text is 5%. The total number of English words in all of the translation texts was 12,284 words translated from Arabic texts, while the mean length of each translated English text was 116. Table 5.1 below shows the length and mean length of the written translation samples as well as the number and mean number of errors in the students' texts. The 524 semantic lexical errors have been classified into five main types subdivided into 17 subtypes and the frequency of each type and subtype have been presented. Some semantic lexical error types were common; others were relatively infrequent (see Table 5.1). This indicates that certain lexical error types appear to be particularly problematic for the students while writing in English.

Figure 5.2 shows the percentage distribution of the main categories of semantic lexical errors in the translations.

The confusion of sense relations, as a main category of semantic lexical errors, was the most frequent, constituting 51.14% of all errors (see Table 5.2). The subtypes of errors included in this main category, listed based on their frequency of

Table 5.1 Length of the corpus texts and number of semantic lexical errors

1. Total texts	105
2. Total English words	12,284
3. Mean length per text	116
4. Total lexical errors	1035
5. Total semantic lexical errors	524
6. Mean number of semantic lexical errors	5

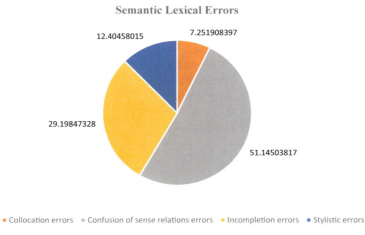

Fig. 5.2 Types of semantic error overall percentage

Table 5.2 Types of semantic lexical error frequency distribution

Error code	Type of semantic lexical error	Number of errors	Frequency percentage
CE	Collocation errors	38	7.25
CSR	Confusion of sense relations	268	51.14
STY	Stylistic errors	65	12.40
IE	Incompletion errors	153	29.19
Total		524	100

occurrence, were direct translation from L1, wrong near synonyms, words with inappropriate meaning, general terms for a specific one, overly specific terms, words distorting meaning, inappropriate co-hyponyms, and, finally, wrong binary terms. Incompletion errors, as a main semantic category, were next in frequency after confusion of sense relations, with a total number of 153 lexical errors followed by stylistic errors occurring 65 times. Collocation errors were the least frequent semantic related errors taking place 38 times, while no incorrect choice of words were found under the semantic category of connotation errors.

As shown in the above table, the confusion of sense relation lexical errors occurred with much higher frequency than the collocation, connotation, and stylistic lexical errors: 268 errors (53%) compared with 153 incompletion errors (29%), 65 stylistic errors (12%), and 38 collocation errors (7%). The types of semantic lexical errors identified during the data analysis are discussed in detail below starting with the confusion of sense relation errors.

5.2.1.1 Confusion of Sense Relation Lexical Errors

Direct translation from L1 was the most frequent type of error in this subcategory, appearing 101 times out of the total of 268 confusion of sense relation errors, with the percentage of 27% of all semantic errors. The subtype wrong near synonym was the second in position of frequency occurring 81 times in the 105 translation texts analysed, and lexical choice with inappropriate meaning were found to be problematic for Saudi English major students with a total number of 64 errors.

As shown in Fig. 5.3, the other subtypes of confusion sense relation errors—general term for specific one, overly specific terms, distortion of meaning errors, inappropriate co-hyponym, and binary terms—were rather infrequent in comparison with the previous subtypes in this category. The subcategories are discussed in detail below.

1. Direct Translation from L1

The findings showed that the students have a more serious problem in choosing the correct lexical item that fully conveys the intended meaning of the source text due to direct translation from L1. Lexical errors due to translation from L1,

5.2 Quantitative Analysis and Description of Semantic Lexical Errors

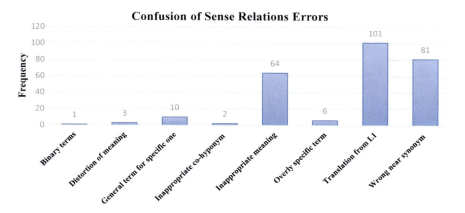

Fig. 5.3 Types of confusion of sense relations error frequency distribution

which can be also classified as interlingual errors, were the most frequent semantic errors, occurring 101 times (27%). Examples of lexical errors due to direct translation from L1 that were found in the translation texts of the students (at the word, phrase, and sentence levels) can be seen in the following:

1. The Arabic source text *hafid ealaa nazafat madinatik wala tulq bialqamamat fa alturuqat* حافظ على نظافة مدينتك ولا تُلق بالقمامة فى الطرقات was translated into English as follows: '*Save your city clean and don't throw rubbish on the streets.'

In this sentence, the student translated the Arabic word (حافظ *hafid*) into an equivalent word in English *save, which is an incorrect choice in this context. The Arabic word حافظ is derived from the root word (حفظ *hafdah*) meaning *'save'* or *'memorise'* something in English in which the student literally translated this lexical item into the L2 regardless of the context. The appropriate lexical choice is *keep* in the context (*Save *keep* your city clean). The difference between the English words *save* and *keep* as nouns or verbs is that *keep* is to maintain or take care of something, while *save* is to help or to survive.

The same lexical error occurred again when a student attempted to translate the same word in the sentence: *yjb 'an nuhafid ealaa albiyat biqadar almustatae* يجب أن نحافظ على البيئة بقدر المستطاع, 'We should try to *save *conserve* the environment as much as possible.' The Arabic word (نحافظ *nuhafid*), which originated from the root word (حفظ *hafdh*), is literally translated again as *save which is incorrect based on the L1 context. The correct lexical choice is *conserve* which relates to the wilderness where human growth is prohibited as indicated in the source text (We should try to *save *conserve* the environment as much as possible, so our children and grandchildren can enjoy the world we live in), meaning to take care of the environment, over the long term, for future generations.

104   5 Semantic Lexical Error Analysis

2. The Arabic source text *suqut awraq al'ashjar fi fasl alkharif* سقوط أوراق الأشجار في فصل الخريف was translated in English as follows: 'The tree *papers fall in autumn.'

In this sentence, the student translated literally the Arabic word (أوراق *awraq*) into an equivalent word in English *paper, which is an incorrect choice in this context. The Arabic word *awraq* is derived from the root word (ورقة *waraqah*), meaning a sheet material for writing 'paper' or a flat organ of a plant 'leaf' in English. This explains the student's incorrect lexical choice in the current context. Due to the student's limited knowledge of the L2 words, he literally translated the L1 lexical item to another lexical item in the L2 that sounds inappropriate. The correct lexical choice in the current context is the word *leaves* (The tree *papers *leaves* fall in autumn).

Another student attempted to translate the same sentence, but he made an incorrect choice of a lexical item when translating the source text into English due to L1 transfer. The Arabic source text *suqut awraq al'ashjar fi fasl alkharif shklaan min ashkal alhimayat aldhdhatiat lilnabat* سقوط أوراق الأشجار في فصل الخريف شكلاً من أشكال الحماية الذاتية للنبات was translated as 'The falling of leaves in autumn are *shape of shapes of self-security for plants." In this sentence, the student translated the Arabic lexical phrase (شكل من أشكال *shklaan min ashkal*) into an equivalent lexical phrase in English *shape of shapes, which is an incorrect choice in this context. The Arabic word *shklaan* is originated from the root word *shkil* which means 'form' or 'shape' in English, and the plural form of the word *shkil* is *ashkal* which means 'forms' or 'shapes' in English. Therefore, the correct lexical choice is *form* in the context (The falling of leaves are *shape of shapes *a form* of self-protection).

3. The source Arabic text *hnak alkthyr min 'ashkal alhayat ealaa al'ard lm yaktashifha al'iinsan ba'ad* هناك الكثير من أشكال الحياة على الأرض لم يكتشفها الإنسان بعد was translated in English as follows: 'There are a lot of *the life faces on earth which not discover it yet by human.'

In this sentence, the student translated the Arabic lexical phrase (أشكال الحياه *ashkal al hyah*) into an equivalent word in English *life faces, which is an incorrect choice in this context. In the Arabic language, the word *ashkal* is the plural form of the word *shakl* which also means 'someone's or something's appearance or face', which clarifies why the student used the wrong lexical item in this context due to the influence of his L1. Thus, the correct lexical choice is *forms of life* in the context (There are many *life faces *forms of life* on earth which not discover it yet by human).

4. The source Arabic text *la shaka 'ana allughat tueadu wasilatan aitisal bayn alshueub w albldan'* لا شك أن اللغات تعد وسيلة اتصال بين الشعوب و البلدان was translated in English as follows: '*Without discussion that languages is a way of communication between people and countries.'

The student in this sentence translated the Arabic lexical phrase (لا شك *la shk*) into an equivalent word in English *without discussion, which is an incorrect choice in

5.2 Quantitative Analysis and Description of Semantic Lexical Errors   105

this context. The Arabic lexical item used (لا شك *la shk*) means that 'something cannot be discussed or questioned,' therefore the student has directly translated the meaning of the L1 lexical item in this sentence into the L2. The appropriate lexical choice in the English language is the lexical phrase *no doubt/without a doubt*> (*Without discussion *No doubt*, languages are means of communication).

5. The source Arabic text *ealayna 'an nahtam bial'tfal min alnawahaa alsihiya w aleaqlia w al'iijtmaeia* 'علينا أن نهتم بالأطفال من النواحى الصحية و العقلية و الإجتماعية' was translated in English as follows: 'We should care for children *brain, *healthy and socially.'

The Arabic lexical item (العقليه *aleaqlia*) is originally derived from the Arabic root word *aql* meaning '*mind' or 'brain*' in English. The student in this sentence has literally translated this lexical item into an equivalent word in English *brain, which is an incorrect choice in this context. The appropriate lexical choice based on the source text context is *mentally* 'we have to care for children *mentally* and socially,' which is derived from the root word *mental* relating to the mind and intellectual status of a person. The L1 transfer in this example is obvious and maybe the lack of lexical knowledge of the L2 has led the student to use an alternative lexical item that is semantically related. In addition, in the same sentence there is another incorrect choice of word which is *healthy. The Arabic lexical item (الصحيه *alsihiya*), which is originally derived from the word (صحه *siha*) meaning 'health' in English, has been translated into an equivalent word in English *healthy. Therefore, a direct translation of L1 meaning occurs again which is considered a problematic issue that English major students need to be aware of. The correct lexical choice is *physically* in the context (we have to care for children *physically*, mentally and socially).

There is some kind of overlap in classifying such errors as mentioned by Shalaby et al. (2009). In other words, the two lexical errors in this example can also be classified as wrong near synonyms of the English words. However, L1 transfer appears to have an influential role in the occurrence of these errors which fits best under the direct translation from L1 subcategory.

6. The Arabic source text *yumaris alnaas hawayat mukhtalifatan kalqura'at w jame altawabie w aleumlat* يمارس الناس هوايات مختلفة كالقراءة و جمع الطوابع و العملات was translated in English as follows: 'People practice different hobbies such as reading and collecting *print and coins.'

In this sentence, the student translated the Arabic lexical item (الطوابع *altawabie*) into an incorrect equivalent lexical phrase in English *print. In the Arabic language, the word *altawabie* means 'stamps' which is the plural form of the root word (طبع *tba'*) that means' print' in English, which explains why the student used the wrong lexical item in this context owing to the transfer semantic features of the L1 lexical item in the source text. Therefore, the correct lexical choice is *stamps* in the context (People practice different hobbies such as reading and collecting *print *stamps* and coins).

106 5 Semantic Lexical Error Analysis

7. The source Arabic text *la shaka 'ana allughat tueadu wasilatan aitisal bayn alshueub w albuldan* لا شك أن اللغات تعد وسيلة اتصال بين الشعوب و البلدان was translated in English as follows: 'No doubt that languages are a way of *call among countries and cities.'

The student in this sentence translated the Arabic lexical item (اتصال *aitisal*) into an equivalent word in English *call*, which is an incorrect choice in this context. The Arabic lexical item used (اتصال *aitisal*) has several meanings in English based on the context it is used in as 'connect', 'connection', 'call', 'joint (two combined items),' or 'communicate', 'communication'. In the current source text context, the word *aitisal* means 'communication' as a way to connect nations and people together. However, the student has directly translated the meaning of the L1 lexical item that he is familiar with without taking into account its semantic association in the L2 context. This type of error occurred due to the student's limited lexical knowledge of the English language. The appropriate lexical choice in the L2 is as follows (No doubt that languages are a means of *call *communication* among countries and cities).

8. The Arabic source text *ahfuz qurshak al'abyad liawmik al'aswad* احفظ قرشك الأبيض ليومك الأسود was translated in English as follows: 'Save *your white money for *your black day.'

In this sentence, the student translated the Arabic idiomatic phrase (قرشك الأبيض *qurshak al'abyad*) literally into equivalent words in English *white money, which is an incorrect choice in the English context. The student translated another Arabic idiomatic phrase (ليومك الأسود *liawmik al'aswad*) literally into English * your black day, because the correct corresponding idiomatic expression for this source text is 'save for *a rainy day*.' Idiomatic expressions are a source of difficulty for both L1 and non-L1 speakers. Therefore, the student's limited knowledge of the L2 words and its common idiomatic expressions are a potential source behind the occurrence of such lexical errors. The correct lexical choice is *a rainy day* in the context (Save your *white money *pennies* for *your black day *a rainy day*). Since it is a common idiomatic expression, it is not necessary to translate every single word in the source text, otherwise it will sound peculiar to the L2 audience.

9. The Arabic source text *iina altuyur ealaa 'ashkaliha tqe'* إن الطيور على أشكالها تقع was translated in English as follows: 'Birds *in their forms fall.'

At the sentence level, the student translated the Arabic proverbial expression (إن الطيور على أشكالها تقع *iina altuyur ealaa 'ashkaliha tqe'*) into equivalent words in English 'Birds *in their forms fall*', which is an incorrect translation in this context. This proverbial lexical sentence is a common Arabic saying which means individuals with similar interests, characteristics, or values often congregate with each other. The student has literally translated the L1 lexical items into several English words that he is familiar with regardless of the context. According to Ghazala (2012), using such a strategy of translation disturbs the intended meaning of the source text since the translated words are understood in 'isolation, not in

5.2 Quantitative Analysis and Description of Semantic Lexical Errors 107

combination with other surrounding words' (p. 6). In the English language, the proverbial expression (birds of a feather flock together) reflects exactly the intended meaning of the Arabic proverb which would be the correct lexical sentence in this context. This example is similar to the previous one in which the student failed to choose the correct corresponding lexical idiomatic expression in the L2 due to his limited vocabulary knowledge. The appropriate translation for this idiomatic sentence is as follows (Birds *in their forms fall* of a feather flock together).

10. The source Arabic text *al'ukul walshurb tawal alyawm madarun bialsh* الأكل والشرب طوال اليوم مضر بالصحة was translated in English as follows: 'Eating and drinking *long day is harmful to health.'

The student translated the Arabic lexical phrase (طوال اليوم *tawal alyawm*) into an incorrect equivalent lexical phrase in English *long day. The lexical item *long* is translated literally for the Arabic word (طوال *tawal*) which derived from the word (طويل *tawal*) meaning 'long' in English. The student transferred the basic meaning of the L1 word into the L2 despite the semantic features associated with the L2 word chosen in this context. The correct lexical choice in this sentence is the adverbial phrase *all day* in the context (Eating and drinking *long day all day* is harmful to your health).

11. The Arabic source text *altabib wasaf dawa' lilmarida* الطبيب وصف دواء للمريض was translated in English as follows: 'The doctor *described a medicine for the patient.'

In this sentence, the student translated the Arabic lexical item (وصف *wasaf*) into an equivalent word for word in English *described, which is an incorrect choice in this context. In the Arabic language, the verb *wasaf* means literally 'describe', which explains why the student used the wrong lexical item in this context due to the transfer of the L1 word's primary meaning to the L2 context. However, in the English language context the correct word choice is the lexical item *prescribe* for a doctor to say what medical treatment an individual should have. Thus, the correct translation is as follows 'The doctor *described *prescribed* medicine for the patient.'

12. The source Arabic text *alwald sirun 'abih* الولد سر أبيه was translated in English as follows: '*The son is his father's secret.'

Another student has literally translated, at the sentence level, the Arabic proverbial expression *alwald sirun 'abih* into an equivalent word for word in English '*The son is his father's secret,' which is an incorrect choice in this context in terms of the semantic features associated with the words selected. This proverbial lexical sentence is a common Arabic saying which means a son's character can be expected to be similar to that of his father. The student, however, has literally translated the L1 lexical items to several English words that he is familiar with regardless of the context, thereby failing to fully convey the intended meaning of the source text. The English language has a similar corresponding lexical idiomatic expression to that of the Arabic expression which is *like father, like son*, or *he is his father's son*. This idiomatic expression reflects exactly the intended meaning of the source text. This finding shows that Saudi students encounter difficulties in choosing the correct corresponding lexical idiomatic expression in the L2 owing to the direct translation strategy of L1 words and to the limited vocabulary knowledge of the L2. Hence, the appropriate translation for this idiomatic sentence is as follows (*<u>The son is his father's secret</u> *Like father, like son*).

2. Wrong Near Synonyms

The next subcategory in frequency of occurrence after direct translation from L1 was 'wrong near synonyms,' unlike Shalaby et al.'s (2009) study which found inappropriate lexical choice more frequent than near synonyms lexical errors. It seems that the students of the current study encounter more difficulties in the use of near synonyms in English while translating. The similarities in meaning between two or more words in the English language cause some kind of confusion for ESL learners with limited lexical knowledge. There are some differences, when two or more words are used to describe one thing in a language. According to Ghazala (2012), there are some words in English that are perfectly identical in meaning and other words that share similar semantic features but are used differently based on context. The problem is that some students in this study were unaware of the semantic difference of some synonymous words and believed that all L2 lexical items similar in meaning have the same identical meaning in the L1. This type of error occurred 81 times, with 30% frequency percentage of all lexical errors in the confusion of sense relations category, and 21.83% of the total number of semantic errors. The examples used in this section illustrate this problem in detail:

1. The Arabic source text *ynbaghaa 'alaa nudie' alwaqt althamin w 'alaa nuajil eamal alyawm 'iilaa alghad* 'ينبغى ألا نضيع الوقت الثمين و ألا نؤجل عمل اليوم إلى الغد' was translated in English as follows: 'We should not *lose the *great time and don't postpone today's word till tomorrow.'

The student translated the Arabic lexical item (نضيع *nudie'*) into an equivalent word in English *lose, which is an incorrect choice in this context. In the Arabic language, the verb (*nudie'*) is derived from the root word (ضيّع *dia'*) meaning 'losing' or 'wasting' something. However, in the English language context the correct word choice is the lexical item *waste*. The meaning of the synonym used *lose and the correct synonym *waste* are not precisely the same. The key difference would be that an individual can *lose* time unintentionally, whereas *wasting* time is mostly on purpose which is indicated in the source text. Thus, the intended meaning is not expressed by the synonym used in the sentence (We should not *lose *waste* time).

Another wrong near synonym occurred in the same sentence which can be found in the lexical phrase *great time. The student translated the Arabic lexical item (الثمين *althamin*), which means something is precious or has 'a great value', into the L2 lexical item *great. However, the meaning of the synonym used *great

5.2 Quantitative Analysis and Description of Semantic Lexical Errors

and the correct synonym *precious* are not identical. Therefore, the intended meaning is not correctly expressed by the synonym used to mean time has a great value in the context (we should not waste the *precious time*).

2. The Arabic source text *alqiam bialrihlat alaistikshafiat yazid min khibrat w muteat almar'* القيام بالرحلات الاستكشافية يزيد من خبرة و متعة المرء was translated in English as follows: 'Going on expeditions increases our *information and enjoyment.'

The student in this sentence translated the Arabic lexical item (خبرة *khibrat*) into an equivalent word in English *information, which is an incorrect choice in the L2 context. In Arabic, the noun *khibra* means 'a past event', 'knowledge', or 'feelings' that influence an individual life or character. Therefore, the correct lexical choice in the English language context is the lexical item *knowledge*. The meaning of the word used *information and the correct synonym *knowledge* are not precisely identical. As a result, the intended meaning is not fully conveyed by the assumed synonym used by the student translator in the sentence (Going on expeditions increases our *information *experience* and enjoyment).

3. The Arabic source text *yumaris alnaas hawayat mukhtalifatan kalqara'at w jame altawabie w aleamlat* يمارس الناس هوايات مختلفة كالقراءة و جمع الطوابع و العملات was translated in English as follows: 'People *do different hobbies like reading and collecting stamps and coins.'

The student in this sentence translated the Arabic lexical item (يمارس *yumaris*) into an equivalent word in English *do, which is an incorrect choice in this context. The Arabic lexical item used (يمارس *yumaris*) is derived from the root word (ممارسة *mumarsah*) which has several meanings in English based on the context it is used in as *practise, training,* or *exercise*. In the current source text context, the word *yumaris* means 'practise' referring to an activity or hobby that is being done regularly which is not exactly identical in meaning with the synonym used *do*. Thus, the intended meaning is not fully expressed by the synonym used to regularly engage in an exercise, activity, or a hobby in the sentence 'People *do *practise* different hobbies like reading and collecting stamps and coins.'

In another translation of the same text, the student used the lexical item *exercises* as an equivalent word for (هوايات *hawayat*) which originally means hobbies based on the source text in the sentence (People practise different *exercises *hobbies* like reading, collecting stamps, and coins). As nouns the difference between *exercises* and *hobbies* is that exercise refers to an activity which requires physical effort, while hobby is a regular activity or interest that is being done for pleasure.

4. The source Arabic text *la shaka 'ana allughat tueadu wasilatan aitisal bayn alshueub w albldan* لا شك أن اللغات تعد وسيلة اتصال بين الشعوب و البلدان was translated in English as follows: 'Without doubt, languages are a means of *contact between people and countries.'

In this sentence, the student translated the Arabic lexical item (اتصال *aitisal*) into an equivalent word in English *contact, which is an incorrect choice in this context. As explained earlier, in the Arabic language, the noun *aitisal* is derived from the root word (اتصل *itsala*) meaning 'call', 'contact', 'communicate,' or 'join'. However, in the current context, the correct English word choice is the lexical item *communication*. As nouns, the semantic features of the synonym used *contact and the appropriate synonym *communication* are not exactly identical in the current context. The key difference would be that communicate is to impart or exchange ideas, knowledge, or information between individuals while contact is to come in physical contact with someone as in the sentence 'Without doubt, languages are a means of *contact *communication* between people and countries.'

5. The source Arabic text *yjb 'an natakhalas min aleadat alsayiyat fahaa 'iieaqa fa tariqina liltaqadum* يجب أن نتخلص من العادات السيئة فهى إعاقة فى طريقنا للتقدم was translated in English as follows: 'We must get rid of bad habits because it's stop our way to *ahead.'

In this sentence, the student translated the Arabic lexical item (للتقدم *liltaqadum*) into an equivalent word in English *ahead, which is an incorrect choice in this context. The Arabic lexical item *liltaqadum* means 'moving forward' or 'progress' in English based on the current context.

Another student translated the same text as follows: 'We must get rid of the bad habits because it is *disable our way to move forward.' The student translated the Arabic lexical item (إعاقة *'iieaqa*) into an incorrect equivalent word in English *disable. In the current source text context, the word *'iieaqa* means 'hamper', 'obstruct,' or 'be a hindrance to' which is not exactly identical in meaning with the adjective used *disable referring to the lack of ability. Thus, the intended meaning is not fully expressed by the near synonym used to indicate that bad habits hold us back as in the sentence (We must get rid of bad habits because they are *disable 'a hindrance to' moving forward).

3. Lexical Choices with Inappropriate Meaning

The use of a lexical item that carries an inappropriate meaning was next in frequency after a wrong near synonym. However, it occurred at a much lower proportion than either translation from L1 or a wrong near synonym, taking place only 64 times at a frequency percentage of 24% of the confusion of sense relations category and represents 17.25% of the total number of semantic errors. The following are examples of this type of error:

1. The Arabic source text *ealaa kl dawlat 'an* tuhawil *tajanub talawuth albiyat 'akthar min dhlk fa alqarn alhadaa waleishrin* على كل دولة أن تحاول تجنب تلوث البيئة أكثر من ذلك فى القرن الحادى والعشرين was translated in English as follows: 'Every country should *above destroy polluting the environment any more in the twenty-first century.'

In this translation example, the use of the lexical phrase *above destroy gives an inappropriate meaning in this context hampering the intended meaning of the source text. The correct lexical choice based on the source text is *try to avoid* as an

5.2 Quantitative Analysis and Description of Semantic Lexical Errors 111

equivalent to the Arabic lexical phrase (أن تحاول تجنب *'an tuhawil tajanub*) (Every country should *above destroy *try to avoid* polluting the environment in the twenty-first century).

2. The Arabic source text *ynbaghaa 'alaa nudie' alwaqt althamin* ينبغى أن لا نضيع الوقت الثمين was translated in English as follows: 'We should not *get off our precious time.'

In this sentence, the student translator used the lexical phrase *get off giving an inappropriate meaning in this context. Based on the source text, the student selected the wrong lexical item as a corresponding translation for the Arabic lexical item (نضيع *nudie'*) which actually means 'losing' or 'wasting' something. Therefore, the correct lexical choice based on the source text is *waste* in the sentence (We must not *get off *waste* the precious time.)

3. The Arabic source text *ealaa kl dawlat 'an tuhawil tajanub talawuth albiya 'akthar min dhlk fa alqarn alhadaa waleishrin* على كل دولة أن تحاول تجنب تلوث البيئة أكثر من ذلك فى القرن الحادى والعشرين was translated in English as follows: 'Every country must try to avoid environment *clear of dirty in the twenty-first century.'

In this example, the inappropriate lexical items *clear of dirty used by the student are meant to be a corresponding translation for the Arabic word (تلوث *talawuth*) meaning 'pollution'. However, the correct lexical choice based on the source text is *pollution* (Every country must try to avoid *polluting* the environment in the twenty-first century). There might be several reasons for the occurrence of such errors. The limited lexical entries of the L2 could possibly have led the students to use alternative words that they believed to be close in meaning, but which sound inappropriate to English L1 speakers.

4. The Arabic source text *yjb 'an natakhalas min aleadat alsayiya fahaa 'iieaqat fa tariqina lltaqadm* يجب أن نتخلص من العادات السيئة فهى إعاقة فى طريقنا للتقدم was translated in English as follows: 'We must get rid of the bad *values because they obstruct our way to *front.'

In this sentence, the student made two incorrect lexical choices when translating the Arabic text. The use of the word *values is inappropriate in this context, because based on the source text the Arabic word (عادات *adat*) meaning 'habits' is the correct lexical choice in the L2 text. In addition, the lexical item *front is an inappropriate English language choice based on the original source text (للتقدم *lltaqadm*). The correct translation in this context is as follows: (We must get rid of bad *values *habits* because they are a hindrance to our *progress*).

More examples of this subcategory of lexical error are illustrated below with the correct intended word in brackets based on the source text:

5. 'The Kingdom of Saudi Arabia exerts every possible *ability *effort* to promote peace in the Middle East.'
6. 'The government does its best to provide *eats *food* for every citizen.'

7. 'People practice different hobbies like reading and collecting *stable *stamps*.'
8. 'People practice different *identities *hobbies* such as reading, collecting stamps and coins.'
9. 'Languages are *internet *a means of communication* between people and the international world.'
10. 'The two *managers *ministers* discussed political and economic issues.'

In this subcategory, most of the incorrect word choices could be attributed to the students' insufficient knowledge of the L2 words. However, some lexical items with inappropriate meanings could be related to the influence of the student's L1. An example of this is the use of the word *eats* in sentence no. 6: 'The government does its best to provide *eats *food* for every citizen.'

In this example, the inappropriate lexical item *eats occurred due to the literal translation of the Arabic lexical item (يأكل ya'kul) which refers to the act of eating food in English. The Arabic word (يأكل ya'kul) is derived from the root word (أكل akil), which is used as a noun in the colloquial Arabic to mean 'food'. Therefore, the meaning associated with the L1 word was translated directly to the L2.

4. Other Subtypes of Confusion of Sense Relation Errors

The use of a general lexical item for a specific one, overly specific terms, words distorting meaning, inappropriate co-hyponym, and confusion of binary terms were less common in the corpus text analysed in comparison with the previous subtypes in this category. Hypernym for a hyponym errors occurred at a much lower proportion than inappropriate meaning errors, taking place only 10 times at a frequency percentage of 3.7% for the confusion of sense relations category. The following are examples of this type of error, with the correct intended word in brackets based on the source text.

1. The Arabic source text *suqut 'awraq al'ashjar fi fasl alkharif yuead shklaan min 'ashkal alhimayat aldhdhatiat lilnabat* سقوط أوراق الأشجار في فصل الخريف يعد شكلاً من أشكال الحماية الذاتية للنبات was translated as 'The falling of leaves in autumn are a form of *gardens *plant* self-protection.' In this context, the intended meaning of the lexical item used is underspecified in which the hypernym *gardens is used for the hyponym *plant*.
2. The same Arabic source text *suqut 'awraq al'ashjar fi fasl alkharif shklaan min 'ashkal alhimayat aldhdhatiat lilnabat* سقوط أوراق الأشجار في فصل الخريف شكلاً من أشكال الحماية الذاتية للنبات was translated by another student as 'The falling of *trees *leaves* in autumn are a form of plants self-protection.'

The next subcategory in frequency was 'overly specific term', taking place only six times with the proportion of 2.2%, as seen in the following examples:

1. 'In the twenty-first century, every country should work more to avoid *air *environment* pollution.'
2. 'No doubt that languages are considered a way of communication among *tribes and *cities *peoples and countries*.'

5.2 Quantitative Analysis and Description of Semantic Lexical Errors 113

This was followed by distortion of meaning errors (1.1%) as in:

1. 'We must *keep pollution *conserve the environment*, so our children and grand-children can enjoy the world we live in.'
2. 'Languages are a way of *conflict *communication* between peoples of the world.'

Inappropriate co-hyponym was uncommon in the students' translations with the proportion of (0.7%). For example, 'Leaves fall in autumn as a form of plants *safety *self-protection*.' Furthermore, the most infrequent subcategory of confusion sense relation errors was binary terms (0.4%) as in 'The Kingdom of Saudi Arabia is doing its best to promote peace in the Middle *West *East*.' These last subcategories of sense relations errors are mostly attributed to the students' limited knowledge of the L2.

5.2.1.2 Incompletion Errors

The findings show that incompletion errors were pervasive in the students' translations in which they deleted lexical items in the L2 that affected the meaning of the sources text negatively. Unlike Shalaby et al.'s (2009) study, this subcategory was next in frequency after the confusion of sense relations category, taking place 153 times, with the frequency percentage of (14.7%) of the total number of errors in all categories.

Omission of L2 lexical items were not limited to the nature of the source text's sophisticated words, but also involved very simple lexical items that should not be challenging for beginner translators. The omitted lexical items, however, contributed to the loss of valuable information of the source text that hampered the intended meaning. Below, a few examples of omission errors are illustrated. The presumed deleted lexical items are put in brackets for comprehension purposes.

1. The source Arabic text *ealaa kl dawlat 'an tuhawil tajanub talawuth albiyat 'akthar min dhlk fa alqarn alhadaa waleishrin* على كل دولة أن تحاول تجنب تلوث البيئة أكثر من ذلك فى القرن الحادى والعشرين was translated in English as follows: 'Every country must try to avoid *... *polluting the environment in the twenty-first century*.'

In this example, several lexical items were eliminated by the student translator distorting the intended meaning of the source text, even though they do not represent complex items. Important information was missing in the L2 text. The student may have omitted these lexical items because he could not find the equivalent accurate words for translation. There might be other factors behind this type of error such as exam anxiety, the complexity of the source text, or the text genre. Word for word translation approach would be useful for students with inadequate lexical knowledge, since these lexical items could easily be rendered into English equivalence at word level.

114   5 Semantic Lexical Error Analysis

More examples are listed below:

2. The Arabic source text *hafid ealaa nazafat madianatik wala tulq bialqimamat fa altarqat* حافظ على نظافة مدينتك ولا تُلق بالقمامة فى الطرقات was translated into English as follows: 'Keep your city clean and don't throw *... *rubbish* on the streets.'

3. The Arabic source text *yumaris alnaas hawayat mukhtalifatan kalqara'at w jame altawabie w aleamlat* يمارس الناس هوايات مختلفة كالقراءة و جمع الطوابع و العملات was translated in English as follows: 'People practice different *... *hobbies such as reading*, collecting stamps and coins'.

4. The Arabic source text *la shaka 'ana allughat tueadu wasilatan aitisal bayn alshueub w albldan* لا شك أن اللغات تعد وسيلة اتصال بين الشعوب و البلدان was translated in English as follows: 'No doubt that languages *... *are a means of communication between people and countries.'*

5. The Arabic source text *alrajul walmarat kilahuma yukmil alakhr* الرجل والمراة كلاهما يكمل الاخر was translated in English as follows: 'Men and women both *... *complement* each other.'

5.2.1.3 Stylistic Errors

Stylistic lexical errors were next in frequency after incompletion category errors and were identified 65 times, at the rate of 17.5% of all semantic errors and 10% of the total number of errors. Style in translation is an essential part of meaning and to some extent it could affect the intended meaning of the source text. According to Ghazala (2012, p. 222), 'a change of style means a change of meaning of some kind.'

Stylistic errors in this study include three subcategories: verbosity, misuse of compounds, and circumlocution errors. The most frequent type of error in this category was that of circumlocution. This error occurred 49 times out of the total of 65 stylistic errors, at the rate of 13% of all semantic errors, and 4.7% of the total number of errors. The subtype verbosity was the second in position of frequency occurring 10 times in the 105 translation texts analysed, and the incorrect use of compound lexical items was found to be less problematic for the students with a total of six errors.

As shown in Table 5.3, the subtypes of stylistic errors verbosity and misuse of compounds were infrequent in comparison with the circumlocution subcategory. The subcategories are discussed in detail below with examples.

1. Circumlocution Errors

In this subcategory, some of the students in this study had the tendency to use a paraphrase strategy instead of providing the correct lexical items that best conveyed the intended meaning of the source text. Such a strategy is useful in spoken form, but in written translation it could result in inaccurate use of the L2 lexical items. Examples of circumlocution errors in the students' translations are illustrated below:

5.2 Quantitative Analysis and Description of Semantic Lexical Errors

Table 5.3 Types of stylistic errors frequency percentage distribution

Error Code	Type of stylistic error	Number of errors	Percentage Frequency
SC	Circumlocution	49	75.3
SV	Verbosity	10	15.3
SMC	Misuse of compounds	6	9.2
Total		65	100

1. The Arabic source text *yanbaghaa 'alaa nuajil eamal alyawm 'iilaa alghad* ينبغى ألا نؤجل عمل اليوم إلى الغد was translated in English as follows: '**Don't say we will do that work* tomorrow.'

The students used several lexical items in the target text to convey the source text message, however, the intended meaning is still vague where fewer words would suffice as in (*Don't put off until tomorrow what you can do today*).

2. The Arabic source text *tabdhul almamlakat alearabiat alsaeudiat kl aljuhud almumkinat liasud alsalam fa mintaqat alshrq al'awsat* تبذل المملكة العربية السعودية كل الجهود الممكنة ليسود السلام فى منطقة الشرق الأوسط was translated in English as follows: 'Kingdom of Saudi Arabia is doing its best *to make the Islam fun.'

In this example, the student used several lexical items to convey the intended meaning of the source text, but he failed to do so and the meaning is distorted by the lexical items used in the current context. The correct translation should be as follows: (The Kingdom of Saudi Arabia is doing its best to *make the Islam fun *promote peace in the Middle East*).

3. The Arabic source text *min jid wajad wamin zara' hasad* من جد وجد ومن زرع حصد was translated in English as follows: '**Who works hard gains hard*.'

In this example, the source text is a common Arabic proverb which could be translated into an equivalent English proverb. Unlike the other examples of literal translation of proverbs and idioms, the student translated this sentence using the paraphrase strategy choosing several lexical items to convey the intended meaning of the source text, but still the meaning is not completely clear. The appropriate equivalent translation of this proverb should be as follows: *Seek and you shall find and as you sow, so shall you reap*. This type of error does not reflect the structure of the L1, but it could be traced back to the student's inadequate knowledge of the L2.

4. The source Arabic text *ahfud qurshak al'abyad liawmik al'aswad* احفظ قرشك الأبيض ليومك الأسود was translated in English as follows: '**Save the best for last*.'

This translation is another example of circumlocution error in which the student translated the idiomatic sentence into several lexical items that deviated from the meaning of the source text. Some Arabic idioms actually have equivalent idioms in

English, but with different lexical items. Most idioms in both Arabic and English are fixed metaphors with different metaphorical meanings in which saying something means something else. Therefore, having a sufficient background of the common idioms in both the L1 and the L2 is essential for accurate translation. The correct translation for the current source text is as follows: (*Save for a rainy day*).

Another example of paraphrasing an idiomatic sentence into English leading to circumlocution error was: The Arabic source text *alwald sirun 'abih* الولد سر أبيه was translated in English as '*The son made his father happy.*' The translation did not convey the meaning of the source text in the target text correctly. In this example, several lexical items were used in a deliberate manner to be evasive. The correct translation, however, is the idiom (*Like father like son* or *he is his father's son*) which clearly has a different meaning.

2. Verbosity

Sophisticated language use in various contexts could impede the reader's comprehension. In other words, simplicity in writing could lead to comprehension while complexity sometimes leads to stylistic problems such as verbosity. One of the primary objectives of translation is to transmit the message of the source text clearly to the L2 without any complexity that could hamper the intended meaning (Ghazala, 2012). A few cases of verbosity were found in the students' translation texts. Verbosity errors were the second in position of frequency after circumlocution occurring 10 times, with (15%) of the total number of stylistics errors. Below are a few examples of verbosity found in the students' translations:

1. The Arabic lexical phrase *alqiam bialrihlat alaistikshafia* القيام بالرحلات الاستكشافية was translated in English as follows '*when you do trip to see anything*.'

In this example, the target text contains more lexical items than are necessary for communication. The student could use the lexical phrase *going on expeditions* instead of '*when you do trip to see anything*' to convey the meaning of the source text in the context (*Going on expeditions* increases our experience and enjoyment).

2. The Arabic lexical phrase *alnabatat dayimat alkhadra* النباتات دائمة الخضرة was translated in English as follows: '*the garden that is always green*.'

The language construction in this example contains more words than is necessary to convey the message of the source text. The appropriate translation for this Arabic lexical phrase is *evergreen plants* instead of *the garden that is always green*. This type of error could be attributed to the L1 transfer of the semantic features associated with the Arabic lexical items. In addition, it could reflect the student's inadequate knowledge of the L2's vocabulary. Since the student was unfamiliar with the scientific lexical items *evergreen plants*, he had to use several words to convey the meaning of the source text which led to this stylistic problem.

3. The Arabic source text *yjb 'an nuhafiz ealaa albiya* يجب أن نحافظ على البيئة was translated in English as follows: 'we must *keep our world clear*.'

5.2 Quantitative Analysis and Description of Semantic Lexical Errors

In this example, the student translator also used many words where fewer would do to convey the intended meaning of the source text effeciently. The correct translation should be as follows: (We must *keep our world clear* conserve the environment).

4. The Arabic source text *naqash alwaziran alqadaya alsiyasiat walaiqtisadia* ناقش الوزيران القضايا السياسية والاقتصادية was translated in English as follows: (*These persons who take care of anything* The two ministers discussed the political and economic issues).

In this example, it appears that the student was not able to find the right equivalent lexical items in the L2 when translating the Arabic news text-type. His unfamiliarity of the equivalent L2 words could be the reason that led him to have a stylistic problem where he used several lexical items that did not deliver an exact intended meaning of the source text. The correct translation, however, is as follows: (*The two ministers* discussed the political and economic issues).

5. The Arabic source text *min jid wajad* من جد وجد was translated in English as follows: '*Anyone who work hard he get in the end something good*.'

As previously mentioned, this source text is a common proverb in Arabic which could be translated into an equivalent proverb in English. However, the student translated this sentence using several lexical items to convey the intended meaning of the source text, but still the meaning is vague. Similar to the previous example, the student was not able to find the right equivalent lexical items in the L2 when translating the Arabic proverb owing to his inadequate knowledge of the L2. The appropriate equivalent translation of this proverb should be as follows: (*Seek, and you shall find*).

3. Misuse of Compounds

Incorrect use of the L2 compound words was less frequent in comparison with the previous types of stylistic errors. It occurred at a much lower proportion than either circumlocution or verbosity, taking place only six times at a frequency percentage of 9% of the stylistics category and represents 0.6% of the total number of semantic errors. Some errors found in the translation texts were related to the incorrect order of the lexical units that form a compound, other errors were either inappropriate or unacceptable language form. The examples below briefly illustrate some of the errors found:

1. The Arabic source text *yaetamid alnajah fa alhayat ealaa alsabr waleamal aljad* 'يعتمد النجاح فى الحياة على الصبر والعمل الجاد' was translated in English as follows: 'Success in life depends on patience and *work hard* hard work.'
2. The Arabic source text *hnak alkthyr min 'ashkal alhayat ealaa al'ard* هناك الكثير من أشكال الحياة على الأرض was translated in English as follows: 'There are many *forms life* life forms on Earth.'

5.2.1.4 Collocation Errors

The last category of sematic errors in frequency was collocation errors. The findings in the study indicate that the students encounter some difficulties in the use of English collocations. This category had the fourth highest frequency percentage (10%) of all semantic lexical errors. According to Ghazala (2012), collocation 'is a combination of two or more words that always occur together consistently in different texts and contexts in language' (p. 106). Based on Ghazala's definition, co-occurring lexical items such as a noun with a specific adjective, a verb with a noun, a noun with a noun, phrasal verbs, and so forth were considered in the analysis of the translated corpus texts in this study. Consequently, 38 incorrect choices of co-occurring lexical items while translating to the L2 were identified. Finding the appropriate English equivalent collocation for the Arabic collocation in the source text was problematic for some Saudi students. Below, a few examples of collocation errors found in the students' translation products are illustrated:

1. The Arabic source text *qataeat waead ealaa nafsi* قطعت وعد على نفسي was translated as (I *take *made* a promise to myself.).

The correct lexical choice is the collocation phrase *made a promise* instead of the lexical phrase *take a promise. The incorrect lexical choice in this context could be traced back to the student's L1. The lexical phrase used *take a promise is actually an equivalent translation from the colloquial Arabic collocation phrase (أخذت وعد *akhadtu waead*). However, this translation is rather inappropriate in the L2, which requires the student to expand his lexical knowledge of the L2 and particularly lexical collocations. More examples of collocation errors are listed below:

2. The Arabic source text *tuetabar alhiwayat wasilat lilmuteat w litamdiat alwaqat* تعتبر الهوايات وسيلة للمتعة و لتمضية الوقت was translated as 'Hobbies are interesting means to *go *pass* time.' The correct translation is as follows: (Hobbies help to *pass* the time).
3. The Arabic source text *yjb 'an natakhalas min aleadat alsayiya* 'يجب أن نتخلص من العادات السيئة' was translated as 'We must *get down* get rid of / break the bad habits.'
4. The Arabic source text *min almuetaqad 'ana alshabab la yaemalun binasayih alkabar* من المعتقد أن الشباب لا يعملون بنصائح الكبار was translated as 'It is believed that the youth do not *work with* act on the advice of the old.' The correct translation is as follows: (It is believed that young people do not *act on* the advice of their elders).

5.3 Discussion and Explanation of Semantic Lexical Errors

This section provides a detailed discussion and explanation of the possible sources of the semantic lexical errors made by Saudi English major students in their translation products. In error analysis studies, language errors are usually classified

5.2 Quantitative Analysis and Description of Semantic Lexical Errors

as either interlingual errors or intralingual errors (James, 2013; Richards, 2015). Subsequently, the potential sources of semantic lexical errors in this study were classified according to these two sources which were further subdivided into two groups related to the subtypes of semantic errors and their possible causes. Such categorisation of the sources of lexical errors has been widely used in previous error analysis studies (e.g., Carrió-Pastor & Mestre Mestre, 2014; Mahmoud, 2019; Shin, 2002) since it provides a clear understanding of the reasons behind the occurrence of language errors. Semantic lexical error subcategories related to the two sources (interlingual and intralingual) are summarised in Fig. 5.4.

The first group includes interlingual errors (direct translation from L1, collocation errors). In this group, literal translation of L1 words and transfer of the semantic features associated with L1 lexical items found in the source text played an influential role in the occurrence of some semantic errors in the students' translation products.

The second group includes the intralingual errors in which the students made some semantic lexical errors because of their incomplete lexical entries of the L2 such as binary terms, words distorting meaning, words with inappropriate meaning, general terms for specific ones, inappropriate co-hyponyms, incompletion errors, and stylistic errors (verbosity, circumlocution errors, and misuse of compounds). Other intralingual errors such as near synonym errors were made due to the semantic confusion between L2 lexical items. Some students were unfamiliar with the sematic difference between two semantically related L2 words.

As illustrated in Fig. 5.5, the most significant data point is that almost three quarters of the semantic errors occurred were due to intralingual influence (73.47%) that is the lack of L2 lexical knowledge (LL2LK) (58.01%) and the confusion between L2 lexical items that are semantically related (SCL2) (15.46%) significantly influenced the words used in the translated texts. Interlingual influence (26.53%), on the other hand, made up a considerable percentage of the total

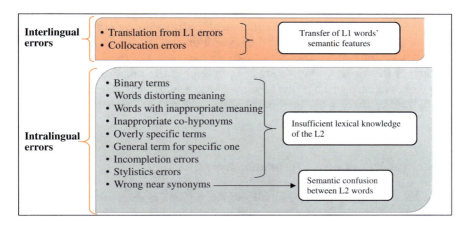

Fig. 5.4 Sources of semantic lexical errors

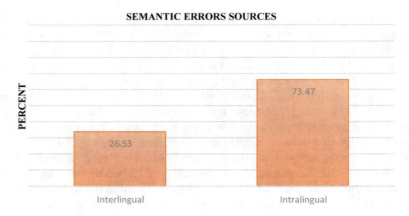

Fig. 5.5 Percentage distribution of semantic errors based on their possible sources

semantic lexical errors due to literal translation of L1 words and the transfer of the semantic features associated with L1 lexical items (TL1S).

Table 5.4 demonstrates in detail the total percentage and frequency distribution of semantic lexical errors in relation to their potential causes.

A discussion of semantic lexical error sources is presented below in detail with error examples taken from the translation texts.

5.3.1 Analysis of Interlingual Errors

Interlingual errors can be understood as lexical errors that emanate from language transfer and occasioned by the L1 of the L2 learner. Interlingual errors are a function of language transfer where the semantic and lexical items of the L1 are inadvertently shifted to the L2 when writing or translating (Qaid & Ramamoorthy, 2011). This is acknowledged by Derrick et al. (2018) who claim that interlingual errors are a consequence of cross-linguistic influence, linguistic interference, or simply interference of the native language. In the context of the current study, the outcome is the tendency by the students to apply their linguistic knowledge of Arabic on a number of linguistic features of the English language, a practice that causes them to make such interlingual semantic errors as direct translation from L1 and collocation errors.

5.3.1.1 Analysis of Direct Translation from L1

Based on the study's findings, interlingual errors due to direct translation of L1 comprised the second largest proportion of the semantic lexical errors observed after incompletion errors. The findings showed a total of 101 errors relating to

5.3 Discussion and Explanation of Semantic Lexical Errors

Table 5.4 Total percentage frequency distribution of semantic lexical errors based on their possible causes

Semantic Lexical Error Source	Possible Cause	Error Category	No	Total Frequency	Percentage	Total %
Interlingual	TL1S	Translation from L1	101	139	26.53	**26.53**
		Collocation	38			
Intralingual	LL2LK	Binary terms	1	304	58.01	**73.47**
		General terms for specific ones	10			
		Words distorting meaning	3			
		Words with inappropriate meaning	64			
		Inappropriate co-hyponyms	2			
		Overly specific terms	6			
		Incompletion errors	153			
		Stylistics errors	65			
	SCL2	Wrong near synonyms	81	81	15.46	
Total				524	100	**100**

direct translation of L1 which is 27% of all the semantic lexical errors committed in the translation texts produced by the students. In terms of errors' frequency, the findings contradict the results of the studies by Shalaby et al. (2009) and Zughoul (1991) which established direct translation from L1 to be the most common type of semantic lexical errors. However, the current study corroborates their results in terms of the source behind this particular semantic error as the most common recurrent form of interlingual transfer error affecting the written works of Arab learners of English. Direct translation of L1 errors can be attributed to several causes. It could be related to the tendency by the students to select and use the L2 word with the closest meaning to the native word being translated. The practice leads to the occurrence of semantic lexical errors at the word level attributable to Arabic language transfer as witnessed in the written and translated texts products of the study population. For instance, when translating the Arabic text *hafid ealaa nazafat madinatik wala tulq bialqamamat fa alturuqat* حافظ على نظافة مدينتك ولا تُلق بالقمامة فى الطرقات the student literally translated the Arabic word (حافظ *hafid*) as *save instead of *keep* thus producing '*Save your city clean and don't throw rubbish on the streets' which overlooks the context in which the word is used and thus fails to convey the intended meaning of the sentence which ought to have been '*Keep* your city clean and don't throw rubbish on the streets.'

Inadequate knowledge of the lexical items of the English language could also lead to direct translation from L1 to compensate for their lexical gaps. In the corpus of the translated texts studied for instance, this type of error was common in the phrase and sentence levels of their products. For example, one of the students translated the Arabic lexical phrase (شكل من أشكال *shklaan min ashka*l) into the equivalent but inappropriate lexical phrase in English *shape of shapes instead of *form of* effectively distorting the actual meaning of the translated text. The effects of this form of L1 transfer confirms the finding by Shalaby et al. (2009) who noted that while transfer of the use of some L1 lexical items may be correct in the L1 language, the use of the same prepositions or words in the L2 may be erroneous. This constitutes a problem as it ignores the context in which a particular lexical item is used effectively leading to production of written or translated texts that do not convey the intended meaning and are low in quality.

5.3.1.2 Analysis of Collocation Errors

The other type of semantic lexical error due to interlingual transfer was collocation errors. In the current study, collocation errors accounted for only 10% of the total semantic lexical errors identified. This proportion of collocation errors was significantly lower compared to previous studies. For instance, in the study by Shalaby et al. (2009) collocation errors accounted for 12% of the total semantic lexical errors identified, while in an earlier study by Hemchua and Schmitt (2006) this form of semantic lexical errors accounted for 26% of all the errors. The difference in the proportion of collocation errors identified in the current study and those of the previous studies could be attributable to the associated classification challenges given that some collocation errors can be appropriately categorised under other subtypes of semantic lexical errors such as near synonyms and inappropriate meaning. Although the collocation errors identified in the translated corpus texts analysed were fewer compared to those found in previous studies, their frequency was relatively higher in comparison to the other semantic lexical errors identified and hence the need to understand how they arise and their effect on the writings and translations produced by Saudi English major students.

As interlingual errors, collocation errors are caused by either the inability of the L2 learner to choose the correct co-occurring lexical items when translating the source text to L2 or their incapacity to find the appropriate English equivalent collocation for the Arabic collocation they seek to translate, thus resorting to L1 transfer. This finding is corroborated by Mahmoud (2005) who cited negative LI transfer as the primary cause of all the collocation errors (61%) identified in his study. Hassan and Hussein (2019) further cite poor proficiency in L2 in addition to L1 interference as contributing factors to grammatical collocation and collocation

5.3 Discussion and Explanation of Semantic Lexical Errors

errors. Thus, unfamiliarity of the Saudi English major students with the grammatical collocations of various adjectives and the prepositions they ought to be associated with cause them to resort to transferring the L1 use of the adjectives and the prepositions they are associated with into English thus making semantic errors. For instance, as established in the study the learners tend to transfer the colloquial Arabic collocation phrase (أخذت وعد *akhadt waead*) into English as *take a promise instead of *make a promise*, and other collocation errors such as *in accordance *on* instead of *in accordance with*, which are inappropriate. The practice is a major problem for the students as it renders their writing and translation inappropriate, impeding their ability to convey the intended meaning.

5.3.2 Analysis of Intralingual Errors

Unlike interlingual errors which occur due to language transfer or interference of the L1, intralingual errors are an outcome of partial or faulty learning of the L2. According to Qaid and Ramamoorthy (2011), intralingual errors are occasioned by inadequate knowledge of the L2 lexical items, a deficit in L2 knowledge that causes learners to inappropriately use and apply the lexical items of the L2 leading to errors. In the context of the current study, the lack of adequate knowledge of the L2, English, and its lexis is the primary cause of semantic lexical errors found among the students. As depicted in Fig. 5.4, the semantic lexical errors with intralingual sources observed in the written translations entail use of binary terms, words distorting meaning, words with inappropriate meaning, hypernym for hyponym, inappropriate co-hyponyms, overly specific terms, incompletion errors, stylistic errors, and wrong near synonym errors.

5.3.2.1 Analysis of Binary Term Errors

Binary terms comprise the least common or infrequent subtype of semantic lexical errors in the corpus text analysed accounting for only 0.4% of the total confusion sense relation errors found. As an intralingual error, errors committed by the students in their use of binary terms could be attributable to their limited knowledge of the English language. In line with the findings of this study, a previous study by Shalaby et al. (2009) found errors relating to confusion of binary terms to be infrequent (at 0.42%) but significant owing to the impact they have on the comprehensibility of the affected text. However, a more recent study by Naba'h (2011) found binary term errors to be more common among English teachers in Jordan with a frequency of 5% of the intralingual errors identified. The discrepancy in the frequency of binary term errors among Arab English students in Saudi and Jordan could be attributed to differences in the national literacy levels. In both contexts, however, unfamiliarity of the learners with the lexical items comprising relational opposites leads them to confuse and use such L2 relations as directional relations (*go-come*), complementary relations (*female-male*), and antonyms (*small-big*) as substitutes. Thus in the analysed texts, confusion of binary terms was evident in sentences such as 'The Kingdom of Saudi Arabia is doing its best to promote peace in the Middle *West *East*' where directional relations *East* and *West* were confused and wrongly used thus producing Middle *West* instead of Middle *East*. While confusion of binary terms could be attributable to the inability of the students to distinguish between English lexical items that are relational opposites, it is worth acknowledging that under differentiation of the L1 items by the learner could also lead to their incapacity to differentiate the equivalent L2 items further informing binary term errors (Naba'h, 2011). Inadequate knowledge of L2 and in particular English lexical items that are relational opposites is a serious issue for students given the significant errors it occasions in their written and translated texts as depicted in the use of *West, teach, sell* where *East, learn, buy* ought to be used.

5.3.2.2 Analysis of Words Distorting Meaning Errors

Words distorting meaning as a subtype of confusion sense relation errors accounted for only 0.99% of all the intralingual errors found in the translation corpus texts. Words distorting meaning errors are commonly caused by insufficient knowledge of the L2 by the students. Lack of adequate knowledge of the L2 lexis leads to confusion between correct and incorrect words and use of the same in the produced texts (Al-Shormani & Al-Sohbani, 2012). The outcome is an example where students select an L2 word that is incorrect and use it in place of the correct L2 word effectively distorting the meaning of the sentence in question. For instance, words distorting meaning are evident in statements such as 'languages are a means of *conflict *communication* between people' as a consequence leading to distortion of the meaning of the text. Rajab et al. (2016) contend the use of words distorting meaning could be due to spelling errors as they found in their analysis of semantic errors committed by Libyan English learners among whom 32.4% of the distortion errors were attributed to spelling issues. This concurs with Al-Shormani and Al-Sohbani's (2012) findings that attributed confusion between words with similar forms such as *wipes* with *weeps* and *sight* with *site* to inadequate knowledge of the spelling of L2 lexical items thus leading to the use of words that distort the meaning of a translated text.

5.3.2.3 Analysis of Words with Inappropriate Meaning Errors

The use of words with inappropriate meanings was also a significant and relatively frequent semantic lexical error among the students at 21% of the total intralingual errors identified and occurring 64 times in the translation corpus texts analysed. These findings are compared closely with those of Shalaby et al. (2009) who found 87 instances of lexical choices with inappropriate meaning accounting for 30% of the total number of errors in that category. Shalaby et al. (2009) attribute the use of

5.3 Discussion and Explanation of Semantic Lexical Errors

words with inappropriate meaning to the Saudi students' inadequate knowledge of the L2 which causes them to confuse sense relations and thus makes incorrect choices of lexical items in their texts. While this is the case, it is worth noting that not all cases of use of English words with inappropriate meaning are due to inadequate knowledge of the L2. L1 transfer also leads to the erroneous choice of English words with an inappropriate meaning, particularly when the students directly translate colloquial and classical Arabic words into L2. For instance, literal translation of such Arabic words as (أكل akil) to *eats instead of *food* and use of the same in a sentence, say 'The government does its best to provide *eats *food* for every citizen,' leads to inappropriate meaning. Thus, as much as incomplete knowledge of the L2 informs errors relating to the use of words with inappropriate meaning, the influence of the L1 transfer in some of those instances cannot be ignored.

5.3.2.4 Analysis of General Term for Specific One Errors

The intralingual error of using a hypernym for a hyponym (a general term for specific one) is also a relatively frequent error observed among the students with an occurrence of 10 times at a frequency percentage of 3.7% of the errors falling under the confusion of sense relations' category. The error of the use of a general term for a specific one in the corpus of the translated texts was characterised by translation of such Arabic source text as *suqut 'awraq al'ashjar fi fasl alkharif yuead shklaan min 'ashkal alhimayat aldhdhatiat lilnabat* سقوط أوراق الأشجار في فصل الخريف يعد شكلاً من أشكال الحماية الذاتية للنبات، to 'The falling of leaves in autumn are a form of **gardens* self-protection' where the intended meaning of the lexical item used is underspecified owing to the use of the hypernym *gardens in place of the hyponym *plant*. In another instance, the same Arabic text was translated by one of the students as 'The falling of *trees in autumn are a form of plants self-protection' also leading to under specification of the intended meaning as the hypernym *trees is used instead of the hyponym *leaves*. According to Widiyati (2018), the tendency to use hypernym for hyponym can be attributed to inadequate knowledge of the L2 among the learners, effectively causing them to settle for lexical choices that not only underspecify the meaning of the translated text but also significantly alter it rendering it ambiguous and incomprehensible. Given the tendency of the semantic field of hyponyms to be included within hypernyms, students who are not fully conversant with the English hypernyms and their various hyponyms tend to use the former thus underspecifying not only the meaning but also the quality and accuracy of their translated texts.

5.3.2.5 Analysis of Overly Specific Terms Errors

Related to this, the use of overly specific terms was also a significant semantic error found in the analysed translated texts. The error occurred six times or 1.97% of the 304 intralingual errors identified. Widiyati (2018) stated that the error is attributed to the tendency by L2 learners to use a hyponym for a hypernym thus over specifying the intended meaning of the translated text. For instance, students could use the overly specific word *cities* to refer to *countries* effectively leading to overspecification of the translated text. The frequency of the use of overly specific terms has, however, been less frequent in previous studies such as the one by Shalaby et al. (2009) where the error occurred only one time at 0.14% of the confusion of sense relation errors. The variation in the frequency of this error subtype between the current study and previous studies could be attributed to the comprehensive nature of the taxonomy this study used comprising translation corpus texts while the other studies employed free production tasks. Like the use of hypernym for hyponym, the use of hyponyms for hypernym is major problem for Saudi English learners as at it undermines the intended meaning of their writing and translations.

5.3.2.6 Analysis of Inappropriate Co-Hyponyms Errors

The use of inappropriate co-hyponyms is another confusion of sense relations error that was evident in the analysed corpus text occurring two times out of the total 304 intralingual errors found. The semantic error is caused by a poor grasp of the L2 by the learner which effectively influences them to choose and use co-hyponyms that are unsuitable for the context in question. For instance, the affected student used the inappropriate hyponym *safety in place of the more appropriate hyponym *self-protection* in the text 'Leaves fall in autumn as a form of plants *safety *self-protection.' Hassan and Hussein (2019) attribute such errors to the tendency by L2 learners to be confused on which correct lexical item to use in a sentence due to their inability to differentiate the relation of inclusion of L2 lexical items. The scholars contend that the limitations of the learner's L1 at the semantic level negatively impact on their semantic competence as they write or translate the text to L2, further contributing to the error. The use of inappropriate co-hyponyms negatively impacts on the translations of the Saudi English major students by hindering the comprehensibility of their productions.

5.3.2.7 Analysis of Incompletion Errors

Incompletion errors were extensive in the analysed texts occurring 153 times and accounting for 29% of the errors in this category. In the analysed corpus texts, the errors were characterised by either deletion or omission of the L2 lexical items from the translated texts. While it could be argued that the complexity of the translation source text was a contributing factor for some of the omitted and deleted words, there were simple lexical items that ought not to be challenging even to novice translators. For instance, in the translated text 'Every country must try to avoid *... *polluting the environment in the twenty-first century'* the words *polluting the environment in the twenty-first century* which are neither sophisticated words

5.3 Discussion and Explanation of Semantic Lexical Errors

nor complex lexical items were omitted. However, owing to the inadequate lexical knowledge of some students, it is plausible to say that their incapability to find equivalent appropriate words for translation may have led them to omit or delete these lexical items. Factors such as exam anxiety, the text genre, or complexity of the source text to the individual learners may also contribute to incompletion errors. However, insignificance of the omitted, deleted, or missing lexical item in the L1 of the student could also inform errors of incompletion. This is clearly captured in the study by Ander and Yıldırım (2010) where one of the students wrote 'students should *… help from their teachers' instead of 'students should *seek* help from their teachers' effectively omitting a critical L2 lexical element which was insignificant in their L1. Incompletion errors are thus a problem for Saudi English major students as it leads to the loss of valuable information as well as hampering the intended meaning of the translated texts.

5.3.2.8 Analysis of Stylistic Errors

Stylistic errors such as verbosity, circumlocution errors, and misuse of compounds occurred 65 times at a frequency of 12.4% of the total semantic lexical errors. The frequency of stylistic errors in the current study compares with that of a similar study by Shalaby et al. (2009) in which the errors occurred 61 times with circumlocution errors occurring 49 and 45 times in the former and the latter study, respectively. The errors were caused by inappropriate use of the paraphrase strategy which led to inaccurate use of the L2 lexical items (circumlocution), the use of sophisticated language thus hampering the comprehensibility of the translated texts (verbosity), and the use of incorrect L2 compound words effectively altering the correct order of the lexical unit that makes up a compound (misuse of compounds). Inadequate knowledge of the L2 causes the students to fail to appreciate how English differs from the spoken form of their L1. This effectively leads to apply a paraphrase strategy, language construction, and word compounding approaches that inform circumlocution, verbosity, and compound misuse in their translations. This is a major problem for students as it renders the translated source text message vague besides rendering the translated lexical items unnecessarily complex.

5.3.2.9 Analysis of Wrong Near Synonyms

At 81 times, wrong near synonym was the third most frequent semantic lexical error accounting for 30% of all the confusion of sense relation errors. The intralingual error can be attributed to students' limited knowledge of the L2 lexical knowledge and in particular their unawareness of the semantic difference between some of the L2 synonyms which led them to think English synonyms with similar meaning carry the same meaning as the equivalent L1 words (Ghazala, 2012; Hassan & Hussein, 2019). For instance, in the context of the translated text 'we should not *lose *the great time', similarities in the meaning of the synonyms of the two English words in the text caused confusion to the student thus leading him to make the wrong lexical choices where (*lose* and *great*) the synonyms of the words (*waste* and *precious*), respectively, were used thus failing to correctly express the intended meaning of the source text; which ought to have been (We should not *waste* the *precious* time). Given the pervasiveness of the error in the analysed corpus text and the impact it has on the expressed meaning of the source text message, the error is a major problem for Saudi English students, hence the need for the appropriate remedial measures.

5.3.3 Comparison of the Study's Findings with Previous Studies in Relation to the Frequency and Sources of Semantic Lexical Errors

This study extends the growing body of knowledge regarding the types of lexical errors made by EFL learners, and by Saudi English learners in particular, in their translation products (e.g., Ander & Yıldırım, 2010; Carrió-Pastor & Mestre Mestre, 2014; Hemchua & Schmitt, 2006; Huaqing, 2009; Llach, 2011; Meara & English, 1987; Shalaby et al., 2009; Zimmermann, 1987). Similarities and differences were found between the findings and results of previous research and this study. The current study shows that lexical errors were pervasive in the translation products which hampers the intended meaning of the source text. Consistent with previous studies (e.g., Hemchua & Schmitt, 2006; Rezai & Davarpanah, 2019; Saud, 2018; Shalaby et al., 2009), semantic lexical errors were found in this study to be common in Arab and non-Arab EFL writings. However, Hemchua and Schmitt (2006) concerning Thai EFL learners and Shalaby et al. (2009) concerning Saudi EFL learners found that near synonyms errors were the most frequent error category. In Rezai and Davarpanah's (2019) study, collocation errors were reported to be the most common type of semantic lexical errors among their Persian EFL students. The findings of the current study, on the other hand, show that incompletion errors are the most frequent type of semantic lexical errors in the students' translations followed by direct translation from L1. Such differences in the frequency of semantic lexical errors might be related to different factors such as the learning context, the type of data elicited, and the lexical error classification system used. This study made use of translation texts to analyse and identify lexical errors and, as a consequence, new categories of lexical errors were identified and added to the error classification system, such as incompletion errors.

Concerning the sources of semantic lexical errors, Hemchua and Schmitt (2006) stated that L1 transfer and difference between L1 and L2 could be the reason behind the occurrence of lexical errors in their Thai ESL learners. Shalaby et al. (2009) also claimed that L1 had an impact on the use of L2 lexical items and the written production of their participants. This study, on the other hand, found that both interlingual and intralingual factors played a major role in the occurrence of most semantic lexical errors in the translation products. The semantic lexical errors occurring as a result of the interlingual influence were owing to literal translation of L1 words and the transfer of the semantic features associated with L1 lexical items. As for the intralingual influence, the findings of the current study indicate that a significant number of lexical errors occurred due to the lack of L2 lexical knowledge and the confusion between L2 lexical items that are semantically related.

5.4 Conclusion

The varied semantic lexical errors, among them confusion of sense relations errors, collocation errors, stylistic errors, and incompletion errors, comprise a significant type of lexical errors commonly observed in the translations of Saudi English major students and originate from either interlingual or intralingual sources due to the interference of the Arabic language and limited knowledge of the English language, respectively.

Discussion and comparative evaluation of the various lexical errors against previous study findings helps characterise error frequency variations. Further, this highlights how the difference in comprehensiveness of the taxonomy of the texts analysed affect how each subtype of the errors is perceived as a significant problem for the students. The analytical approach has demonstrated how the semantic lexical errors are counterproductive to the written translations of the students as they significantly affect not only the intended meaning of the productions, but also the clarity of the message in the L1 and ultimately the comprehensibility of the translated texts by the L2 audience. Although there are different factors that could be the cause of the errors, the significance of L1 transfer and incomplete lexical knowledge of the L2 in the occurrence of the semantically erroneous texts in the writings and translations of the learners is indisputable.

The following chapter provides a discussion of the impact of the current research analysis on the fields of L2 learning, translation, and language teaching.

References

Al-Shormani, M. Q., & Al-Sohbani, Y. A. (2012). Semantic errors committed by Yemeni University learners: Classifications and sources. *International Journal of English Linguistics, 2*(6), 120–139.

Ander, S., & Yıldırım, Ö. (2010). Lexical errors in elementary level EFL learners' compositions. *Procedia—Social and Behavioral Sciences, 2*(2), 5299–5303.

Carrió-Pastor, M. L., & Mestre Mestre, E. M. (2014). Motivation in second language acquisition. *Procedia-Social and Behavioral Sciences, 116*, 240–244.

Derrick, D. J., Paquot, M., & Plonsky, L. (2018). Interlingual versus intralingual errors. In *The TESOL encyclopedia of English language teaching* (pp. 1–6). https://doi.org/10.1002/9781118784235.eelt0079

Ghazala, H. (2012). *Translation as problems and solutions: A textbook for university students and trainee translators* (9th ed.). Konooz Al-Marifa Company for Printing and Publishing.

Hassan, A. Y., & Hussein, Z. A. (2019). Lexical errors in composition writing by 2nd year Iraqi EFL learners at Al-Nisour University College. *Midad Al-Adab Refereed Journal, 1*(17), 803–821.

Hemchua, S., & Schmitt, N. (2006). An analysis of lexical errors in the English compositions of Thai learners. *Prospect, 21*, 3–25.

Huaqing, H. (2009). An analysis of lexical errors in non-English majors' writing: A corpus based study. *Foreign Language World, 3*, 2–9.

James, C. (2013). *Errors in language learning and use: Exploring error analysis*. Routledge.

Llach, M. P. A. (2011). *Lexical errors and accuracy in foreign language writing*. Multilingual Matters.

Mahmoud, A. (2005). Collocation errors made by Arab learners of English. *Asian EFL Journal, 5*(2), 117–126.

Mahmoud, A. (2019). Interlingual transfer of intralingual errors: Lexical substitution from MSA to EFL. *Studies in English Language Teaching, 7*(4), 419–431. https://doi.org/10.22158/selt.v7n4p419

Meara, P., & English, F. (1987). *Lexical errors and learners' dictionaries*. Birkbeck College.

Naba'h, A. A. (2011). Lexical errors made by in- service English language teachers in Jordan. *Damascus University Journal, 27*(1), 49–75.

Qaid, Y. A., & Ramamoorthy, L. (2011). Analysis of intralingual errors in learning English as a foreign language by Yemeni students. *Language in India, 11*(5), 534–545.

Rajab, A. S., Aladdin, A., & Darus, S. (2016). An investigation of semantic interlingual errors in the writing of Libyan English as Foreign Language learners. *SSRN Electronic Journal, 7*(4), 277–296.

Rezai, M. J., & Davarpanah, F. (2019). The study of formal and semantic errors of lexis by Persian EFL learners. *International Journal of Cognitive and Language Sciences, 13*(1), 41–47.

Richards, J. C. (2015). *Error analysis: Perspectives on second language acquisition*. Routledge.

Saud, W. I. (2018). Lexical errors of third year undergraduate students. *English Language Teaching, 11*(11), 161–168.

Shalaby, A. N., Yahya, N., & El-Komi, M. (2009). Analysis of lexical errors in Saudi college students' compositions. *Journal of the Saudi Association of Languages and Translation, 2*(3), 65–93.

Shin, S. C. (2002). Error analysis: Lexical errors produced by Australian KFL learners. *KAREC Discussion Papers, 3*(3), 1–25.

Widiyati, M. (2018). Lexical errors in news item texts written by English education department students. In *ELTiC Conference* (Vol. 3, No. 1). http://eproceedings.umpwr.ac.id/index.php/eltic/article/viewFile/431/377

Zimmerman, R. (1987). Form-orientated and content-orientated lexical errors in L2 learners. *International Review of Applied Linguistics, 25*(1), 55–67.

Zughoul, M. (1991). Lexical choice: Towards writing problematic word lists. *International Review of Applied Linguistics, 29*(2), 45–60.

Chapter 6
Implications for Language Learning, Translation, and Language Teaching

6.1 Introduction

The previous chapters demonstrated the importance of lexis in written translation and how formal and semantic lexical errors could have affected the quality and clarity of the students' translation products. The students' formal and semantic lexical errors were categorised into 31 subtypes and, based on a taxonomy developed specifically for this study, a quantitative frequency analysis was implemented. The chapters provided a detailed explanation of the possible sources of the identified formal and semantic lexical errors. The findings indicated that inadequate knowledge of the L2 formal and semantic aspects and the difference between the linguistic systems of the target and home languages account for the occurrence of lexical errors.

This chapter discusses the implications of the findings for ESL/EFL students, teachers, and researchers. Through analysis of the formal and semantic lexical errors and their sources common among Saudi English major students, the study puts forth practical pedagogical suggestions for improving English language instruction across Saudi universities. This chapter is presented in four sections. The first Sect. (6.2) illustrates the implications of the current study analysis for the field of language learning. The second Sect. (6.3) discusses the contributions of the study to the field of translation. The pedagogical implications for the teaching of English language with respect to vocabulary are provided (6.4). Finally, a summary of the impacts of lexical error analysis on the fields of language learning, translation studies, and language teaching is provided (6.5).

© The Author(s), under exclusive license to Springer Nature Singapore Pte Ltd. 2022
Y. Alenazi, *Exploring Lexical Inaccuracy in Arabic-English Translation*,
New Frontiers in Translation Studies, https://doi.org/10.1007/978-981-19-6390-2_6

6.2 Implications for Language Learning

The findings and analysis of the current study have several important implications for the field of the L2 learning. The findings show a significant degree of different types of formal lexical errors, among them misselection, misformation, and distortion errors and semantic lexical errors including collocation, stylistic, incompletion, and confusion of sense relations errors pervades the translations of the students and is thus a major impediment to effective learning of English as their additional language. Based on the analysis, it is unambiguous that the formal and semantic lexical errors prevalent among the students are characterised by an inability to select the appropriate lexical items and form the correct words and inadvertent shifting of the L1 lexical items to the L2 thus posing a challenge to L2 learning (James, 2013). In this study for instance, the effects of formal lexical errors and in particular misselection of suffixes on language learning were evidenced by the tendency by English major students to write such translated statements as "People have *difference *different* skills ...," while the effects of semantic lexical errors were characterised by the use of such translated texts as "Save for *a black day *a rainy day*" due to direct translation from the Arabic language. This research thus demonstrates how the various types of formal and semantic lexical errors affect the learning of English as an L2 by the Saudi students effectively providing an invaluable basis for understanding, developing, and approaching SLA among L1 Arabic speakers.

The range of lexical errors, both formal and semantic, found in the students' translations of this study is related in one way or another to the field of SLA. Formal lexical errors due to overgeneralisation of L2 rules are linked to the error analysis concept which holds that for a person to learn a language, they must first build a structure of rules based on the information of the L2 they are exposed to and on the basis of which they will use the L2 (Khansir, 2012). In the current study for instance, unawareness of whether to retain or delete the word-final < e > when applying inflectional or derivational suffixes led to distortion errors such as *completeing for *completing* and *operateion for *operation* (the rule requires the retention of the vowel < e > at the end of the word if a suffix starting with a consonant is applied, as in attaching -ly to *complete* to create *completely*, or the deletion of < e > if a suffix starting with a vowel is applied, such as affixing -ion to *operate* to form *operation*).

Linguistic errors are critical in learning as they help predict the challenges associated with language learning. For the students, the analysis of these linguistic errors is essential in that it assists their language instructors to better understand the difficult areas the learners are likely to encounter in the course of their language learning and thus plan on how to address the challenges. The current study analysis does not only link the findings of the study on formal and semantic lexical errors to the field of SLA but also seeks to generate new findings vis-à-vis the field of SLA.

6.2.1 Implications of Error Analysis for Language Learning

The findings of this research in relation to both intralingual and interlingual sources of semantic and formal lexical errors confirm the practicality of the error analysis approach as a tool to study the students' errors. The types of lexical errors witnessed among the students have helped illustrate the nature of linguistic gaps that exist among L1 Arabic speakers attempting to learn and acquire English as a second language. In other words, the errors have helped show what the students do not know and understand about the L2 and the ways in which they try to deal with this knowledge deficit. The undertaking perfectly aligns with the practice of the error analysis approach which not only explains linguistic gaps in the process of SLA but also studies the occurrence, character, sources, and outcomes of ineffective language. The findings of the present study on formal and semantic lexical errors thus contribute to the error analysis field by establishing the frequency, nature, origins, and effects of unsuccessful acquisition and learning of the English language by the students on their translations. The study analysis on the pedagogical implications of lexical errors and the subsequent taxonomy adopted to address the linguistic gaps contributing to the incorrect use of lexis also contribute to error analysis. The analysis demonstrates both English language instructors and students endeavour to discover ways of dealing with their lack of linguistic knowledge which effectively attests to a link between the strategies of the English learners and the concept of error analysis.

From the perspective of the error analysis concept, analysis of lexical errors in the translation products of Saudi English learners helps enhance the description of L2 besides facilitating the contrastive description of the English and Arabic languages which together assists in predicting the potential occurrence of lexical errors in the students' written texts. This study focuses on examining language errors of English majors from L1 Arabic language background, analysing errors manifested in their translation products. Previous error analysis research has been conducted on L2 learners from different L1 backgrounds and focused on analysing free written texts, unlike the current study which focuses on examining lexical errors in the translations of English majors from Arabic L1 background.

Based on the study's analysis, the identified errors reveal the gaps in the students' lexical knowledge of the L2 and demonstrate how they attempt to compensate for these gaps by relying on their L1 lexical knowledge, leading them to make interlingual errors such as direct translation from L1. Furthermore, partial knowledge of the L2 lexical items cause the students to employ different communication strategies. However, such efforts to fill their lexical gaps lead to intralingual errors such as verbosity and circumlocution errors.

This study, by using an error analysis approach, asserts the significance and practicality of using different language samples and employing a comprehensive taxonomy when examining lexical errors to gain more insight into the difficulties experienced by L2 learners and to get a better understanding of their L2 lexical knowledge.

6.2.2 Positive and Negative Transfer in Language Learning

The current study effectively links lexical errors from interlingual sources to differences and similarities between the L1 and L2 of the study population, and hence, its findings and analysis coincide with the perspectives of the language transfer. The phenomenon of language transfer rests on the premise that learners of an L2 have a tendency to transfer meanings and forms of their L1 and the way in which they are distributed to the L2 (Yang, 2019). Frequency analysis of the current study on the lexical errors common in translation products generated by the students found a statistically significant trend in the content and form of the students' L1 Arabic language transference. These included word level lexical errors such as translation of the Arabic word (ظفاح hafid) as *save instead of *keep* due to literal translation of the Arabic source text and the transfer of L1 phonetic features such as <b>,<f>,<p> to L2 lexical items and thus writing words such as *stambs, *facation, *hapit, and *possiple in place of *stamps, vacation, habit,* and *possible.* As claimed by the concept of language transfer, the errors could be attributable to differences between the Arabic and English languages. While such negative forms of language transfer may be inadvertent, as Qaid and Ramamoorthy (2011) posit, their effects on acquisition of the L2 may be considerable given the consequences associated with an incorrect language choice and as evidenced by the effects of the lexical errors on the quality of the written translations produced by the students. Figure 6.1 illustrates the influence of this phenomenon on the process of Saudi students' translations.

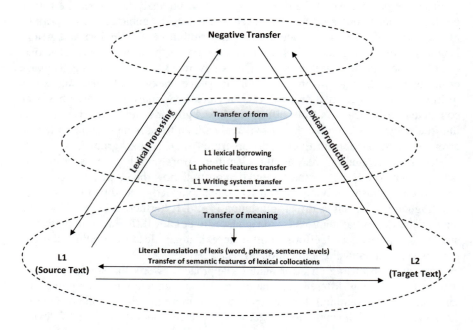

Fig. 6.1 Influence of negative transfer on the process of translation

6.2 Implications for Language Learning

Translation is a complicated cognitive process in which a translator first needs to analyse the semantic features of the source text through processing its lexical items and then re-analyse these semantic features producing formally correct lexical items in the L2. The student translator, therefore, needs to interpret the linguistic features (form/content) associated with the source text lexical items and re-encode these features with the same depth in the L2 using the right words to deliver a comprehensible message.

The translation process could be simpler if the L1 text and L2 text share similar linguistic systems, but in the case of English and Arabic the process is challenging. Based on the study's findings, the students' L1 is the main source behind the occurrence of various types of lexical errors in their L2 translation products. The students' L1 (Arabic) differs from English in that they come from unrelated language families. Therefore, the students in this study tend to produce English texts with incorrect lexical items due to negative transfer and as a result of their insufficient knowledge of the L2. The Arabic language has words with very complex meanings and certain formal relations that do not exist in the English language. Student translators with insufficient L2 lexical knowledge will rely on their L1 lexical knowledge as a strategy to finish the translation process.

The students tend to transfer formal and semantic features of their L1 while processing lexical items in the source text. When the students fail to retrieve the appropriate equivalent L2 words in their mental lexicons, they rely more on their L1 to produce words in the target text regardless of the context. Students sometimes add Arabic words in the target English text without modifying these words to fit the L2 structure, producing borrowing and orthographic errors. Students also tend to translate L1 words literally using formally correct L2 words, but they neglect the semantic features associated with the words chosen distorting meaning of the original text, and thus, the written language produced is semantically incomprehensible. Based on the study's findings, transferring the meaning of the source text lexical items directly to the L2 led to errors in the use of L2 collocations. Students' lack of knowledge of the L2's collocational fixed expressions forces them to depend on their L1 to produce equivalent expressions although they may be inappropriate.

In its analysis of formal and semantic errors, the current study limits itself to negative transfer as illustrated in the type of interlingual errors presented. The study explores the effects of negative transfer of L1 phonological system on L2 lexical items in-depth as illustrated by substituting English consonants $<b>$ for $<p>$ and $<v>$ for $<f>$ leading to distortion of the respective L2 words among other numerous instances of L1 transfer by the English major students (Hui, 2010; Shalaby et al., 2009). Even though the transfer concept envisages both negative and positive transfers, there is no evidence of positive transfer found in the data set of the current study. According to Gass and Selinker (2008), positive transfer (facilitation) referred to "the use of the first language (or other languages known) in a second language context resulting in a target-like second language form" (pp. 517–518). They furthermore stated that negative transfer (interference) is "the use of the first language (or other languages known) in a second language context when the resulting second language form is incorrect." Thus, while language transfer, through its concept of positive transfer, seems to imply that learners of an L2 could enhance their learning of the L2, it is apparent that such occurrences are not applicable to all instances of foreign language learning or SLA.

6.2.3 The Implications of a Systematic Error Taxonomy for Language Learning

A wide range of research attempts to agree on an error analysis classification system to be implemented for lexical error analysis purposes (Llach, 2011). Several classification criteria are considered in lexical error taxonomies: formal/semantic distinction, descriptive criterion, psycholinguistic criterion, origin of influence taxonomy, linguistic criterion, word-class distinction, product-/process-oriented categorisation, and miscellaneous classification. Systematising taxonomies into these criteria is a complicated task, since error classification could be based on more than one categorisation criterion.

Based on the nature of the current study and the type of data collected, miscellaneous classification was designed informed by previous taxonomies. Lexical error taxonomies are usually developed for an error analysis study based on the data collected. Therefore, the current study taxonomy of lexical errors was mainly adopted from Shalaby et al. (2009). Previous studies conducted their analysis of lexical errors using free production data of L2 learners, whereas this study used translated corpus data. Thus, the analysis and findings of the study have contributed to this linguistic area in developing a comprehensive list of lexical error categories based on form, content, and origin of influence regarding translation products. It is important to mention that the translation corpus used for the analysis was useful in examining learners' language since it reveals how the learner conveys the L1 words in their L2, and accordingly how the learner interprets the semantic relations between words in the L1 and L2. Translation texts provide a significant advantage in providing a clear picture of the L2 learner's intended meaning to the researcher. It is much easier to determine the relationship between L1 and L2 vocabulary if the intended meaning is available. Therefore, linguistic categories in the error taxonomy adopted have been expanded by including new subcategories such as in the formal distortion lexical error category (capitalisation, word segmentation, grapheme substitution, unique distortion errors) and adding a new semantic lexical error category such as incompletion errors (see Fig. 6.2). This study shows that the taxonomy of lexical errors can be modified, and new categories can be added to it based on the type of language sample collected and the learning context. Taxonomies of language errors can be also designed from a pedagogical point of view to explain learners' errors and improve language instruction.

6.3 Implications for the Translation Studies 137

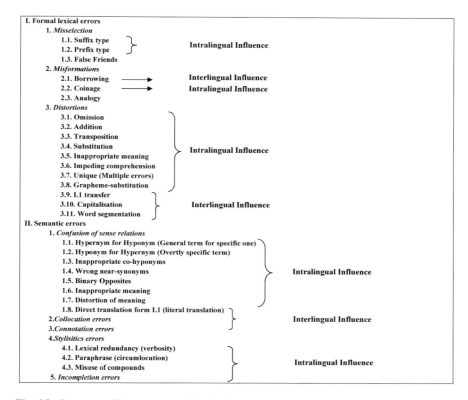

Fig. 6.2 Summary of the current study lexical error taxonomy

This classification system of lexical errors allows for fine-grained analysis of L2 learners' language production with respect to vocabulary by employing error specifications in terms of linguistic categories and origin of influence. The taxonomy hence can be useful as a groundwork for corpus-based studies of ESL learners in different contexts. It can also serve as a basis for effective feedback for the students about their language development in classroom practice.

The implications for language learning established by this research are summarised in Fig. 6.3.

6.3 Implications for the Translation Studies

6.3.1 Impacts of Lexical Errors on Translation Quality

In the translation field, it is not uncommon for translators to focus more on the whole discourse of the translation and thus to some degree neglect finer details such as individual lexemes and the effects they are likely to have on the entire

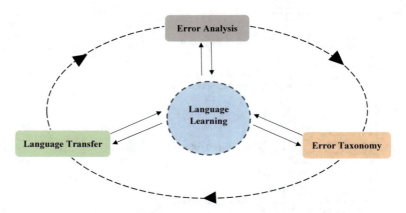

Fig. 6.3 Implications of the analysis of lexical errors for language learning

discourse. The error analysis is important in the field of translation as it draws attention not only to the manner in which the translated L2 vocabulary conveys meaning of the source text but also to the accuracy of the smallest meaningful linguistic units used. Morphemes as the smallest meaningful units of language make up words which are then collated into vocabulary (Usman, 2015). Variously put, morphology is a part of grammar which deals with word forms further highlighting the fact that grammar and vocabulary are closely related. Therefore, the importance of the accuracy of the small blocks of the language used in a translation cannot be ignored. By drawing attention to the inaccurate word usage in the translated texts, the error analysis underscores the importance of using a method of vocabulary instruction such as grammar-translation method (GTM) which is effective for teaching vocabulary and grammar as it integrates grammar activities that enable teachers to promptly correct errors made by the learners (Liu, 2020). Adoption of the GTM in teaching translation would thus be critical in ensuring the student translators and others in the field pay attention to both the whole discourse and the small blocks of language during translation given that it deductively teaches grammatical structures and rules for translating from L1 to L2, thus ensuring accuracy in both L2 word usage and conveyance of source text meaning. The outcome would be correct translation and accurate usage of the smallest meaningful linguistic units of the L2 which would then have a positive effect on the whole discourse.

Translators tend to judge the translation script starting from the discourse before reviewing the sentence structure and lastly the vocabulary. As evidenced in the foregoing error analysis, a bottom-up approach should be used when teaching and reviewing translation, that is, start with the vocabulary or words, then move to sentence structure, and conclude with discourse. In the purview of the GTM, the approach is critical in that it would ensure students are first taught the vocabulary and the applicable grammatical structures and rules of the L2 with emphasis put not only on mastering and memorising the words but also the rules of the language. This will enable the instructor to assess the level of understanding the students have of the L2 vocabulary based on their usage as well as their comprehension of the applicable structures and rules based on the grammatical and lexical errors they produce. Having mastered the L2 vocabulary, instruction should then focus on syntax to equip the students with the requisite knowledge on how to arrange the mastered L2 words and phrases into sentences that are coherent and well-formed. This will help the students learn how to adjust the sentence structure of the L1 source text to the syntactic conditions of the L2, thus ensuring accurate translation. Only after teaching the L2 vocabulary and sentence structure should translation instruction move to the discourse level where issues of the appropriateness, transparency, and fidelity of a translation come to bear. Instruction on translation discourse will help familiarise the students with the applicable concepts and most importantly learn how to convey the meaning of the L1 source text accurately and use the applicable idioms and grammar correctly. By highlighting common lexical errors, the error analysis highlights the importance of using the bottom-up approach in teaching of translation as it progressively helps build up the L2 knowledge thus averting distortions that often impede the fidelity and transparency of translated texts.

Lexis is a core aspect in translation given the fact a good translation cannot be attained devoid of words that correctly and accurately express the message in the source text. The current analysis of lexical errors lays bare the centrality of adequate knowledge of the L2 lexis among Saudi English major students without which appropriate translation of the source texts is difficult to achieve. Most translation and pedagogic theoreticians, among them Michael Lewis, concur that vocabulary plays an integral function in helping learners acquire and develop native-like translation and language capabilities (Koletnik, 2012). It is thus imperative that translation instruction incorporates activities that promote learning of the L2 vocabulary including common phrases and idioms. The classroom activities should entail exercises that support vocabulary learning both contextually and through translation from the L1. To be a good translator, however, a student should have not only adequate knowledge of the L2 vocabulary but also good mastery of the grammar and hence the need to use an instruction method such as GTM that combines vocabulary and grammatical learning and is thus likely to be highly effective in producing excellent translators.

6.3.2 Impacts of Lexical Errors on Translation Practice

The analysis of the current study addresses the diverse lexical errors made by the students in their efforts to translate corpus texts from their L1 (Arabic) to the L2 (English). First are formal lexical errors including misselection, misformation, and distortion errors made by the students in the translation texts as identified and described in Chap. 4. Based on the findings, distortion errors comprised the most prevalent form of lexical errors in the translated texts and were characterised by capitalisation and spelling omission errors which were caused by limited orthographic knowledge of the L2 thus leading to inappropriate translations. For instance, the translated texts featured such capitalisation errors as *Life where the L2 lexical item *life* was inappropriately capitalised; and spelling omission errors such as *midde, *mentaly, and *shoud were written in the translated texts in place of *middle, mentally,* and *should* omitting the respective vowels and consonants—a problem that was common especially where the end consonant in a lexical item needed to be doubled; a further indication of inadequate orthographic knowledge of the L2 among the students. The findings highlight the need for improving teaching of translation with regard to vocabulary by incorporating instructional techniques aimed at enhancing the orthographic knowledge of the students. Baker (2011) argues that there is no direct connection among orthographic lexical items and their meanings both across different languages and within the same language. Translation instruction should thus not only seek to clarify variation between orthographic words and their meanings but also to demystify the view that words comprise the least element of meaning by emphasising the potential of a small section of a word to carry meaning. For instance, inappropriate translations resulting from spelling omission errors where the rule requiring the use of double consonants when certain suffixes are used led to distortion of the meanings of the words *mentally, stopped, and running* thus indicating the variation between orthographic words and their meanings and hence the need to use translation instruction strategies that holistically enhance the orthographic knowledge of the English language among the affected Saudi students.

Distortion errors found are also relevant to the field of translation in that orthographic competence enhancement has a direct impact on the L2 lexical processing and more specifically vocabulary acquisition among L2 learners. As illustrated by the type of formal lexical errors including impeding comprehension errors such as the use of *geun and *habbite in place of *gain* and *hobby* respectively made by the students, the critical role played by orthographic knowledge in lexical processing especially during translations is evident. These lexical errors rendered it difficult to comprehend the translated texts without going back to the source texts and could be attributable to the students' limited orthographic knowledge of the English language and their tendency to translate without consideration of the context. Vocabulary studies have shown that correlation exists between translation proficiency of L2 learners and their capacity to employ context in their attempt to infer meaning of unfamiliar L2 vocabulary (Baker, 2011; Coady & Huckin, 2000). Consequently, it is not uncommon for the L2 learners to misidentify certain L2 words, an occurrence which effectively causes them not to base their lexical inference on the context. In the current study, the limited orthographic knowledge of the L2 among the students creates a situation where some learners erroneously presume to know a vocabulary, thus ignoring the different contextual clues that draw attention to the semantic inappropriateness caused by the misidentification. Coady and Huckin (2000) attribute such identification errors to inadequate data retrieved from orthographic processing. During translation, orthographic processing inadequacies manifest in the form of poor comprehension

6.3 Implications for the Translation Studies

and inaccurate lexical retrieval leading to inappropriate translations and hence lexical errors highlighted in translated texts produced by the students. It is thus essential that translation instruction incorporates components aimed at teaching L2 learners to use context when inferring meaning of L2 words that are unknown to them. The approach will help inculcate among the students the habit of always basing their lexical inferences on the source text context thus enabling them to take note of contextual clues that draw their attention to any forms of semantic incongruity that may be informed by misidentification of unfamiliar L2 words. Translation instructors are encouraged to employ teaching strategies that enhance orthographic pattern knowledge and support mental grapheme representations (MGRs) acquisition among the learners to ensure they not only understand the patterns and rules of orthotactics, letter position, spelling, and sound-letter correspondence but also store accurate mental representations of particular L2 vocabulary (Apel, 2019). The outcome will be the enhanced ability of the students to retrieve context appropriate words from the grapheme representation stored in their minds thus leading to more accurate lexical retrieval and hence more accurate and high-quality translations.

The current study also highlights misformation errors such as borrowing and coinage as some of the significant issues in the translated productions. Borrowing was characterised by such translations as *min jid wajad wamin zara'a hasad* من جد وجد ومن زرع حصد 'Who *jid *works hard* will get great benefits' where the word *jid* is directly borrowed from L1 and written in Arabic while coinage manifested in the translated text in the form of *tueadu alsiyaha min 'ahami masadir aldakhl alqawmaa fa misr* تعد السياحة من أهم مصادر الدخل القومى فى مصر '*The coinsc is an important source of income in Egypt' where the incomprehensible word *the coinsc was coined in place of the L1 word *alsiyaha* to mean 'tourism.' These lexical errors are pedagogically useful given their correspondence with the transfer competence, subject-related competence, and linguistic competence of both the students and their L2 instructors (Elmgrab, 2013). The identified misformation errors could be attributed to limited lexical knowledge among the students, effectively highlighting the need to use instruction strategies aimed at enhancing the learners' knowledge of the L2 lexis when teaching translation. This may entail creation of vocabulary lists for the students to use in their revisions and writing practice as well as provision of opportunities for students to translate specific source texts into L2 as a group while actively correcting one another. The approach will help the students build a sufficient knowledge and repertoire of problematic L2 words thus ensuring they are able to find suitable words in their English lexicon when translating texts from L1 to L2 and therefore averting instances where they revert to their L1 lexicon or invent odd words in an attempt to bridge the gap in their L2 lexical knowledge.

The findings attribute some of the lexical errors identified to the failure to grasp the differences between the English and Arabic writing systems. Word segmentation errors including the use of words such as *with out, *onearth, and *every thing in the translated texts in place of *without, on earth,* and *everything* are indicative of unawareness of the variation in word space rules in the two writing systems. While normal word spaces are essential in the English writing system where there are two separate lexical items, e.g., *on earth* and unnecessary where compound words are used, e.g., *without*, word spaces tend to be unnecessary at the lexical level in the Arabic writing system, hence the tendency by the Saudi English students to commit word segmentation errors. Similarly, grapheme substitution errors such as writing *expirians, *knoldg, and *beard instead of *experience, knowledge,* and *bird* could be attributed to the inability to understand the difference between English and Arabic phoneme-graphemes correspondence. Teaching of translation should address this linguistic gap by emphasising the distinction in the respective rules of the two languages and especially the fact that while Arabic letters and words are written as they are pronounced, English writing has more complex spelling rules and hence any attempt to apply the L1 spelling rules to the L2 will lead to misspellings and consequently grapheme substitution errors (Watson, 2002). This will enable the L2 learners to become more familiar with the phoneme grapheme correspondence rules of the two languages and therefore more cautious with their translations leading to improvements in the quality of their translation productions.

The current research also contributes to the translation field by highlighting how such stylistic semantic errors as circumlocution affect the written translations produced by Saudi English major students. The study characterises circumlocution as the most frequent type of stylistic errors committed by the L2 learners, occurring 49 times out of the total 65 stylistic errors found. An analysis of the errors highlights the tendency of the Saudi students to employ a paraphrase strategy when translating Arabic texts into English as opposed to giving the correct lexical items which best convey the intended meaning of the source text. Although the paraphrase strategy works in speaking, it tends to be counterproductive in written translation in that it leads to inaccurate use of the L2 lexical items. To illustrate, when translating the Arabic source text *tabdhul almamlakat alearabiat alsaeudiat kl aljuhud almumkinat liasud alsalam fa mintaqat alshrq al'awsat* تبذل المملكة العربية السعودية كل الجهود الممكنة ليسود السلام فى منطقة الشرق الأوسط using the paraphrase strategy, the inaccurate and unclear translation was produced as follows: "The Kingdom of Saudi Arabia is doing its best *to make the Islam fun*." This could be attributable to the use of inaccurate lexical items in an attempt to convey the intended meaning of the original text, the outcome of which is the distortion of the source text meaning. However, had the students provided and used the correct lexical items to convey the intended meaning of the original text, the correct translated text would have been 'the Kingdom of Saudi Arabia is doing its best *to promote peace in the Middle East*' thus effectively relaying the intended meaning of the source text. The analysis of these findings demonstrates the need to not only enhance the L2 knowledge of the Saudi English major students but also sensitise them on the importance of using the correct lexical items to accurately convey the intended meaning of any source texts they translate so as to minimise the associated translation equivalence errors (Elmahdi & Moqbil, 2016). This will have positive implications for the translation field by preventing instances where L2 learners use the counterproductive paraphrase strategy in written translations and ensure

6.3 Implications for the Translation Studies

appropriate equivalent translation thus precluding confusion of the meanings of the written target texts.

The findings demonstrate the significance of collocations and translation of idiomatic phrases in the translation of source texts to target texts. In the analysed written translations produced by the students, such idiomatic errors due to literal translation from L1 as the translation of the Arabic source text *ahfud qurshak al'abyad liawmik al'aswad* احفظ قرشك الأبيض ليومك الأسود to English text 'Save your money for *your black day' were frequent. Literal translation of the Arabic idiomatic expression ليومك الأسود *liawmik al'aswad* leads to an incorrect use of the L2 phrase *black day in the target text instead of 'save for *a rainy day*' which is the correct corresponding English idiomatic expression. From the findings, the errors are also prevalent when translating such common Arabic proverbial expressions as *iina altuyur ealaa 'ashkaliha taqaeu* إن الطيور على أشكالها تقع and *alwald sirun 'abih* الولد سر أبيه which were literally translated into L2 as '*Birds in their forms fall' and '*The son is his father's secret' instead of *Birds of a feather flock together* and *He is his father's son,* respectively. Ghazala (2012) attributed the idiomatic errors to the literal translation of L1 lexical items into several individual L2 lexical items they are familiar with without due consideration of the collective meaning of the combination of the lexical items in the sentence. The students thus translate the idiomatic phrases in the source text word for word and in total disregard of the context effectively producing lexical sentences and written translations which hardly reflect the intended meaning of the original texts. By assessing the use of co-occurring lexical items such as a noun with a specific adjective, a verb with a noun, a noun with a noun, and phrasal verbs in the translated corpus texts produced by Saudi English major students, the current study analysis has implications for the translation field (Ghazala, 2012). The analysis highlights the tendency by the learners to make incorrect choices of co-occurring lexical items when translating texts from Arabic to English due to difficulties identifying the appropriate L2 equivalent collocation for the L1 collocation in the source text. Consequently, Arabic collocation such as (*'ukhidhat waead* أخذت وعد) was written in L2 as *take a promise instead of *made a promise* due to difficulty in making the correct choice causing the learner to resort to his L1 and thus the equivalent translation of the colloquial Arabic collocation. This is also the case in the Arabic source texts as *tuetabar alhiwayat wasilatan lilmutieat w litamdiat alwaqt* تعتبر الهوايات وسيلة للمتعة و لتمضية الوقت, *yjb 'an natakhalas min aleaddat alsyy'h* يجب أن نتخلص من العادات السيئة, and *min almuetaqad 'ana alshabab la yaemalun binasayih alkibar* من المعتقد أن الشباب لا يعملون بنصائح الكبار which appear in the translated corpus text as 'Hobbies are interesting means to *go *pass* time,' 'We must *get down *get rid of /break* the bad habits,' and 'It is believed that the youth do not *work with *act on* the advice of the old,' respectively—translations which are inappropriate in L2 due to incorrect lexical choices of the co-occurring lexical items. The analysis of these findings is critical in the translation field as they underscore the need to enhance not only the L2 lexical knowledge of translation students but also their understanding of their L1 collocations and the equivalent L2 collocations.

6.3.3 Impacts of Lexical Errors on Translation Principles

As can be discerned from the foregoing analysis, the findings coincide with translation principles in various ways. Klaudy (2006) asserts that the need to train translators and teach translation was the impetus behind the emergence of translation studies. As an applied and descriptive translation inquiry, the current study plays a critical role in shedding light on the linguistic difficulties marring translation efforts by Saudi English major students, effectively laying a theoretical foundation for design of the most effective approaches for translation training and teaching translation to EFL learners. The findings on the effects of the L1 of the learners and the limited lexical, morphological, and orthographical knowledge and how these elements render them susceptible to different types of formal and semantic lexical errors have implications for the translation field in that they help lay the scientific background and the professional context necessary for the conception and advancement of translation principles.

The findings also coincide with such translation principles as the communicative approach. The communicative approach principle of translation is premised on the perspective that what ought to be translated is the meaning and not the actual words since language is merely a medium through which messages are passed and undue focus on language may impede comprehension (Chang, 2011). Under the communicative approach to translation, the goal is always to deliver the exact contextual meaning of the source text in such a manner that both the language and content become readily appropriate (Ali, 2018). In the current study, misformation errors such as coinage (use of *atteiaed instead of *effort*) and borrowing (use of *the slam instead of *peace*) highlight the students' tendency to focus more on the language and thus engage in the practice of transcoding L1 words to L2 which ultimately renders the translated text incomprehensible. An analysis of the findings emphasises these lexical errors can only be avoided if the students choose the correct lexical items which fully convey the intended meaning of the original text. This is affirmed by Ghazala (2012) who stated that the primary goal of translation is usually to clearly transmit the source text message to the L2 devoid of complexities that could hinder its intended meaning. The analysis emphasises the significance of translating the original text without altering the intended meaning, coinciding with the perspective of the communicative approach which emphasises the need to give the accurate contextual meaning of the source text in a manner that renders both the language and content agreeable.

Given its focus on the lexical errors and in particular the analysis of the manner in which the students use English vocabulary and the effect of incorrect lexical choice on their written translation production, the current study and its findings correspond with the linguistic approach of translation. The perspective rests on the premise that all translations ought to be examined from the standpoint of its basic units among them the sentence, syntagm, and the word (Hodges, 2009). In the current study, the written translation productions by the students have been considered from the viewpoint of their fundamental elements including the source text and the L2 lexical items, the resultant translated sentences, and the syntagm effectively allowing for the analysis of such elements as text purpose, shift, equivalence, form, and meaning (Kenny, 2012). The outcome has been a better understanding of how the lexical errors made by the students arise, the contributing factors, and their effects on the comprehensibility of the translated source texts. The findings provide insight on how the English language is used in the Arabic cultural context by examining how Saudi English students shift meaning from their L1 to L2 when translating Arabic texts to English and the lexical errors they produce, thus contributing to the advancement of the functional linguistic facet of the linguistic approach concept.

The findings contradict the linguistic perspective as espoused by Nida (1991) in that in addressing the linguistic aspects of the art of translating its focus is solely on formal relations rather than on meaningful ones. Semantic and formal processes of translation such as convergence, divergence, substitution, and equation as depicted in the analysis of formal and semantic lexical errors commonly made by Saudi English major students hardly assume a transformational orientation. Thus, while the focus of the current study pays more attention to the pragmatic features of the source text and context and how appropriately these are captured in the translated texts, due consideration of the semantic and formal aspects within which the translation process would be more productive. The findings also contradict a key premise of the communicative perspective in that it pays more attention to the form and content of the translation production, thus ignoring other core aspects of written communication. According to Nida (1991), communicative theory-based written translation approaches should duly consider both the extralinguistic and paralinguistic features of written communications. In oral messages, these entail both verbal and non-verbal cues while in written messages these include quality, format, and style. Accordingly, although the current study analyses errors prevalent in the translation productions of the Saudi English major students based on both form and content, the attendant paralinguistic and extralinguistic features ought not to be ignored given their effect on the appropriateness and quality of the written communication.

The implications of lexical error analysis for translation studies presented in this section are summarised in Fig. 6.4.

6.4 Implications for Language Teaching

The current study analysis and its findings on the types of formal and semantic lexical errors common among translation productions generated by the students have varied implications for the field of language teaching. As highlighted in the previous section on the pedagogical implications of the lexical error analysis, the linguistic errors affect not only the accuracy and meaning of their translations but also the overall quality of their written productions. The current study findings indicate such interlingual errors as collocation (e.g., *take a promise instead of

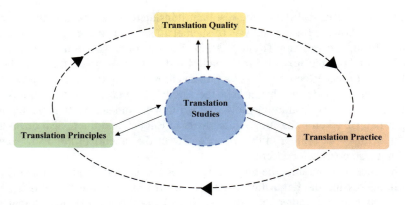

Fig. 6.4 Implications of lexical error analysis for translation studies

made a promise) and direct translation from L1 (e.g., translation of the Arabic lexical phrase (شكل من أشكال) *shakal min 'ashkal* into the near-equivalent but inappropriate L2 lexical phrase *shape of shapes* instead of *a form of* occurred at the sentence, phrase, and word levels. This highlights the need to adopt pedagogical approaches that focus more on how L1 transfer influences the use of L2 words, phrases, and sentences. To illustrate, failure to understand the difference between the English words *save and *keep* as verbs leads to L1 transference where, due to the close meaning between the two lexical items, they make the incorrect lexical choice by literally translating the word to the near-equivalent but incorrect L2 word, effectively making semantic errors. The current study analysis establishes the need for English language instruction to discourage the common practice by Saudi students of English to first compose sentences in their L1, translate, and then write it in L2 given that the approach leads to L1 transfer and ultimately literal translation errors. The applied linguistic findings highlight the need for adoption of language instruction strategies that enhance the knowledge of the students in the English lexis and the way it differs from the Arabic lexis so as to preclude their susceptibility to L1 transfer.

The findings and analysis of the current study also recognised intralingual formal and semantic lexical errors as a function of partial or faulty learning of the L2 and demonstrated the need for adoption of language teaching approaches that safeguard against the errors by ensuring complete and accurate learning of the English language. The findings thus resonate with Qaid and Ramamoorthy's (2011) findings that insufficient knowledge of the L2 lexical items prompts learners of the L2 to use the lexical items of the language in an inappropriate manner and hence the errors. Thus, semantic lexical errors (such as the use of binary terms, words distorting meaning, words with inappropriate meaning, hypernyms for hyponyms, inappropriate co-hyponyms, overly specific terms, incompletion errors, stylistic errors, and near synonym errors) and formal lexical errors (such as omission errors, substitution errors, transposition errors, addition errors, unique errors, impeding comprehension errors, and errors resulting in inappropriate meaning) witnessed among the students are an indication of the current English teaching practices and methodologies to equip the student with adequate knowledge of the English lexical items and hence the need for more effective instructional approaches. The English language instruction techniques adopted in response to the intralingual sources of formal and semantic lexical errors should be aimed at both promoting the familiarity of the students with the L2 orthographic rules and enhancing their phonological and morphological knowledge of the L2. By highlighting the significance of the level of lexical knowledge and in particular how incomplete L2 lexical entries contribute to intralingual errors in translation productions by Saudi English students, the implications of the current study analysis and its findings for the English language instruction and the field of applied linguistics in general cannot be clearer.

6.4.1 Content

6.4.1.1 Improving the L2 Instruction Curriculum

To improve English language instruction curriculum, efforts can be made to develop vocabulary instructional programmes whose instructional goals are to enhance the knowledge of the English language lexis. The instructional programmes can entail courses that target and are implemented at both the English teacher training level and the English student learning level. By ensuring L2 instructor training programmes incorporate curricula aimed at equipping the instructors with core linguistic competences in English language morphology, phonology, and syntax as well as other English language critical pragmatics, the approach will be helpful in honing the ability of the teacher to promote and support the efforts of their learners to become knowledgeable in the English lexis. In the same way, incorporation in the curriculum of specialised vocabulary instructional programmes whose central aim is to improve the competence of the Saudi students of English in the L2 vocabulary will help specify and incorporate in classroom instruction L2 learning activities and approaches that promote the orthographical, morphological, syntactic, and lexical knowledge of the L2. This will help ensure more direct instruction of word comparisons, associations, and morphological structure effectively enhancing the knowledge of the students in the English lexis and ultimately their capacity to produce English writings and translations that have minimal or no formal and semantic errors caused by inadequate knowledge in these areas.

The lexical errors found in the current study attributed to interlingual and intralingual sources can also be traced back to the use of instructional materials that are mostly based on the English language neglecting the leaners' L1. This is demonstrated by the special issues apparent among Saudi learners of English such as the tendency to produce word segmentation errors (such as writing *my self instead of *myself*, (due to variations in word space usage in the L1 and L2 writing systems, and producing capitalisation errors (such as the use of *saudi arabia instead of Saudi Arabia* because of the nature of Arabic alphabets). This is also evidenced by literal translation of L2 lexical items' meaning, an occurrence that manifested in the translation of both lexical collocations and very simple lexical items as in their translation of the lexical phrase *yaemalun be* ـب يعملون *<u>work with</u> *act on* and *awraq al ashjar* الأشجار أوراق 'tree *papers *leaves.*' These lexical errors that are unique to the students highlight the need for the development of English instruction materials that are based on the learners' L1 to ensure clarity in the difference of the L1 and L2 lexicons and writing system during content delivery. The outcome will be combined English teaching resources that will be suitable for the cultural and linguistic backgrounds of the L2, effectively minimising the susceptibility of their translation to intralingual and interlingual errors. The approach will also ensure non-Arabic English instructors who have minimal knowledge about the effects of the Arabic language and culture on English language development efforts of the Saudi students have access to teaching resources they can use to effectively deliver the content and mitigate the undesired outcomes. Thus, a good balance between the imported L2 instruction materials and the combined language teaching materials designated for English writing and translation courses will help ensure the content of English language instruction is not only properly aligned with the instructional goals of the courses but also that the content is structured in a manner that supports successful learning and acquisition of the L2 vocabulary and the pertinent writing and translation skills.

The findings of this study also point to the need by the educators bestowed with the responsibility of designing English instruction syllabus and curriculum to come up with programmes that employ a task-based approach (TBA) and which are both proactive and reactive in addressing the identified linguistic mistakes (Rahimpour, 2010). The origin of the type of formal and semantic lexical errors common among the students cannot be exclusively attributed to instructional inadequacies at the university level as it also signifies gaps in teaching and learning of the language at the preceding levels of education—both primary and secondary. It is thus important that English instruction syllabus designers and curriculum planners at all levels of education in the country incorporate tools and components aimed at enhancing the learners cognitive understanding of the L2 rules they commonly learn erroneously so as to enhance their competence in the language (Tabari, 2013). This may include such components as activities requiring English language instructors to use the Arabic language in their explanation of the lexical and grammatical features of the L2, exercises that require teachers to give clues and not direct corrections of the lexical mistakes noticed, as well as extensive reading initiatives and remedial courses aimed at increasing the exposure and contact of the students with the English language. To further enable the English language instructors to promote and support the students in their L2 learning, the language learning and teaching activities and tasks incorporated in the syllabus and curriculum can be structured in a way that encourages the teachers to have a positive attitude towards the linguistic errors and how they treat them. This will

6.4.1.2 Teaching Vocabulary in Context

The analysis in the current research draws attention to the importance of context when teaching and using vocabulary by demonstrating the potential of Saudi learners to better learn the L2 vocabulary by coming across the new vocabulary within the context of English texts and sentences. As Alroe and Reinders (2015) affirm, the essence of context is not only learning vocabulary but also using it, asserting the need for weaker students to be equipped with strategies for utilising context in their efforts to learn L2 words and acquire new vocabulary. Context is thus critical in learning and using new words as it enables L2 students to find out the meaning of the unfamiliar vocabulary based on the context of the related L2 sentences and thus gain skills in how to use them. Given that context allows for incidental learning of the vocabulary of an L2, its importance in helping students develop familiarity with new words and enhancing their capacity to use them cannot be understated.

Shalaby et al. (2009) argued contextual instruction is particularly important when teaching problematic L2 words in that it helps the students to understand the context in which the words are used, thus enhancing their ability to retain their meaning and retrieve them when appropriate. The findings have implications for language teaching in that they draw attention to the need of language instructors involved in the education of the students to adopt a contextual approach during the creation and teaching of the list of problematic words to the L2 learners. Contextual instruction will not only help enhance the students' understanding of the unfamiliar English lexis but also their capacity to accurately use them in their written productions.

The findings also stress the importance of context by demonstrating how lexical errors associated with literal translation of L1 come about and how they can be avoided through contextual teaching of the English vocabulary. The study attributes instances of direct translation from L1 among the students to their tendency to select and use L2 lexical items that have the closest meaning to the L1 word being translated. For instance, when translating the Arabic word (حافظ *hafid*) the students selected and used the English word *save* instead of *keep,* thus producing the erroneous sentence '*Save* your city clean and don't throw rubbish on the streets' instead of the correct sentence '*Keep* your city clean and don't throw rubbish on the streets.' The lexical error is triggered by disregard of the context in which the source Arabic word is used, and hence, its translated form fails to convey the intended meaning of the sentence. Thus, contextual teaching of the English vocabulary does not only empower learners to avoid specific lexical errors but also to infer the accurate meaning of L2 words from the contexts in which they are used.

In teaching a second language, it is critical that students are taught how to establish the meaning of any unfamiliar L2 vocabulary on the basis of the sentence contexts in which they are utilised. The instructional technique will not only enable students to learn new words but also acquire skills on how to use context to decipher the meaning of any strange vocabulary they encounter in their interaction with the L2. Consequently, neglecting teaching the application of L2 words in different contexts can negatively affect the written production of L2 as it denies them the chance to learn how to contextually determine the meaning of L2 vocabulary. The outcome is often a situation where the learners tend to make lexical choices that are not appropriate for both the applicable cultural context and the communicative purpose for which the translation is being produced. The essence of teaching the use of L2 vocabulary in context is not to avert the use of inaccurate linguistic forms but rather to ensure the students are able to make lexical choices that are suitable for the contexts in which they are used. It is thus vital for language teachers to use instructional strategies that equip students with techniques on how to better use context to learn new words and appropriately apply them.

6.4.2 Assessment: Evaluation and Learning Outcomes

The research findings have implications for language teaching and in particular how the assessments and tests aimed at measuring the learning outcome of the teaching process are designed and administered. Rodríguez-Bonces and Rodríguez-Bonces (2010) emphasise the need to use both formal and informal assessments in determining the outcomes of vocabulary teaching in which the latter adopts a self-evaluation format and the former uses rubrics. To accurately assess learning outcomes using both informal and formal tests, the assessment activities ought to be formulated in a manner that allows the students of English to demonstrate that they adequately understand how various features of the L2 occur in different written texts and how they ought to correctly apply them in their writings and translations to avoid formal and semantic lexical errors. For instance, following a language lesson on the way various adjectives and superlatives apply in noun phrases and how omission of superlatives and adjectives may lead to incompletion errors, the study demonstrates the importance of testing the relevant L2 knowledge of the learners by way of test items that accurately assess the competence of the students in the L2 features learnt.

The findings also highlight the need for the adoption of language exams with components that accurately test knowledge, retention, and the ability of the students to retrieve specific problematic lexical items. The problematic lexical items may include such technical and semi-technical vocabulary as words that have a high frequency of occurrence in English writing but are absent in the students' L1 (Arabic). Assessment tasks that are focused in this area will be integral in testing the extent to which the students are able to avoid lexical errors by recognising L2 lexical items absent in their L1 lexicon and accurately segmenting these words in their written productions. The assessment approach will also enable the teachers to

6.4 Implications for Language Teaching

determine the extent to which the goals of the vocabulary instructional programme are being attained by examining how the students use error-prone L2 lexical items and the influence this has on the quality and integrity of their writings and translations. As the current study found, and as Alenazi (2018) suggested, the use of test items that entail provision of English translated and written texts full of lexical errors and which require the L2 learners to point out the errors and correct them would also help to accurately test the learning outcomes of vocabulary instruction. Accuracy is thus a critical aspect in checking the learning outcome of a programme for teaching vocabulary.

6.4.3 The Teaching Process

6.4.3.1 Learning Activities and Task-Based Approach

The current study's analysis offers insights into the morphological, orthographical, phonological, and syntactic origins of formal and semantic lexical errors common among the students, effectively establishing a basis for exploring the process of teaching and learning vocabulary. The strategies used to teach English vocabulary should exploit the techniques the students use to acquire L2 lexemes as well as generate and select the L2 lexical items to use in their written texts. One of the key techniques entails making associations and comparisons of the L2 words they learn with those in their L1. Shalaby et al. (2009) suggest that the tendency by language instructors to help their students associate and compare the L2's lexical items with the L1—especially in classes with learners with a common L1—assists in eliciting associations and comparisons that support L2 learning. In the context of current study, the approach can be implemented by encouraging English language teachers to make reference to the Arabic language in their English instruction so as to assist the learners to make meaningful comparisons and associations between the English and Arabic lexicon. A review of the current instructional strategies in which the L1 is primarily used to teach English is, however, crucial to ensure its effects are duly considered and measures for discouraging learners from directly translating their thoughts from Arabic to English when writing in L2 are adopted.

The analysis of lexical errors established in the current study also highlights the need for vocabulary teaching methodology which incorporates special classroom activities aimed at precluding the occurrence of lexical errors. Given its tendency to integrate special activities that should be performed in classrooms during L2 teaching, TBA is recommended as the best method for teaching vocabulary and addressing the identified formal and semantic lexical errors. This is corroborated by Sarani and Sahebi's (2012) findings that the approach has better learning outcomes in teaching of technical vocabularies in comparison with other traditional approaches. According to Rozati (2014), TBA seeks to instil among L2 learners the skills to convey meaning based on the contexts and to excite their intrinsic self-regulating processes leading to enhanced communicative and grammatical competence.

The approach is thus useful in teaching English vocabulary in that instead of sequencing language items it specifies a sequence of interactive activities that are carried out in the L2. The approach ensures that the focus on specific lexical items and various forms of the L2 as well as confrontation of the target by the learners occurs unintentionally during classroom activities (Rozati, 2014). The technique helps lessen the pressure on the learner to grasp the specific language forms of the L2, thus facilitating innate acquisition of communicative and lexical competence in the L2. On the basis of the TBA, teachers can design learner-centred lessons in which tasks such as storytelling and group problem-solving activities are geared towards assisting the learners to purposefully communicate in L2 by finding suitable inputs and making new meanings. This enables them to develop meaning systems they can reliably tap into their application of the learned and acquired L2 (Rodríguez-Bonces & Rodríguez-Bonces, 2010). The fact that the approach puts emphasis on learner-centred lessons provides an opportunity for language teachers to use differentiated teaching strategies in acknowledgement of the reality that different students employ different language forms and techniques to build a meaning system. By employing the task-based framework for designing lessons, language instructors can be able to encourage students to prepare for the task by engaging with the various L2 phonology, syntax, morphology, lexis, and semantics and emphasise the accurate use of lexical items thereby encouraging learners to focus not only on meaning but also the form and structure of their written texts. As Lee (2011) argued, a combination of written vocabulary exercises and an authentic task ensures better receptive and productive retention of L2 lexical items. However, form recall as evidenced in the type of semantic and formal lexical errors produced by the students is by and large the most intricate category of lexical knowledge, the method of vocabulary instruction notwithstanding. As demonstrated in the study analysis, formal errors (such as *mast and *must, knowledge* and *Knoldg) are a function of inadequate knowledge of the spelling of L2 lexical items which then leads to distortion of meaning.

6.4.3.2 Shortcomings of Task-Based Approach

Although TBA is recommended as the best method for teaching vocabulary during L2 learning due to the associated better language learning outcomes, the technique is not without its fair share of shortcomings. As its name implies, the approach entails integration of special activities for language learning that the students are required to perform in the classroom so as to acquire the L2 vocabulary. This attribute of the TBA is in itself a limitation as it calls for careful planning of the tasks that the learners of language should perform in a given lesson besides requiring such planned classroom activities to meet the established criteria. This level of planning tends to be taxing to language teachers in addition to being time-consuming given the amount of time it takes to have a series of carefully planned classroom activities for task-based learning. The effectiveness of the task-based learning is also likely to be negatively affected by linguistic deficiency among the learners of a second language. The ability to perform task-based learning activities

6.5 A Summary of the Analysis Impacts on Language Learning ...   153

incorporated in a classroom is dependent on the linguistic proficiency of the students expected to compete the task. As a result, students who lack the linguistic resources necessary to successfully complete the task have difficulties not only performing but also participating in the task. Such students find it difficult to for instance participate in speaking tasks given their inability to express themselves which could end up discouraging them from performing the task or even cause them to lose confidence in their ability to master the L2.

6.4.3.3 Integrating Task-Based Approach and Grammar-Translation Method in Vocabulary Teaching

Given the current study analysis and in particular the effectiveness of translation in promoting vocabulary acquisition through intentional learning, GTM could also be a useful technique in the teaching of vocabulary. GTM entails deductive teaching of the grammatical structures and rules for translating from L1 to L2. The technique encourages learners to not only memorise the vocabulary of L2 but also the applicable grammatical rules, thus ensuring accurate use of the language. As such, GTM should not be abandoned because it was an old method of teaching, given that it could still be useful in language learning if GTM and TBA are combined in vocabulary instruction. Integration of these two approaches would ensure teachers emphasise accurate application of the grammatical structures and rules of the L2 by the students in their performance of the special classroom activities, thus promoting their mastery of the vocabulary and grammatical rules of the L2 being taught. The integrated approach to L2 teaching would also ensure performance of such tasks as description of pictures and role play incorporating grammar drills that allow teachers to assess the extent to which the students correctly use grammatical structures and make corrections where necessary, further supporting both vocabulary and grammatical learning among the students. Integration of the two approaches would also ensure both accurate and appropriate use of the L2 vocabulary and grammar by teaching the students how to correctly put grammatical labels on the L2 vocabulary and the appropriate application of the L2 vocabulary.

The implications of the current study analysis for language teaching are summarised in Fig. 6.5.

6.5 A Summary of the Analysis Impacts on Language Learning, Translation Studies, and Language Teaching

The error analysis undertaken in the current study has significant implications for translation, language learning, and language teaching (see Fig. 6.6). The analysis of lexical errors significantly impacts on language learning by highlighting

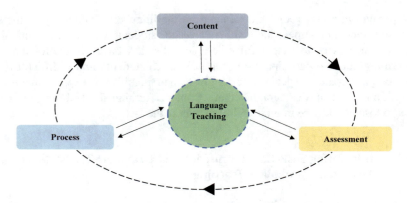

Fig. 6.5 Implications of lexical error analysis for language teaching

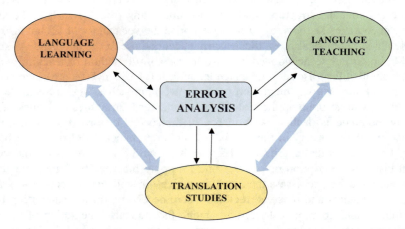

Fig. 6.6 Impact of lexical error analysis on language learning, translation studies, and language teaching

the practicality of the error analysis approach as a tool to study the L2 learners' errors. The types of lexical errors witnessed among Saudi English major students have helped demonstrate the nature of language gaps that exists among L1 Arabic speakers attempting to learn and acquire English as a second language. The identified formal and semantic lexical errors thus contribute to the error analysis field by establishing the frequency, nature, origins, and effects of unsuccessful acquisition and learning of the English language by the students in their translations.

The current analysis effectively links lexical errors from interlingual sources to differences and similarities between L1 and L2 of the Saudi students, and hence, its findings coincide with the perspectives of the language transfer. Frequency analysis lexical errors common in the translations produced by the students found a statistically significant trend in the content and form of the students' L1 (Arabic) transferred. The analysis of the study has also contributed to the field of language learning in developing a comprehensive list of lexical error categories based on form, content, and origin of influence regarding translation products. The taxonomy of lexical errors designed can be very useful from a pedagogical point of view to explain learners' errors and improve language instruction. It can be used as a basis for corpus-based studies on ESL learners in different contexts.

With regard to translation, the current analysis demonstrates the effect that the tendency to focus too much on the translation discourse while ignoring the small blocks of the L2 on both the translation capacity of the learner and their acquisition of the language. The analysis thus draws attention to the importance of the L2 words used in the translated texts by highlighting the common lexical errors that could occur at the vocabulary level, thus compromising both the quality and comprehensibility of written translations. This also accentuates the need for translators to assess translation texts beginning from vocabulary, before moving to sentence structure and finally to the discourse; an approach that helps focus on how correctly the words are translated, the sentences formed, and thus the influence this has on the appropriateness and accuracy of the whole discourse.

The analysis also significantly impacts on language teaching by highlighting the tendency by L2 learners to make lexical errors as a result of using the L2 vocabulary out of the context. The analysis thus reiterates the importance of teaching vocabulary in context by providing ample opportunities for the students to encounter the L2 vocabulary within the context of the L2 texts and sentences. Language teaching should therefore incorporate teaching practices that equip learners with techniques for utilising context in their endeavour to familiarise themselves with new words as well as learn and acquire the L2 vocabulary. This approach to L2 instruction will have a positive effect on the lexical knowledge of the learners as will be demonstrated by improvements in the quality and accuracy of their written productions. Furthermore, the analysis draws attention to the need to use the most effective approaches for L2 learning so as to reduce or even eliminate lexical errors among EFL/ESL students. The inaccurate use of L2 vocabulary warrants an investigation into, and the need to use, language teaching methods such as GTM that emphasises mastery of both the vocabulary and the applicable grammatical rules. The integration of the TBA and GTM in vocabulary instruction can positively influence L2 learning by ensuring mastery of vocabulary and grammatical rules and hence promoting accurate use of the L2 in the performance of various language learning activities.

6.6 Conclusion

This chapter presented a discussion of the theoretical and practical implications of the study analysis and findings for the field of language learning, translation studies, and language teaching research. The analysis of the different types of lexical errors helped in understanding how the various subtypes of these errors constitute a problem for the students and the way they alter form, meanings, and comprehensibility of their translations. While the negative transfer of the L1 form and semantic features accounted for a significant number of the formal and semantic lexical errors, the importance of Arabic in teaching English writing and translation to the L1 speaking Saudi students cannot be understated. In addition, the lexical error taxonomy used in this study could serve as a useful tool to raise the students' awareness about the L2, and it could be useful as an instructional tool for teachers to employ in vocabulary teaching. It could also serve as a groundwork for error analysis studies in other EFL/ESL contexts.

The findings in this study highlighted the need for the adoption of language instruction strategies that enhance the knowledge of the students in the English lexis and the way it differs from the Arabic lexis so as to prevent their susceptibility to L1 transfer. Revision of the current English teaching strategies as well as materials for writing and translation courses and incorporation of written vocabulary exercises in the instructional strategy were suggested as some of the most consequential pedagogical solutions to the problem. Adoption of the contextual approach, TBA, GTM, and intensive instruction on L2 concepts and rules at the preparatory year level could be very helpful to tackle the issue of lexical errors among the university students.

References

Alenazi, O. S. (2018). Spelling difficulties faced by Arab learners of English as a foreign language. *Arab World English Journal, 9*(2), 118–126.

Ali, W. I. (2018). Communicative translation as a new approach in translation with reference to English and Kurdish. *A Special Issue for Cihan University-Erbil Second International Conference on Linguistics and Arts (CIC-LITART'18),* (1), 142–150.

Alroe, M. J., & Reinders, H. (2015). The role of translation in vocabulary acquisition: A replication study. *Eurasian Journal of Applied Linguistics, 1*, 39–58.

Apel, K. (2019). The development of orthographic knowledge and its relation to reading and spelling. *Twenty-Fourth Annual SSSR Meeting.* Society for the Scientific Study of Reading (SSSR).

Baker, M. (2011). *In other words: A coursebook on translation* (2nd ed.). Routledge.

Chang, S.-C. (2011). A contrastive study of grammar translation method and communicative approach in teaching English grammar. *English Language Teaching, 4*(2), 13–24.

Coady, J., & Huckin, T. (2000). *Second language vocabulary acquisition: A rationale for pedagogy.* Cambridge University Press.

Elmahdi, O., & Moqbil, A. (2016). *Errors in translation equivalence.* Integrity Media.

Elmgrab, R. A. (2013). Implication for translation teaching pedagogy: A case of Benghazi University. *Procedia-Social and Behavioral Sciences, 70*, 358–369 (S1877042813000748). https://doi.org/10.1016/j.sbspro.2013.01.073

Gass, S., & Selinker, L. (2008). *Second language acquisition: An introductory course* (3rd ed.). Routledge.

Ghazala, H. (2012). *Translation as problems and solutions: A textbook for university students and trainee translators* (9th ed.). Konooz Al-Marifa Company for Printing and Publishing.

Hodges, P. (2009). Linguistic approach to translation theory. Retrieved December 19, 2020, from https://www.translationdirectory.com/articles/article2019.php

References 157

Hui, Y. (2010). The role of L1 transfer on L2 and pedagogical implications. *Canadian Social Science, 6*(3), 97–103.

James, C. (2013). *Errors in language learning and use: Exploring error analysis.* Routledge.

Kenny, D. (2012). Linguistic approaches to translation. In Carol A. Chapelle (Ed.), *The Encyclopedia of applied linguistics.* Blackwell Publishing Ltd. https://doi.org/10.1002/9781405198431.wbeal0713

Khansir, A. A. (2012). Error analysis and second language acquisition. *Theory and Practice in Language Studies, 2*(5), 1027–1032.

Klaudy, K. (2006). The role of translation theory in translator training. *European Master's in Translation DGT, Brussels, 19*(20), 1–19.

Koletnik, M. (2012). Learning vocabulary through translation - An eclectic approach. *Scripta Manent, 7*(1), 2–12.

Lee, S.-O. (2011). Using post-task written vocabulary exercises in task-based instruction. *Language Education in Asia, 2*(1), 15–27.

Liu, G. (2020). An attempt to integrate grammar translation method, communicative language teaching, task-based language teaching: Rationale and evaluation. *Journal of Educational Research and Policies (JERP), 2*(8), 99–104.

Llach, M. P. A. (2011). *Lexical errors and accuracy in foreign language writing.* Multilingual Matters.

Nida, E. A. (1991). Theories of translation. *TTR: Traduction, Terminologie, Rédaction, 4* (1), 19–32.

Qaid, Y. A., & Ramamoorthy, L. (2011). Analysis of intralingual errors in learning English as a foreign language by Yemeni students. *Language in India, 11*(5), 534–545.

Rahimpour, M. (2010). Current trends on syllabus design in foreign language instruction. *Procedia-Social and Behavioral Sciences, 2*(2), 1660–1664.

Rodríguez-Bonces, M., & Rodríguez-Bonces, J. (2010). Task-based language learning: Old approach, new style. A New Lesson to Learn. *Profile, 12*(2), 165–178.

Rozati, S. M. (2014). Language teaching and task based approach. *Theory and Practice in Language Studies, 4*(6), 1273–1278.

Sarani, A., & Sahebi, L. F. (2012). The impact of task-based approach on vocabulary learning in ESP courses. *English Language Teaching, 5*(10), 118–128.

Shalaby, A. N., Yahya, N., & El-Komi, M. (2009). Analysis of lexical errors in Saudi college students' compositions. *Journal of the Saudi Association of Languages and Translation, 2*(3), 65–93.

Tabari, A. G. (2013). Challenges of language syllabus design in EFL/ESL contexts. *Journal of Language Teaching and Research, 4*(4), 869.

Usman, A. H. (2015). Teaching vocabulary through grammar-translation method. *EDUKASI-Jurnal Pendidikan, 13*(2), 299–312.

Watson, J. (2002). *The phonology and morphology of Arabic.* Oxford University.

Yang, X. (2019). A review of negative language transfer regarding the errors in English writing in Chinese colleges. *Journal of Language Teaching and Research, 10*(3), 603–609.

Chapter 7
Summary, Conclusion, and Recommendations

7.1 Introduction

This chapter presents the conclusions reached in this study, acknowledging some limitations and suggestions for further research. The chapter is presented in seven sections. The first Sect. (7.2) provides a brief overview of the research project. The second Sect. (7.3) demonstrates a summary of the major findings based on the research questions and analysis. The third Sect. (7.4) presents the contributions of the study. The fourth Sect. (7.5) offers two pedagogical frameworks as a set of recommendations to improve ESL/EFL teaching/learning with respect to language errors and writing skills. The chapter concludes (Sects. 7.6 and 7.7) by presenting the limitations of the study and suggesting areas for further research.

7.2 Overview of the Research Project

The study provided a comprehensive analysis of the lexical errors made in the translations of Saudi English major students. The research was conducted for the purpose of enhancing the written products of Saudi learners of English at the university level. There have been calls for error analysis studies to investigate the challenges encountered by Saudi learners while learning English (e.g., Javid et al., 2013; Khan, 2011; Rahman & Alhaisoni, 2013). It is evident from the literature (e.g., Elmahdi, 2016; Khalifa, 2015) that Saudi English major students have difficulties communicating in written language while translating from Arabic to English language and particularly in the appropriate use of English lexis. Lexical errors are problematic and pervasive in the students' written products which negatively affects the quality of their translations. This problem calls for English language teachers and translation trainers in KSA to have a better understanding of

---

© The Author(s), under exclusive license to Springer Nature Singapore Pte Ltd. 2022

Y. Alenazi, *Exploring Lexical Inaccuracy in Arabic-English Translation*, New Frontiers in Translation Studies, https://doi.org/10.1007/978-981-19-6390-2_7

the types of errors made in the students' written translations and find appropriate pedagogical solutions.

There have been a few recent error analysis studies exploring the common lexical errors in the written products of Saudi university students and the possible reasons behind them (e.g., Al-Jabri, 1998; Shalaby et al., 2009; Sheshsha, 1993). However, these studies are restricted within limited categories of lexical errors and have not reached an agreeable conclusion about the potential sources of errors. Furthermore, none of the studies identified has endeavoured to examine the different lexical error categories apparent in the translation products of English majors during their university study. This study investigated Saudi students enrolled in an English language and Translation programme, analysing their skills and knowledge in relation to their L2 (English) lexicon. This was undertaken by exploring the types of incorrect lexical choice by students in their translation products, determining the frequency distribution of the types of lexical errors identified and which of these errors could be traced back to interlingual/intralingual influences.

The study targeted the whole population of male Saudi English major students who were enrolled in the English language and Translation programme at one of the Saudi public universities at the time of the study (2019). A total of 105 translated texts written by the students at the university level were collected. The corpus texts were mainly the students' responses to the translation courses' exams.

Consequently, lexical errors were analysed using a quantitative method to describe them and reveal their sources. Additionally, their frequency distributions were calculated using frequency statistics. The use of quantitative analysis provided the researcher with both depth and breadth of insight into the data. Furthermore, the study followed the main steps in the EA approach as acknowledged mostly by SLA researchers (e.g., Ellis, 2008; Gass & Selinker, 2008; James, 2013). These main steps included the collection of a language sample, identification, description, and explanation of errors. The approach was used to examine the different patterns of lexical errors and provide a detailed analysis of these lexical errors made by students and identify possible reasons for the errors being made.

7.3 Summary of the Major Findings

The analysis of lexical errors presented in this research offered a significant insight into the nature of difficulties in English translation encountered by Saudi English major students. The main findings of the study are summarised in this section in relation to the research questions and its objectives. It first summarises the characteristics of lexical errors made in the translation texts according to their linguistic categories. Then, it provides a summary of the potential sources of the lexical error made at the different categories.

This section addresses the first research question: What are the types of lexical errors distributed in Saudi English major students' translation texts?

7.3 Summary of the Major Findings

The analysis of lexical errors conducted in this study showed that 1035 words were incorrectly translated in a corpus consisting of 12,284 individual words. The lexical errors identified have been classified into two groups, formal and semantic lexical errors. These two groups were divided into eight major types which were further subcategorised into 31 subtypes and the frequency of each type and subtype then determined. Some lexical error types were common; others were relatively infrequent. The number of semantic lexical errors was slightly higher than that of the formal lexical errors, with 524 errors compared with 511 errors respectively. The major types of the formal and semantic lexical errors varied in their frequency of occurrence as demonstrated in Fig. 7.1, except for one major type that did not occur at all which is the connotation type of error.

This section addresses the second research question: What is the frequency distribution of lexical errors prevalent in the students' translations?

The study found that there were a variation between the types within each major category of the formal and semantic lexical errors, however, some subtypes of lexical errors did not occur such as false friends; analogy; connotations, or only occurred a few times such as the prefix type; binary terms; borrowing; or inappropriate co-hyponyms. On the other hand, some types of lexical errors occurred rather frequently, such as distortions which occurred 452 times (43%). This subtype of error was the most frequent among the other subcategories of formal and semantic lexical errors. It was followed by confusion of sense relations lexical errors under the semantic category which occurred 268 times (25%). The incompletion lexical error category was next in position with a proportion of 14.65%.

Among formal and semantic lexical error subcategories, the incompletion lexical error subcategory was the most frequent of all errors occurring 153 times (14.70%). This was followed by capitalisation errors which were the common type of distortion errors found in the students' translation texts, with a frequency percentage of 12.4%. Direct translation from L1 subcategory of lexical errors was next in frequency occurring 101 times (9.7%), followed by omission spelling errors which occurred 86 times (8.20%), and wrong near synonyms with a total number of 81 errors (7.80%).

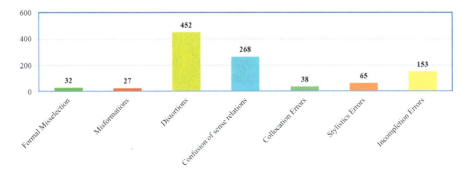

Fig. 7.1 The frequency distribution of the major types of lexical errors

This section addresses the third research question: What are the reasons behind the occurrence of these lexical errors in Saudi English major students' translation texts?

The results of the analysis indicated that formal and semantic lexical errors were related to two major sources which are interlingual and intralingual influences. Lexical errors witnessed among the students were not homogeneous. More than half of the lexical errors were due to intralingual influence. The lack of L2 morphemic, syntactic, orthographic, phonologic knowledge, and the lack of L2 lexical knowledge and the confusion between L2 lexical items that are semantically related significantly influenced the students' words choice in the translated texts. Interlingual influence, on the other hand, made up a considerable proportion of the total lexical errors due to literal translation of L1 words, the transfer of the semantic features associated with L1 lexical items, interference between the students' L1 and the L2 writing systems, and the transfer of the L1 phonological system.

7.4 Contributions of the Study

The results of the study provide a theoretical background for the design of a translation module for university-level English language and Translation programmes. This study examined the lexical aspects that are supposed to be challenging for English L2 learners, especially those who are majoring in English. It suggests a framework for analysing the lexical errors in the translations of students who are translating from Arabic to English. It reveals the gaps in the students' lexical knowledge of the L2 and demonstrates how they attempt to compensate for these gaps.

The study contributes to the field of language learning, and particularly to the field of error analysis research by examining language errors of English majors who each has an Arabic language background, analysing lexical errors manifested in their translation products. It extends the growing body of knowledge on the phenomenon of negative transfer. The findings indicated that students tend to transfer formal and semantic features of their Arabic while processing lexical items in English language. The students relied more on their L1 to produce words in the target text regardless of the context owing to some kind of difficulty they had in retrieving the appropriate equivalent L2 words in their mental lexicons.

The study expands the lexical error classification system used in previous error analysis studies by developing a comprehensive list of lexical error categories based on form, content, and origin of influence regarding translation products for the purpose of analysis. Furthermore, most of the error analysis investigations with respect to vocabulary used free written products as the basis for their analysis. This study, however, used translation products to analyse the different types of lexical errors. The type of language samples collected provided a clear understanding of the L2 learner's intended meaning to the researcher since it is easier to determine the relationships between L1 and L2 vocabulary if the intended meaning is available. Therefore, linguistic categories in the error taxonomy adapted from the previous research (e.g., Hemchua & Schmitt, 2006; Shalaby et al., 2009) have been expanded by including new subcategories such as in the formal distortion lexical error category (capitalisation, word segmentation, grapheme substitution, unique distortion errors) and adding new semantic lexical error categories such as incompletion errors.

The analysis in this research contributes to the translation field by highlighting how lexical errors affect the quality of written translations produced by English learners. The analysis showed the importance of the L2 words used in the translated texts by highlighting the common lexical errors that could occur at the vocabulary level thus compromising both the quality and comprehensibility of written translations. The analysis also indicated that there is a tendency by the students to employ a paraphrase strategy when translating Arabic texts into English as opposed to giving the correct lexical items which best convey the intended meaning of the source text. Although the paraphrase strategy works in spoken form, it tends to be counterproductive in written texts in that it leads to inaccurate use of the L2 lexical items.

By providing an understanding of the morphologic, orthographic, phonologic, and syntactic origins of the lexical errors commonly made by the students, the findings of this study contribute to the field of language teaching. They can be useful for educators in the enhancement of ESL/EFL teaching in the Saudi context and the improvement of English major students' writing and translation skills. The detailed analysis and explanations of lexical errors provided in this study can be valuable for English instructors as a guide to address their students' weaknesses in the L2 and to develop pedagogical solutions to address the issue of lexical errors in their students' translations.

The analysis of lexical errors and their sources in this research has shown that Saudi English major students encounter difficulties in writing skills, particularly when using words of the L2. This highlights the need for consideration of pedagogical approaches that can help address the related English writing problems among Saudi learners of English. In the following section, based on the results and conclusions reached from the analysis of formal and semantic lexical errors, the study puts forth practical pedagogical solutions and recommendations for remedying language errors and improving English language teaching with respect to vocabulary and writing skills. If properly implemented, these will help diminish if not eliminate lexical errors in the written translations of the Saudi students, a trend that will ultimately set them on a path towards excellence as English language experts and professional translators.

7.5 Recommendations for Teaching Vocabulary and Alleviating the Related Language Errors

The range of lexical errors witnessed among the written translation products of Saudi English major students and rightly attributed to both interlingual and intralingual sources can be remedied by realigning not only the way English as an

L2 is taught but also the way the students learn the language. In other words, the adoption of instruction strategies aimed at addressing the common lexical errors and enhancing the writing proficiency of the learners has the potential to remedy the errors found among the students. This section thus provides recommendations for both teachers and learners on how vocabulary can be effectively taught and the related language errors witnessed in the written products of the Saudi English students can be avoided.

7.5.1 Pedagogical Strategies for Remedying Lexical Errors

From the analysis in the foregoing chapters, it is apparent that the answer to the common lexical errors made by the students may lie in the way in which instruction of the L2 is undertaken. Consequently, pedagogical strategies comprise the most appropriate basis upon which suggestions for improving vocabulary instruction and learning for both teachers and learners ought to be derived. In the context of this research, the pedagogical strategies suggested by the researcher will be twofold, with each comprising teaching/learning proposals through which the language errors can be avoided. The first section entails instructional approaches for teaching vocabulary and tackling the language errors using a unique model of teaching vocabulary. The second section concerns ways in which writing skills of the students can be improved. Future research can be conducted to elaborate more on these two learning/teaching frameworks.

7.5.1.1 The Proposal of "ERROR": A Framework for Teaching Vocabulary and Dealing with Language Errors

To effectively teach vocabulary and overcome lexical errors, L2 instructors and learners are advised to consider five important elements: Education, Revision, Retention, Observation, and Resolution (see Fig. 7.2). The suggested framework may afford the instructors a chance to inspire, represent, master, expand, and sustain knowledge of the appropriate vocabulary while providing meaningful responses to students during the instruction. It could be useful in assisting students to avoid common lexical errors. Below is a brief explanation of each element of this proposed framework.

The First Element: Education

It is suggested that language instructors develop a strategy for teaching the spelling system of the L2 given the strong correlation between vocabulary and spelling. The ability of a student to spell new words impacts their capacity to access, retrieve, and use the words in both active and passive contexts. Thus, by equipping

7.5 Recommendations for Teaching Vocabulary …

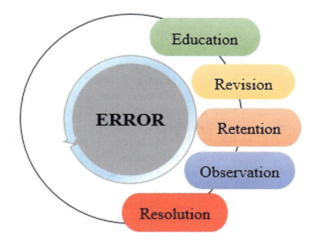

Fig. 7.2 The proposal of "ERROR"

their students with the ability to spell newly taught words, teachers will enhance the capacity of students to access the vocabulary in active and passive contexts. Teachers can also use semantic maps to teach L2 words and demonstrate how the words are semantically used. This can be achieved as follows: pick and mark a new word from a text; write the unfamiliar word in the centre of a blank semantic map; carefully pronounce the word; ask the students to read the word aloud; meaningfully define the word and give relatable examples of the word; list related words with similar meaning; match the words with pictures that symbolise their meaning and add them to the semantic map; ask the students to re-read the text; apply the meaning of the new vocabulary to the text; and share and compare their maps with those of their peers.

It is important to emphasise the value and significance of words by demonstrating multiple meanings and usage of a particular word in different contexts. This will help the students understand the importance of a rich vocabulary knowledge and how handy the skills are to correctly use the rich vocabulary when writing in L2. Instructors are also advised to teach students how to correctly use the words in context by giving several meaningful examples in different contexts as well as asking students to give their own examples of the new vocabulary in context and give meaningful feedback, especially where the vocabulary in question has multiple meanings. It is also recommended to teach students how to use dictionaries by clarifying the concise nature of the word meanings provided in the dictionary, how to interpret it, and how to discern the correct definition of a word. In addition, in L2 teaching, it is important to consider how L1 could influence the use of L2 words by comparing the linguistic characteristics between the two languages. This can be achieved by familiarising students with unknown words and L2 lexicon not present in their L1 as well as by drawing their attention to the differences between the Arabic and English writing systems and how word segmentation and coinage errors may arise due to transference of L1 phonological trends to L2 thus affecting the meaning of the translated text when translating.

The Second Element: Revision

Teachers are also advised to encourage students to develop a habit of revising their English language products once they have written them. Students should be sensitised on the importance of reviewing their written products for linguistic errors which should entail checking the accuracy and appropriateness of the words used in the written texts as well as the spacing and spelling of the words. This can be attained by identifying new vocabulary and phrases in the written products and checking their usage to ensure appropriate L2 equivalent collocation for the L1 collocation in the source text is used in the translated text. Another useful activity during the revision would be to check whether words in the finished written product are properly segmented. This is in cognisance of the fact that space is required at the lexical level in the L2 writing system and not required in the L1 writing system. Thus, when writing in L2, Saudi students are likely to use word space where it is not required and then fail to incorporate word space where necessary. The focused revision and review of the finished written texts will be integral in helping to identify and correct the common formal and semantic lexical errors common in the written products of ESL/EFL learners further enhancing their quality and efficiency in conveying the intended meaning.

The Third Element: Retention

Instructional activities aimed at enhancing retention of the vocabulary taught and peculiarities of the L2 should be incorporated in the language classes to ensure students retain what they learn about both the vocabulary and the language. Teachers are thus advised to provide students with ample opportunities to contextually gain and develop a clear understanding of the new words by seeing, pronouncing, writing, and reading them. To further consolidate the students' remembrance and knowledge of the vocabulary, opportunities for diverse application and usage of the new words should also be provided. It might be best if teachers make connections between the new words and real-world items so as to assist the learners retain, remember, and recognise the new vocabulary. Classroom activities aimed at increasing the number of times the students encounter and use the new words should also be integrated in vocabulary instruction for enhanced retention. Teachers are also suggested to make the use of graphic organisers to enable students to deeply engage with the new words and thus gain a deeper understanding of the vocabulary and their usage which will lead to better retention and thus better remembrance and retrieval of the vocabulary when writing in the L2.

The Fourth Element: Observation

During language instruction, teachers should be observant of their students by particularly checking their practice in relation to the vocabulary being taught as well as monitoring their general progress vis-à-vis the acquisition of the vocabulary knowledge being instilled through the lessons. This can be achieved by incorporating both teacher-student supervision, where they personally monitor the engagement of the individual learners with the new language, as well as peer-to-peer monitoring, where students are asked to check and correct their fellow learners' usage of the L2. Teachers are also encouraged to enlist the support of their colleagues to help observe teacher-learner interaction during language instruction and to assist in enhancing student learning and teacher practice to ensure improved performance and better learning outcomes for their students. Observation of the classroom during language learning will be integral in making learning and teaching more visible besides providing an opportunity for constructive feedback which helps teachers discern ways for enhancing their language instruction techniques. The approach will thus be critical in enabling teachers to gauge the performance of their students during language instruction, assess the ability of the students to contextually and accurately use L2 vocabulary in their written products, and measure and take note of the behaviour of the students as well as their mastery of the L2 vocabulary through systematic observation of the classroom during the language instruction and learning sequence. Systematic observation could further help the teacher to gauge the frequency of occurrence of certain language usage behaviours in the classroom and how to best mitigate practices that could lead to inappropriate usage of the L2 and hence avoid related lexical errors in the written texts produced by the students.

The Fifth Element: Resolution

It is important for both teachers and students to be determined to eliminate the lexical errors common in the written products. Arriving at such a resolution requires teachers to encourage each of their students to recognise and acknowledge the language errors they commonly make when writing in the L2. This should be followed by a commitment by both the teacher and the learners to do all it takes to avoid committing the errors in their subsequent written tasks by seeking and developing the requisite lexical knowledge as well as asking for assistance from their peers whenever they are in doubt of the accuracy of the usage of a particular lexical item or phrase. Moreover, it would be useful if the teacher encouraged the learner to continue developing their knowledge of the L2 by clarifying that language learning is not an event but rather an incremental process and hence the need to not despair for committing a lexical error or overlooking some rules of the L2 writing system in their initial stages of learning the new language. Teachers are advised to push their students to keep learning the differences and similarities between their L1 and L2 writing systems, practice translation with different source texts, and to engage peer learning to enhance their masterly of the L2.

7.5.1.2 "WRITE": A Proposed Pedagogical Strategy to Improve Writing Skills

In this section, a pedagogical strategy to improve writing skills is suggested. As shown in Fig. 7.3, the strategy to improve writing skills includes five aspects (Word, Review, Involvement, Tasks, and Encouragement). This suggested teaching strategy could be useful for language teachers to enhance the writing proficiency of their students. The five aspects of this teaching strategy are explained below.

The First Aspect: Word

Students are recommended to develop a habit of paying attention to words and how to use them accurately in different contexts when writing. A focus on words and expressions will enhance the familiarity of the students not only with the words and expressions but also with their different meanings in various contexts. Consequently, the students will, with time, develop the proficiency to determine the varied meanings of the L2 expressions and words and the ability to correctly apply them in diverse contexts. Students are also recommended to extensively practise with context exercises aimed at establishing the different meanings of L2 expressions and words so as to further familiarise themselves with the vocabulary and become more aware of the importance of their meanings. L2 learners are also advised to pay attention to semantic features of the L2 and how these vary from those of their L1. The approach will help students in making correct lexical choices thus averting instances where students transfer semantic features of their L1 lexical items in the source context to the translation products written in L2. To expand students understanding of vocabulary, teachers are recommended to explore the origin of words with their students, explain the connotation of new words, illustrate the context in which the usage of the word is appropriate

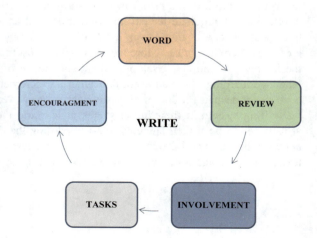

Fig. 7.3 A proposed writing pedagogical strategy

and inappropriate, show connection between words, demonstrate collocations, illustrate how affixes (suffixes and prefixes) alter meaning, and design activities that will together help promote a word-rich classroom environment. Furthermore, increasing exposure to the various English language texts, such as creative writing, reports, and articles could help in expanding the students' knowledge of the L2 words. Finally, it is important that teachers ensure learners frequently practise with and revise the new vocabulary to maintain the knowledge of the vocabulary they learn.

The Second Aspect: Review

Language teachers are advised to ask their students to frequently review their written products as key components of the writing process. By incorporating in-depth review in the sequence of writing, students can develop the habit of always revising their work whenever they complete a writing task. Through reviewing, the students should be able to pick out words that have been incorrectly used, segmented, collocated, and affixed among other lexical error-producing applications thus allowing them to promptly correct them and hence improve the quality and comprehensibility of their written products.

The Third Aspect: Involvement

To further enhance their writing proficiency, students should be involved in checking the texts produced by their colleagues. Instead of having teachers and students as the only ones involved in checking the written products, peers should also be allowed to partake in the exercise. Involvement of peers will allow for peer correction techniques where learners will check each other's written works for lexical errors, correct one another, learn from each other's mistakes, and offer instant feedback to one another. The strategy will be integral in not only promoting learner autonomy by ensuring students are responsible for their own language learning but also in helping the students learn to assist one another to become proficient writers. The approach also promotes improvement of writing skills by allowing language instructors, students, and their peers to participate in the efforts to identify and eliminate language errors.

The Fourth Aspect: Tasks

Language students are also advised to pay more attention to the nature of the writing tasks and employ the appropriate techniques to finish the task in order to minimise chances of them making common lexical errors. When translating, for instance, teachers may recommend their students to desist from translating L1 lexical items in the source texts word for word into the equivalent L2 lexical items as doing so may lead to the incorrect choice of words given the context and effectively alter the intended meaning of the original text. Instead, a translation strategy that emphasises understanding the translated lexical items in combination with the other surrounding words should be employed. When it comes to translation of L1 proverbial expressions, the approach probably will ensure correct choice of the L2 lexical idiomatic expressions that best correspond with the idiomatic sentence being translated. The learners can also engage with their peers and instructors as to which writing strategies they use and pick the ones likely to work best for them and for the nature of the task they are dealing with.

To further enhance their writing skills, students can also broaden their knowledge of the L2 vocabulary and idiomatic expressions so as to have an expansive repertoire of the L2 lexicon from which they can readily draw from when writing. English language lessons may feature exercises that encourage multiple retrieval of specific L2 lexical items to promote syntax and meaning recognition among the learners and writing of sentences that expose the learners to diverse word usage contexts to support their ability to produce correct illustrations of the encountered new words. The task performed should then be repeated or an equivalent task given to allow the students to apply the lexical knowledge gained. Form-focused vocabulary tasks could provide learners of an L2 with ample opportunities for language-focused learning.

Teachers are advised to motivate students to learn new vocabulary by clarifying the value of rich lexical knowledge, inculcating a classroom culture of word exploration, nurturing a classroom environment that is word-rich, exploring interesting ways of enhancing student engagement during vocabulary studies, and incorporating challenges such as word-of-the-week which requires learners to creatively use a particular word in their written products. To model the understanding and skills needed to develop the rich lexical knowledge, teachers can: pronounce the vocabulary being taught circumspectly and employ syllabification to properly articulate each section of the vocabulary; write the vocabulary on the board so as to equip the students with the correct spelling and enable them to correctly retrieve it when writing; give a concise and meaningful definition of the word; provide meaningful examples of the usage of the word and ask the students to give their examples.

The Fifth Aspect: Encouragement

Endeavours to eliminate errors should involve encouraging and supporting learners to become better writers as opposed to criticising them. In their efforts to reduce errors, it is recommended that language teachers desist from demanding or expecting error-free writing from their learners and instead focus on reducing language errors by supporting students to acquire the necessary lexical knowledge, giving positive feedback where needed, and reinforcing correct usage of L2. This approach will help give students the confidence to learn and use the L2, gradually building the necessary lexical knowledge and motivating them to seek ways of having increased contact with, and mastering the L2.

7.6 Limitations of the Study

The current research contributes to the literature regarding the analysis of lexical errors in translation products of English major students in the Saudi context. However, there are some limitations that need to be acknowledged regarding the study. First, this study is limited to lexical errors in specific linguistic areas made by second-, third-, and fourth-year English major students of one public university in their written translation tasks only. It disregards the spoken texts of translation 'interpreting' which calls for further research, since it requires different sample methods and data collection. The study also attempted to analyse language errors in specific linguistic areas with specific regard to vocabulary. Other types of language errors found in this research, which are not related to the scope of the study, such as grammatical errors, are not included in the analysis.

This study is limited to the English language and Translation programme affiliated to one public university in KSA. The data for the study was collected from male students only at the university, due to cultural consensus. In the Saudi context, male and female students are separated at different campuses and it is difficult for a male researcher to have access to the female campus and vice versa for a female researcher.

Similar to all error analysis studies, the study is likely to have limitations related to the error analysis approach that is used in the research. The identification, categorisation, and explanation of language errors is not an easy task, and therefore, the analysis is not always accurate. However, the researcher sought consultation from an English lecturer with an L1 Arabic speaker and an L1 English speaker both holding a higher degree in linguistics and with English second/foreign language teaching experience in order to make the process of the analysis as accurate as possible.

7.7 Suggestions for Future Research

The findings of this study can be complemented by further research regarding the use of translation corpus texts to conduct in-depth analysis of the lexical errors made by English and translation majors in other EFL contexts. Future research may replicate or extend the current study by including a wider range of language samples, representing different groups at different educational levels.

Similar studies may scrutinise lexical errors in translation products from female English major students. The gender factor may show variations in the types and frequency of lexical errors in the learners' language production since the current study's translation samples were collected from male English major students only. In addition, this study has focused on lexical errors made in written translation products, therefore, future research may investigate the lexical errors made in spoken translation products or other language samples such as short stories, reports, and essays. Other studies may make a comparison between the lexical errors made in written translation production and those made in spoken translation, which could provide information about the differences in the types of lexical errors based on the type of language product. Furthermore, future longitudinal studies investigating the L2 learners' errors are recommended to better understand the complex relationships between lexical errors and the L2 learning and teaching process.

References

Al-Jabri, S. M. H. (1998). *An analysis of lexical errors in written English of Saudi college freshman female students* [Unpublished Master's thesis], Girls College of Education.

Ellis, R. (2008). *The study of second language acquisition*. Oxford University Press.

Elmahdi, O. E. H. (2016). Translation problems faced by Saudi EFL learners at university level. *English Literature and Language Review, 2*(7), 74–81.

Gass, S., & Selinker, L. (2008). *Second language acquisition: An introductory course* (3rd ed.). Routledge.

Hemchua, S., & Schmitt, N. (2006). An analysis of lexical errors in the English compositions of Thai learners. *Prospect, 21*, 3–25.

James, C. (2013). *Errors in language learning and use: Exploring error analysis*. Routledge.

Javid, C. Z., Farooq, M. U., & Umer, M. (2013). An investigation of Saudi EFL learners' writing problems: A case study along gender-lines. *Kashmir Journal of Language Research, 16*(1), 179.

Khalifa, M. (2015). Problem in translating English and Arabic languages' structure: A case study of EFL Saudi students in Shaqra University. *European Journal of English Language and Literature Studies, 3*(4), 22–34.

Khan, I. (2011). Role of applied linguistics in the teaching of english in Saudi Arabia. Retrieved June 20, 2018, from https://ssrn.com/abstract=2857575

Rahman, M., & Alhaisoni, E. (2013). Teaching English in Saudi Arabia: Prospective and challenges. *Academic Research International, 4*(1), 112–118.

Shalaby, A. N., Yahya, N., & El-Komi, M. (2009). Analysis of lexical errors in Saudi college students' compositions. *Journal of the Saudi Association of Languages and Translation, 2*(3), 65–93.

Sheshsha, J. A. (1993). Lexical error analysis in learning English as a foreign language. *Social Science Research Series, 24*, 5–30.

Printed in the United States
by Baker & Taylor Publisher Services